HIGH-FREQUENCY FINANCIAL MARKET DATA

SOURCES, APPLICATIONS AND MARKET MICROSTRUCTURE

Owain ap Gwilym

and

Charles Sutcliffe

RISK
BOOKS

Published by Risk Books, a division of Risk Publications
Haymarket House
28–29 Haymarket
London SW1Y 4RX
Tel: +44 (0)171 484 9700
Fax: +44 (0)171 930 2238
E-mail: books@risk.co.uk
Home Page: http://www.riskpublications.com

© Financial Engineering Ltd, 1999

ISBN 1 899332 49 9

British Library Cataloguing in Publication Data
A catalogue record for this book is available from the British Library

Commissioning Editor: Laurie Donaldson
Project Editor: Avril Eglinton
Desk Editor: Lindsey Hofmeister
Copy Editor: Derek Atkins
Typesetter: WordWise, Lee-on-the-Solent, Hampshire

Printed and bound in Great Britain by Selwood Printing Ltd,
Burgess Hill, West Sussex
Covers printed by Lea Printers, Bromley

Contents

About the authors

Owain ap Gwilym is a lecturer in finance at the Department of Management at the University of Southampton. Previously, he spent two years working on a research project on intraday empirical regularities in the Liffe futures and options markets. Owain's PhD studies at the University of Wales, Swansea, involved empirical investigations of index options markets. He currently teaches in the areas of quantitative finance, portfolio theory and corporate finance for MSc programmes in international banking and international financial markets and for undergraduate courses. Owain's research interests include derivatives, market microstructure and asset pricing, and he has published widely in international journals, including the *Journal of Banking and Finance*, *Journal of Futures Markets*, *Journal of Derivatives* and *Journal of Fixed Income*. He is a joint editor of *Financial Times Credit Ratings International* and *Financial Times Credit Ratings in Emerging Markets*, and an academic advisor for the Investment Management Certificate of the Institute of Investment Management and Research.

Charles Sutcliffe graduated in economics from Reading University, after qualifying as a chartered management accountant. As well as working for International Computers Ltd, Unilever and Reading University, he was the Northern Society Professor of Accounting and Finance at the University of Newcastle. For the last nine years Charles has been a professor of finance and accounting at the University of Southampton, and in 1995–96 was a visiting professor at the London School of Economics. He has published in a wide range of refereed journals, and is also the author of six books. Charles has also acted as a consultant to the Securities and Investments Board, HM Treasury, the United Nations, the London Stock Exchange, and Liffe; he has had research grants from the Social Science Research Council, the British Council, the Institute of Chartered Accountants in England and Wales, and the Chartered Institute of Management Accountants. He is a member of the editorial boards of the *Journal of Futures Markets* and the *European Journal of Finance*, and his current research interests centre on the empirical investigation of financial markets.

Paul MacGregor joined Liffe in 1994 as Statistical Manager, and extended his responsibilities to Marketing Manager for all aspects of Liffe Market Data in 1997. He has since been made of head of Third Party Sales, the department responsible for managing Liffe's Independent Software Vendors, Quote Vendors and Historical Data Vendors. Paul has been instrumental in the launch of Liffe Tick Data (1995), LIFFE*data* on the LIFFEnet website (1995), and the release of the LIFFE*style* historical data analysis software (1998). During his time at Liffe, Paul has worked closely with the alternative investments industry worldwide, to develop and continuously improve Liffe's market data products. He is a graduate in economics, holds a diploma in marketing from the London School of Economics, and is a member of the Society of Technical Analysts. Paul has previously worked at BP and the British Plastics Federation.

Acknowledgements
The authors wish to thank Laurie Donaldson, Avril Eglinton and Lindsey Hofmeister of Risk Books, and Richard Olsen of Olsen & Associates for their help in the production of this book. We are also grateful to Paul MacGregor of Liffe for contributing Panel 2.1, and Julie Cardy of the University of Southampton for help in coping with the large number of references. We are indebted to the many researchers whose work is surveyed in this book. Any survey of a relatively new and rapidly developing subject is bound to be incomplete, and we hope that those authors whose contributions to the literature on high-frequency data have inadvertently been omitted will understand.

1 Introduction and overview

In modern financial markets, news and prices are disseminated across the globe almost instantaneously, a situation which requires competitive institutions to analyse and react to market events at high speed. Recent years have witnessed an ever-increasing interest in the potential for developing trading strategies and risk-management solutions from the analysis of high-frequency financial market data. This Executive Report considers the sources, management, manipulation and uses of this powerful commodity.

The term "high frequency" is defined here as financial time series sampled at least on an intra-day basis, ie within the trading day. This excludes analysis using only daily open/close and high/low data. "Tick by tick" data (sometimes referred to as "time and sales" data) typically includes a record of price movements and associated information on timing and volumes. High-frequency financial datasets consist of varying degrees of detail on the trading process, depending on the source. Real-time datafeeds also fall into this category, but detailed research and analysis typically requires a historical archive of data.

Advances in this area during the late 1990s have encompassed computer technology, improved databases and progress in modelling the markets – for instance, in the area of non-linear analysis. In response to demand from market participants, many data suppliers have released high-frequency price data in convenient formats (see Chapter 2). The availability of such data has resulted in tremendous interest from researchers from a number of different disciplines, and has stimulated model development for data analysis, trading, forecasting and risk management (see Chapters 4–10). Over one thousand published studies of financial markets have employed high-frequency data, and the vast majority of these have appeared during the 1990s.

High-frequency data enables improved understanding of market behaviour and microstructure (ie the fine detail of the trading process), and allows exploration of strategies and hypotheses over very short time horizons. Conversely, for a vast range of applications, low-frequency data sampled discretely does not allow an adequately comprehensive analysis of a market which trades continuously throughout a day; research and analysis based on daily data risks ignoring large amounts of important information.

This Report focuses on the issues and applications related to high-frequency data in financial markets. It aims to be a guide to many aspects of high-frequency data by covering a broad set of information ranging from data suppliers to detailed research angles.

Overview and background

Historically, the use of paper-based systems implied that anyone gathering financial market datasets encountered severe problems with collection, storage and manipulation; this inevitably involved considerable time, space and expense. As electronic systems have developed, the opportunities for data collection have exploded and the data is now far more manageable. This type of data is nevertheless a valuable commodity, particularly on a real-time basis, and therefore purchase costs can still be relatively high.

Analysis of macroeconomic data typically involves sampling over monthly or quarterly time intervals, and the testing of asset-pricing models normally employs daily or lower-frequency data. In contrast, far higher data frequencies – up to the tick-by-tick level – are desirable for the majority of financial market applications. This naturally leads to a massive amount of data when examining liquid assets over long periods. The increased availability of transaction datasets, combined with advances in computing power, has resulted in a rapidly developing resource for financial research and analysis.

Much of financial theory was developed during the 1960s and 1970s on the basis of traditional statistical techniques, early computers and low-frequency databases. Advances in the 1980s and 1990s have resulted in the availability of large high-frequency datasets which allow for the analysis of financial time series at the frequency that is most suitable for the specific application. These developments challenge the traditional models and dictate the need for new modelling techniques. Academics and practitioners are now working closely together in the field of financial economics, and especially so in the area of high-frequency data (Goodhart, 1999).

The globalisation of finance has resulted in extremely active and liquid markets. As a guide, some foreign exchange markets can have over 5,000 newly quoted prices displayed per working day, and active futures markets typically have an even greater number of daily transactions. Such figures imply that an archived database can easily have millions of data items. As a consequence of the availability of such datasets, there has been great interest in the econometric and statistical techniques required to handle and exploit them. Innovative approaches have developed to extract quality information from the mass of data available.

Preparing, managing and modelling high-frequency data is a challenging yet rewarding task. The design of appropriate methodologies using relevant data is necessary to uncover the underlying trends and properties. The data assists researchers and traders to explore and verify patterns in market behaviour. In many applications, the benefits from successful exploitation of the data are often substantial. The above issues are discussed in detail in Chapter 3.

The motivation and demand for high-frequency data

During the 1990s, rapid advances have been made in trading, risk control and asset management. Simultaneous progress in computing technology has facilitated the process of collecting, storing and manipulating high-frequency datasets. In the context of increasingly competitive and volatile financial markets, daily prices and models based upon low-frequency data are insufficiently accurate to meet the demands of traders and risk managers. Dunis and Zhou (1998) suggest that in the field of asset management, the arrival in Europe of more aggressive styles of management, the pressure for performance and the increasing attention to risk have prompted some fund managers to use higher-frequency data, with more quantitatively oriented firms using real-time datafeeds.

Greater instability in global financial markets has increased uncertainty, which in turn has motivated the development of new hedging tools and considerable growth in derivatives trading. While uncertainty is perceived to have increased, new techniques that rely heavily on the analysis of non-linearities in high-frequency data now assist the process of risk taking and management in different markets. Modern financial markets are characterised by a large number of participants, with various levels of risk tolerance, a range of investment horizons, and differing reactions to unexpected news. It is argued by many that such a situation can only be explained through non-linear modelling techniques (Dunis and Zhou, 1998).

Financial economists believe that high-frequency data provides them with a micro-perspective on the markets, while fund managers – equipped with the insights gained about the movements of speculative prices – can exploit them in their asset allocation or trading models (Gaviridis, 1998). The empirical literature using high-frequency data has uncovered patterns and relationships that would be impossible to find using data sampled at daily or lower frequencies (see Chapters 4–10). The discovery of any pattern in a price or volatility series has important consequences since it implies predictability. Since information arrives in the market continuously, the use of only low-frequency data implies ignoring a large portion of the available information. Using high-frequency data can therefore reduce the lag between actual market information flow and its analysis.

In terms of examining empirical puzzles in financial time series and investigating the evidence for non-linearities and chaotic dynamics, it is clear that low-frequency analysis could lead to incomplete or misleading inferences. Investigation of how prices evolve, in the context of the dynamic interaction between heterogeneous agents, is a key area of interest. However, the data currently publicly available does not allow for robust testing of the interactions between agents with differing information sets, investment horizons and objective functions (Goodhart and O'Hara, 1997). Future research is likely to consider how market participants react to various sets of information and respond to each other's actions.

The uses of high-frequency data

There are many features of financial markets that can only be investigated using high-frequency data. These include:

✦ time of day seasonals in volume, volatility, and other key variables (see Chapter 5);

✦ short-run leads and lags between markets (see Chapter 6);

✦ the speed of the response to information arrival and price discovery between rival markets (see Chapters 5 and 6);

✦ market depth and liquidity, and the price response to a block trade (see Chapter 10); and

✦ tick size and price clustering (see Chapter 8).

In addition, high-frequency data can be used to improve the analysis of market effects that can also be studied using data at a daily or lower frequency. These include:

✦ arbitrage (see Chapter 4);

✦ market efficiency (see Chapter 9);

✦ relative volatility of spot and derivatives markets (see Chapter 7);

✦ programme trading and spot market volatility (see Chapter 7);

✦ the effect of derivatives expiration on spot volatility and volume (see Chapter 7);

✦ dual capacity (see Chapter 8); and

✦ hedging (see Chapter 5).

It is often the case that high-frequency data is much better suited to analysing these problems. For instance, the expiration effect only lasts about an hour, so that any effect is much diluted in daily data. Chapters 4–10 discuss various studies that have used high-frequency data to investigate these phenomena.

Large datasets can have many important advantages. For example, they are necessary for obtaining reliable estimates of the tails of the returns distribution, because there are very few observations in the tails when small datasets are used. A key benefit of intra-day data is the large number of independent observations that are available to improve the statistical significance of any study. Another use of high-frequency data is that some regulators require organisations to make sure that they trade at the best available price. This can be done by comparing transactions' prices around the time of a trade with the price actually achieved by the trading organisation; such information can also be used to monitor the performance of traders.

High-frequency data and market microstructure theory are natural complements. The theories of market microstructure concern the detailed operation of organised markets: bid–ask spread, tick size, inventory control by market-makers from trade to trade, how market prices impound new information, etc. High-frequency data is usually essential to test these theories. The very large sample sizes that can be produced using high-frequency data permit the use of estimation methods that are not feasible for lower-frequency datasets, eg testing for chaos. Gaviridis (1998) notes that the insights from high-frequency analysis are being used by a range of market participants for asset allocation, trading, valuation and risk-management decisions – for instance, in the integration of high-frequency methodologies in near-automatic asset management or trading systems.

Not only does the availability of high-frequency data enable researchers to understand past market behaviour, but it can also alter the subsequent behaviour of traders. For example, the analysis of a large dataset of high-frequency data by researchers may reveal a short-term market anomaly. Consequently, traders will analyse high-frequency data in real time in order to detect and exploit this anomaly, thus leading to its disappearance.

Market microstructure differs between securities – for instance, exchange-traded derivatives use a clearing house with novation and the associated daily margining procedures, while equities do not. Market microstructure can also differ between exchanges trading the same security: some use open outcry while others use screen-based trading. In addition, the market microstructure can change substantially over time, as shown by the recent switches of trading mechanism for the London International Financial Futures and Options Exchange (Liffe), the London Stock Exchange, the French stock exchange (Matif), the Sydney Futures Exchange, etc. These differences in market microstructure imply that it may not be possible to generalise empirical findings for one exchange, security or time period to other exchanges, securities or time periods.

Asset pricing, options pricing, risk management and hedging all depend crucially upon the accuracy with which volatility can be modelled. An obvious advantage of employing high-frequency data is that it enables a more detailed examination of both the sources and characteristics of return volatility. Probability theory indicates that it may be possible to substantially improve volatility estimates by using very frequent observations.

Lequeux (1999) notes how the analysis of high-frequency data has generated a wealth of information about market behaviour and has led to new perspectives in risk management and forecasting. Market practitioners use such data to test hypotheses and new trading strategies as well as to generate correlation and volatility estimates for input into pricing and risk models. Exploiting the link between trading and real-time information has emerged as a result of analysing high-frequency data. Real-time trading models epitomise the practical application of such research, with neural networks and genetic algorithms representing the latest modelling tools gaining wide acceptance among market practitioners.

Trading performance is now typically rewarded subject to the constraint that predetermined risk limits are adhered to. Fund managers are required to report their risk levels and incorporate risk considerations in their forecasting and model-building procedures, and this may well require high-frequency data. The objective is to maintain real-time risk control through techniques such as value-at-risk (VAR).[1] These techniques aim to establish the maximum losses that may be suffered as a result of adverse price movements.

High-frequency data is well suited for VAR calculations since it overcomes the problem that periodic snapshots may not provide an accurate reflection of the risk inherent within dynamic trading strategies. Gaviridis (1998) notes that more precise measures of risk will also enable more efficient asset allocations. A greater understanding of market behaviour as a result of using high-frequency data is likely to improve risk management.

Some empirical studies have used high-frequency data to provide input to models with longer data intervals. For example, Brennan and Subrahmanyam (1996) used trade and quote data for US stocks in 1984 and 1988 to estimate the illiquidity of each stock. These illiquidity numbers were then used as explanatory variables in a cross-sectional analysis of the effect of illiquidity on returns. Similarly, Patel and Wolfson (1981) used stock and options trade and quote data for 1976–77 for 96 US firms to compute daily-implied volatilities. Thus high-frequency data enables a wider set of explanatory variables to be used in models estimated using lower-frequency or cross-sectional data.

Differences between intra-day and inter-day traders

As traders move from holding positions open for days or weeks to circumstances where positions are opened and closed within the day, intra-day data becomes essential. In the simplest terms, traders will want to buy at the lowest point of the day and sell at the highest point. To achieve this, it is essential to identify the most likely timings of extreme prices. Since intra-day seasonalities exist in volume and volatility, there may be liquidity constraints on executing orders when the extreme prices occur. Thus intra-day traders will try to predict both the magnitude and timing of extreme events from high-frequency data. Such short-term (or "noise") traders also attempt to exploit micro-level market inefficiencies.

There are a number of institutional arrangements that differ for intra-day traders ("scalpers" and "day traders", who open and close positions within the day) and inter-day traders ("position traders", who keep positions open for a day or longer). These are as follows.

✦ Dividend and interest payments accrue on a daily basis, and within each day these numbers are fixed, as is the number of days to expiry or maturity. This fact has been used in research on the high-frequency dynamics of mispricings so as to greatly simplify the data requirements.

✦ Price limits are usually reset each day.

✦ Traders may have overnight position limits that are much smaller than their intra-day position limits (Lyons, 1995). In some cases, limits on trading may only be checked after the close of daily trading and so breaches of the limits during the day may not be apparent if the daily closing position is in accordance with the limits.

✦ Payments of variation margin in derivatives markets are usually collected on a daily basis, computed using the settlement price that is determined at the close of daily trading. Hence scalpers and day traders can avoid making variation margin payments.

✦ In some markets there are restrictions on the capacity of a trader (broker or principal) that apply afresh each day.

✦ Various types of limit order may expire at the close of daily trading.

For these reasons, intra-day trading may be different from inter-day trading, and studies using high-frequency data need to take account of these differences.

Structure of this report

This chapter introduces the field of high-frequency financial market data and highlights some of the key issues involved. The remainder of this report consists of the following: Chapter 2 includes details on the potential range of data sources and suppliers, and the different types of data available; Chapter 3 examines the issues involved in data manipulation and exploitation; Chapters 4–10 analyse the uses of high-frequency data and offer detailed descriptions of several application areas; Chapter 11 concludes the report and considers some likely future trends in this area; and Chapter 12 contains a comprehensive bibliography of published literature relevant to the topic.

Notes

1. On this topic, see Risk Books' publications entitled *Risk Management for Financial Institutions* and *VAR: Understanding and Applying Value-at-Risk*.

2 Sources and types of high-frequency data

Realistic intra-day risk management or trading strategies can only be developed and studied if good-quality high-frequency data is available. Decisions on the sourcing of high-frequency data (whether real-time or archived) are central to any research or analysis. The content and quality of the data will determine its worth to the end user, for it must be emphasised that high-frequency datasets are not uniform in their coverage and some have significant limitations. Examples of datasets with limited scope are those containing price-change transactions only, and others that contain indicative quotes only. Further, the vast majority of datasets contain no information on counterparties or principals for the trading activity, nor on market-maker inventory positions.

A key consideration is that data quality varies widely across markets and sources. One reason behind this is the degree of centralisation of the market under examination. As equity and derivatives trading is largely exchange-based and hence very centralised, transactions data can be easily collated (by the exchange) and distributed to interested parties. In contrast, foreign exchange markets are largely decentralised, most trading is still bilateral, and there are no trade reporting requirements; hence, aggregated data is unavailable. It is only with the introduction of electronic trading systems, and therefore increases in market centralisation, that high-quality multi-dealer transactions datasets have become available.

The publicly available stock of high-frequency data is growing substantially over time for four reasons, as follows.

✦ Several existing financial markets are changing their trading systems. This enables easier collection and distribution of high-frequency data. For example, the trend away from floor trading towards electronic systems is likely to ease the process of collecting and auditing market data, as has occurred with Liffe, Matif and the London Stock Exchange.

✦ New financial markets are appearing and being established around the world, and these tend to collect and distribute high-frequency data on their transactions from the outset of trading.

✦ New securities are being listed by existing markets, eg the new European stock-index futures contracts traded at Liffe.

✦ The number of trades (and quotes) in existing financial markets tends to increase over time (ie they become thicker), and this leads to more observations per day.

Some of the reasons underlying the increase in the availability of high-frequency data are set out below.

✦ The costs of data collection and analysis have fallen, because of the important changes in the way that exchanges operate, caused by the impact of new technology and electronic communication.

✦ Until quite recently, only trades were recorded by most centralised exchanges, and this was done largely for legal reasons; there was no need to record quotes. The records that were maintained typically consisted of information on the asset traded, its price, the volume, the counterparties and an estimate of the time of the trade.

Increased market surveillance means that regulators and others wish to record *all* aspects of the trading process, so that an audit trail is generated in case behaviour is subsequently questioned.

✦ There is nowadays a much stronger demand for high-frequency data from many market participants.

Developments in information technology have made the collection, storage and retrieval of financial market data more widespread at levels of increasing detail. With the increasing computerisation of markets, each individual transaction can be recorded and analysed. The data is available from many vendors and is vital for forecasting future price movements and volatility levels. While it has become relatively easy to obtain continuous records of market data, there is still scope for further expansion to cover issues such as the identity, motives and portfolio positions of traders.

Various sources exist for obtaining high-frequency financial data. These include securities and derivatives exchanges, which provide data from their own audit trails; electronic information providers with real-time feeds, such as Reuters and Bloomberg; and specialist suppliers of archived data, for example Tick Data Inc and Olsen & Associates. The choice of supplier will depend on the end use of the data, and whether the need is for current and/or historical data. Some users will require the front-end software offered by some suppliers to enable improved access, search and exporting features, while others will develop their own tailor-made software and systems. Extensive datasets have emerged from the markets in foreign exchange, equities and derivatives, but there is far less coverage of fixed income markets.

Some high-frequency data is released by exchanges in real time, while other data may be released with a delay of a few hours or days. Additional data may be available with a considerable lag, by which time the information is no longer commercially sensitive. Finally, some data may only be available to approved researchers who have signed confidentiality agreements.

Types of data

The data items included in high-frequency datasets vary considerably between sources. For instance, some foreign exchange databases only include indicative quoted prices; some derivatives exchanges only include transactions that involve a price change; others have a full record of all quoted and traded prices, together with traded volumes; and the most comprehensive databases include information on the traders and brokers involved in each trade.

Many exchanges, such as the New York Stock Exchange (NYSE) and the Chicago Board Options Exchange (CBOE), maintain historical records of all trades and all quotes. In contrast, exchanges such as the Chicago Board of Trade (CBOT) and the Chicago Mercantile Exchange (CME) record "time and sales" data that only contains the times and prices of trades if there has been a change from the previously recorded price. Quoted prices will only appear in the database if the bid quote exceeds, or if the ask quote is below, the previously recorded trade price (see Smith and Whaley, 1994). The implications of such an incomplete dataset include problems in estimating bid–ask spreads (see Chapter 3) and in gauging the speed of reaction to news arrivals (see Chapter 6).

The included variables will obviously determine what level of research or analysis is possible with a given dataset, and is thus a very important consideration prior to purchase and implementation. Most publicly released historical datasets do not include information on the underlying parties to a quotation or trade. There are some exceptions (for instance, Reuters' FXFX pages identify the branch of the trader's bank) but even then potentially valuable information, such as inventory positions, may not be disclosed.

Only somewhat limited high-frequency data is available for decentralised over-the-counter markets such as that for foreign exchange or the interbank money market. They tend to provide just quote data, which is widely distributed in real time to facilitate the trading process. Where available, tick-by-tick data from the foreign exchange market consists of a sequence of bid–ask prices quoted by various firms that function as market-makers. Indicative quotes for foreign exchange markets are widely available, eg through Reuters pages. However, these are not the firm quotes on which dealers trade; these indicative quotes are non-binding and do not represent actual transactions. Since the prices are not necessarily tradable, they cannot be used to identify arbitrage opportunities with certainty.

A further problem with data from indicative quotes involves the quoted spread. Lyons (1995) shows that while it is true that the indicated spreads usually bracket actual quoted spreads in the interbank foreign exchange market, they are typically two to three times as wide. Furthermore, the indicative quotes are less likely to bracket true spreads when volatility is highest since there are limits on the frequency with which the indicated quotes can change. Finally, Lyons (1995) suggests that the dealers at major banks pay no attention to the current indicated quotes and collect their high-frequency information through signals transmitted via intercoms connected to inter-dealer brokers. Essentially, the indicative quotes can only provide a guide to current price levels to non-dealer participants in the market.

Foreign exchange trade data is rarely available because this is confidential to the counterparties. There is no public record of all foreign exchange transaction prices and volumes for the interbank market. Nor is much firm quote data available; only a very small number of empirical studies – eg Lyons (1995) and Goodhart and Payne (1996) – have used either trade or firm quote data. The few examples of trade or firm quote data that are available have been specially collected and typically only cover very short periods of time – perhaps a few days. This absence of trade data for foreign exchange markets has led to an interest in estimating trade data from indicative quote data. Goodhart, Chang and Payne (1997) tested the Bollerslev and Domowitz (1993) algorithm using quote and trade data on the US$/DM exchange for seven hours in 1993, and concluded that its performance is poor.

Some applications are concerned with trades of a particular type, assuming the relevant identifiers are part of the dataset. For example, the data may identify arbitrage trades, inter-market-maker trades, programme trades, basket trades, worked principal trades, block trades, etc. The analysis may deal with time-independent features of such trades, such as the size distribution of block trades. However, the analysis may involve an event study of each selected trade, eg the price impact of block trades. In the latter case, the analysis becomes a time series problem, and a time dimension must be chosen (see Chapter 3).

Trade data can also contain some additional information – for instance, trade type identifiers, such as programme trades, and shapes (there are several counterparties to the trade, eg trader A bought 50,000 shares comprising 30,000 from trader B and 20,000 from trader C).

Data supplied by exchanges

All centralised exchanges keep records of trades, including the time, price, volume traded, and the identity of the counterparties. This information is held primarily for audit purposes and for resolving disputes (Goodhart and O'Hara, 1997). In most cases, information on counterparties is removed before the trade data becomes publicly available. Most exchanges store a long history of such data. In response to increasing demands from market participants, many exchanges now supply archived high-frequency data on the instruments that they list. Some exchanges have also developed front-end software to facilitate easier access and organisation of data, and have made considerable efforts to make the data products user-friendly.

Liffe has been one of the more innovative proponents of supplying exchange data, offering CD-ROM titles containing high-frequency data on its traded derivatives contracts. These products include front-end software that allows construction of continuous series and other user-defined options (see Panel 2.1). Annual subscriptions pay for a full data history for the relevant products up to and including the most recent quarter, followed by three quarterly update discs. There is also the possibility of receiving overnight updates via the Internet. The CD-ROM data includes information on the time to the nearest second, derivatives delivery month, price, transaction code, and traded volume.

Most other major futures exchanges, including CME, Eurex and Matif, offer tick-by-tick data products. The preferred delivery media tend to be either magnetic tapes or CD-ROM, due to the size of the datasets. Such data is frequently in ASCII text format with no front-end software. An extensive dataset is maintained by the Commodity Futures Trading Commission (CFTC) in the US, which includes data from exchanges such as the CME. Its computerised trade reconstruction (CTR) records include the identity of the floor trader executing a trade, the price and number of contracts in each trade, and the principals behind each trade. It is thus possible to examine the precise detail of the trading process, including trader strategies.

Stock exchanges have generally followed a different path, and their market data is typically available predominantly on a real-time basis through quote vendors. In addition, they usually provide related services via disk or hard copy, such as turnover reports, dividend data and other company-specific information. Both stock and derivatives exchanges are increasingly focusing on Internet-based data availability.

A major source for archived high-frequency US equity-market data is the Institute for the Study of Security Markets (ISSM) in Memphis, USA. Their database contains all trade and quote records for stocks listed on

Panel 2.1 THE SOURCING AND PREPARATION OF LIFFE TICK DATA

It is now clear that the use of intra-day data for historical analysis gives users a certain "edge" over the more traditional end-of-day data analysis. Also, the growth of electronic trading has improved the quality of data available to the marketplace. The advent of "market depth" – ie the size of bids and offers available below the "best" bid and offer in the marketplace – brings transparency to the electronic market, previously only available to floor traders.

The ability to track accurate volumes per trade is adding a new dimension to the analysis performed on intra-day data. Typically, there are 10 million quotes on the Liffe market in the space of one year (or nearly 40,000 per day), equalling about 170MB of data per contract. As this is not easy to prepare or analyse, exchanges and data vendors have begun to look at ways of viewing and extracting such large streams of data.

In this Panel, an overview is given of the Liffe*data* Historical CD-ROM and Internet update service developed by Liffe to meet the needs of this new marketplace.

Table A. Liffe historical data software product range

New CD-ROM title	Contracts covered
Equity products End-of-day data	All index futures since 1984. All individual equity and index options since 1992, including FTSE Eurobloc 100 Index futures and options since 1999, FTSE Eurotop 300 Index futures and options since 1999, FTSE Eurotop 300 Ex UK Index futures and options since 1999, MSCI Euro Index futures and options since 1999, and MSCI Pan-Euro Index futures and options since 1999.
Financial products End-of-day data	All financial futures and options since 1982, including index futures, Euro Libor and Euribor.
"Euro-In" products tick data	Three-month Euro Libor futures since 1989 (previously ECU futures), three-month Euro Libor options since 1998, three-month Euribor futures since 1998, three-month Euribor options since 1999, five-year EFB futures since 1999, 10-year EFB futures since 1999, Euro Bund futures and options since 1998, Euro BTP futures and options since 1998, FTSE Eurotop 100 Index futures since 1998, FTSE Eurobloc 100 Index futures and options since 1999, FTSE Eurotop 300 Index futures and options since 1999, FTSE Eurotop 300 Ex UK Index futures and options since 1999, MSCI Euro Index futures and options since 1999, and MSCI Pan-Euro Index futures and options since 1999.
"Euro-Out" products tick data	Long Gilt and Short Sterling futures and options since 1986, Five-Year Gilt futures since 1998, Three-Month EuroSwiss futures and options since 1991, JGB futures since 1991, Three-Month Euroyen futures since 1996, FTSE100 Index futures since 1986, FTSE Eurotop 100 Index futures since 1998, FTSE100 Index options since 1992, and FTSE250 Index futures since 1994.
Commodity products intra-day and end-of-day data	All coffee, cocoa and No 5 white sugar intra-day futures since 1995. All commodity futures and options end-of-day data since 1988.

Liffe*data* Historical – Liffe's new product to reflect the birth of the euro

A key event in Liffe's recent history has been the successful conversion of the Euromark and Eurolira futures and options contracts into the Euro Libor and Euribor. Also, the Deutschmark-denominated Bund contract and the lira-denominated BTP contracts have been replaced by the euro Bund and euro BTP contracts. Added to this, Liffe launched a whole new range of equity index products in May 1999.

So how has Liffe's historical data product range been adjusted to reflect these changes? Liffe's view is that the situation has improved. Instead of subscribing to four tick data titles, historical data analysts are now asked to subscribe to just two: *"Euro-In"* Products and *"Euro-Out"* Products. These two CD-ROM titles replace those entitled *Deutschmark Products*, *Lira Products*, *Sterling Products* and *Euro/Swiss/Yen Products*. In addition, Liffe has launched *Commodity Products Historical Data* on CD-ROM, containing both end-of-day and intra-day prices on Liffe's key commodity contracts. A tabular representation of the new historical data product range is given in Table A on page 11.

Liffestyle

Liffe originally developed and pioneered tick datasets on CD-ROM in September 1995. It has subsequently endeavoured to continuously improve its historical data coverage and develop products that meet customer demands. Feedback from customers has focused, it says, on the fact that while data quality is good, the speed and user-friendliness of the viewing and extraction software has been poor. As a result, Liffe contracted Intelligent Financial Systems (IFS) Ltd, a financial software house specialising in the provision of advanced quantitative software,[1] to develop a historical data software package for it, which has since been called *"Liffestyle"*.

Figure A. Viewing all delivery months for June 9, 1998 to March 15, 1999 in the FTSE100 Index future

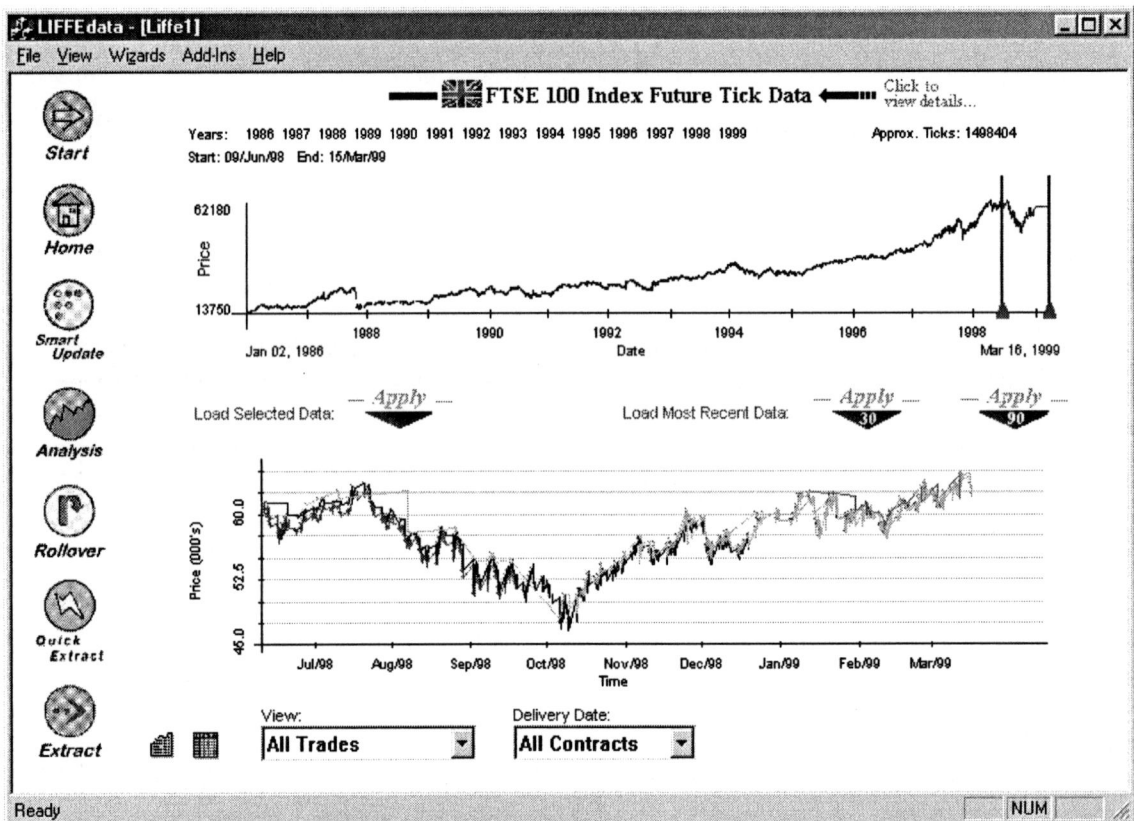

Selecting a period for analysis

In practice, it is extremely hard for an end-user to choose the correct period of tick data to analyse. An end-user may, for example, wish to analyse certain periods of high-volume market activity – but how is it possible to identify these periods without downloading and viewing large amounts of data initially? This can be a long process, but *Liffestyle* is able to provide visualisation at software start-up, so that tick data can be viewed in broad terms immediately upon initiation. In the example above, the user has selected the FTSE100 Index futures contract from June 9, 1998 to March 15, 1999 (see Figure A). The upper chart shows the entire tick history of the FTSE100 futures, while the lower chart shows the section "zoomed in" via the slider bars, broken down by delivery month.

By clicking on the "Apply" icon, the user in our example has selected for analysis the FTSE100 futures tick by tick for June 9, 1998, through to March 15, 1999. The time delay between selecting the data (nearly 1.5 million records) and the construction of the chart for each delivery month is generally found to be 2–3 minutes. To prepare and view historical tick data of such magnitude using traditional methods normally takes considerably longer.

The user is viewing each of the delivery months on the same chart, but this is not the only option available. A continuous time series can be calculated almost instantly, allowing the user to view data in 1-, 5-, 15-, 30- and 60-minute samples. Via an in-built "zoom" function, used by dragging and clicking along the bottom of the tick chart, end-users can view data down to the nearest tick if required.

Analysis of "continuous contract"

Another lengthy process when preparing historical futures data for analysis is the creation of a "continuous contract". This is the method by which individual quarterly expiry months are strung together to make analysis of a long time-series possible.

Normally, a historical data user would download several years of data, choose a rollover strategy, and apply it using some not insignificant data manipulation skills.

But what is a rollover strategy? There are many differing methodologies that can be used, varying from volume crossover (ie the volume in the far contract overtakes that in the near contract), to volume threshold (ie the volume in the far contract rises above a certain threshold level), or a fixed date. These features are fully provided for in the Liffe*style* software.

Figure B. The Liffe*style* Rollover Wizard

As can be seen from the screenshot shown in Figure B, the default rollover strategy used by *Liffestyle* is a daily check on when the far contract volume rises above the near contract volume. When this occurs, the software will automatically roll over the prices. Pushing the "Rollover Analysis" key will deliver a text file letting an end-user know exactly which dates have been used (see Table B).

Table B. Rollover analysis of the daily volume check on the FTSE100 Index futures contract from June 9, 1998 to March 15, 1999

Total rollovers: five

Rollover 1 occurred at date Fri, Mar-21, 1997
Near contract: Mar97   Far contract: Jun97
Near volume: 2539   Far volume: 10178
Near price: 42700.0   Far price: 42850.0
Basis correction required between near and far contracts: 150.00

Rollover 2 occurred at date Fri, Jun-20, 1997
Near contract: Jun97   Far contract: Sep97
Near volume: 3007   Far volume: 6481
Near price: 46550.0   Far price: 46830.0
Basis correction required between near and far contracts: 280.00

Rollover 3 occurred at date Mon, Sep-08, 1997
Near contract: Sep97   Far contract: Dec97
Near volume: 5369   Far volume: 7382
Near price: 49980.0   Far price: 50640.0
Basis correction required between near and far contracts: 660.00

Rollover 4 occurred at date Thu, Dec-18, 1997
Near contract: Dec97   Far contract: Mar98
Near volume: 6507   Far volume: 6674
Near price: 52150.0   Far price: 52700.0
Basis correction required between near and far contracts: 550.00

Rollover 5 occurred at date Tue, Mar-10, 1998
Near contract: Mar98   Far contract: Jun98
Near volume: 6506   Far volume: 10518
Near price: 58000.0   Far price: 58750.0
Basis correction required between near and far contracts: 750.00

Having created a continuous contract and evaluated the rollover points, an end-user may want to do some further analysis prior to exporting data and leaving the *Liffestyle* package. At the time of writing (mid-1999), the *Liffestyle* software includes the following analysis tools to assist in this process.

✦ **Intra-day volume** gives the end-user an analysis of traded volume averaged over each day of the sampling period. This can be particularly useful for intra-day traders who want to enter and exit the market during periods of high activity.

✦ **Returns History** yields instantaneous percentage returns plotted over the sampling period for the most actively traded contract.

✦ **Returns Distribution** is a frequency histogram of percentage returns obtained over the sampling period for the most actively traded contract.

✦ **Historical Volatility** shows the localised standard deviation of returns plotted over the sampling period.

Many users, particularly of high-frequency data, have their own advanced trading packages that evaluate all the technical indicators they require, once they have exported the data. Therefore, for the more advanced end-users, technical indicators are not required. Instead, a "Quick Extract" function allows the data to be downloaded almost instantly. This is also available in Liffe*style*, and a screenshot from it is given in Figure C.

Figure C. The Liffe*style* Quick Extraction Wizard

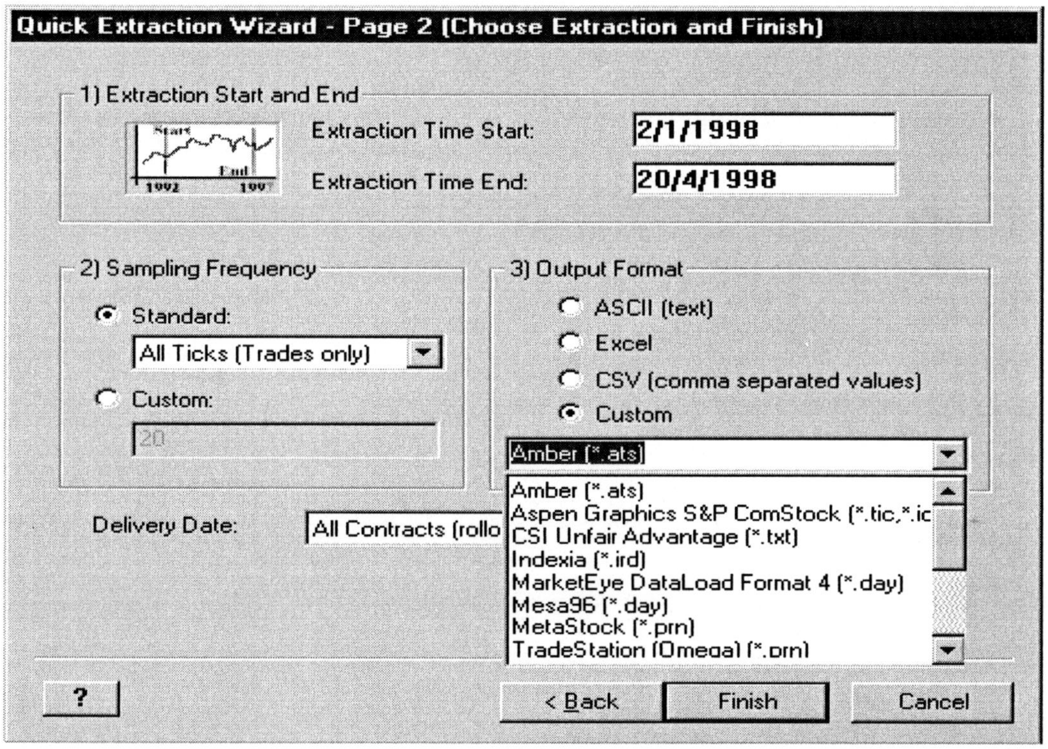

In the example given in Figure C, the end-user has chosen to extract into Amber Software all FTSE100 Index futures tick data for 1998. This "Quick Extraction" facility allows advanced users of tick data simply to go into the software and retrieve the data they require very quickly.

There are a couple more levels of functionality at hand when using the full Extraction Wizard. In the example shown in Figure D, the end-user has defined a 15-minute tick frequency but has also had the opportunity to define the display to be Open, High, Low or Close. Bid–ask spreads and volumes are also displayed. This gives the opportunity for further analysis of the data under scrutiny.

*Liffe*style *software compatibility*

One of the most common questions posed by historical data users to Liffe over the years has been, "Will it work in my favourite trading software package?" Hence Liffe has worked closely with the major trading software application providers worldwide to case compatibility issues. As at mid-1999, Liffe*style* will export into the following custom-built data formats:

Figure D. Defining differing outputs in the Extraction Wizard

- ✦ Amber;
- ✦ Aspen Graphics S&P Comstock;
- ✦ CSI Unfair Advantage;
- ✦ Indexia;
- ✦ MarketEye Dataload Format 4;
- ✦ Mesa;
- ✦ Metastock; and
- ✦ Tradestation (Omega).

Another very common question asked is, "How frequently can I update my data history?" Some data providers offer only quarterly or monthly updates via diskette and/or CD-ROM, which can sometimes be too infrequent for financial analysts. Liffe*style* delivers update capability via its "Smart Update" function (see Figure E), where any Liffe*style* subscriber can update appropriate datasets via the Internet on a daily basis, either by individual contract or by CD-ROM title.

Conclusion

The use of high-frequency data for trading has become increasingly popular over recent years. This has been driven by:

- ✦ the growth of technical trading within the alternative investment industry;
- ✦ the recognition by exchanges of the value of tick data; and
- ✦ the growth in desktop computing power.

Liffe has developed its products in order to adjust its already popular historical data service to reflect the launch of the euro and the change that this has brought about to Liffe's product range. Also, the migration of Liffe's products from an open-outcry trading environment to an electronic marketplace appears to have improved the quality of data available to end-users at the intra-day level – for instance, accurate bid, offer and trade volumes are provided.

Liffe, perceived as a pioneer in the provision of tick data to historical-data users, has seen significant benefits in terms of rising contract volumes in recent years. The clear message from end-users has been that they need speedy provision of clean, well-presented historical tick data for their financial analysis. This is exactly what Liffe is attempting to achieve.

References:

Lequeux Pierre (ed), 1999, Financial Markets Tick by Tick: Insights in Financial Markets Microstructure, *Wiley, Chichester, UK*

1. For more information on IFS, visit its website at <http://www.ifsys.co.uk/>.

Figure E.

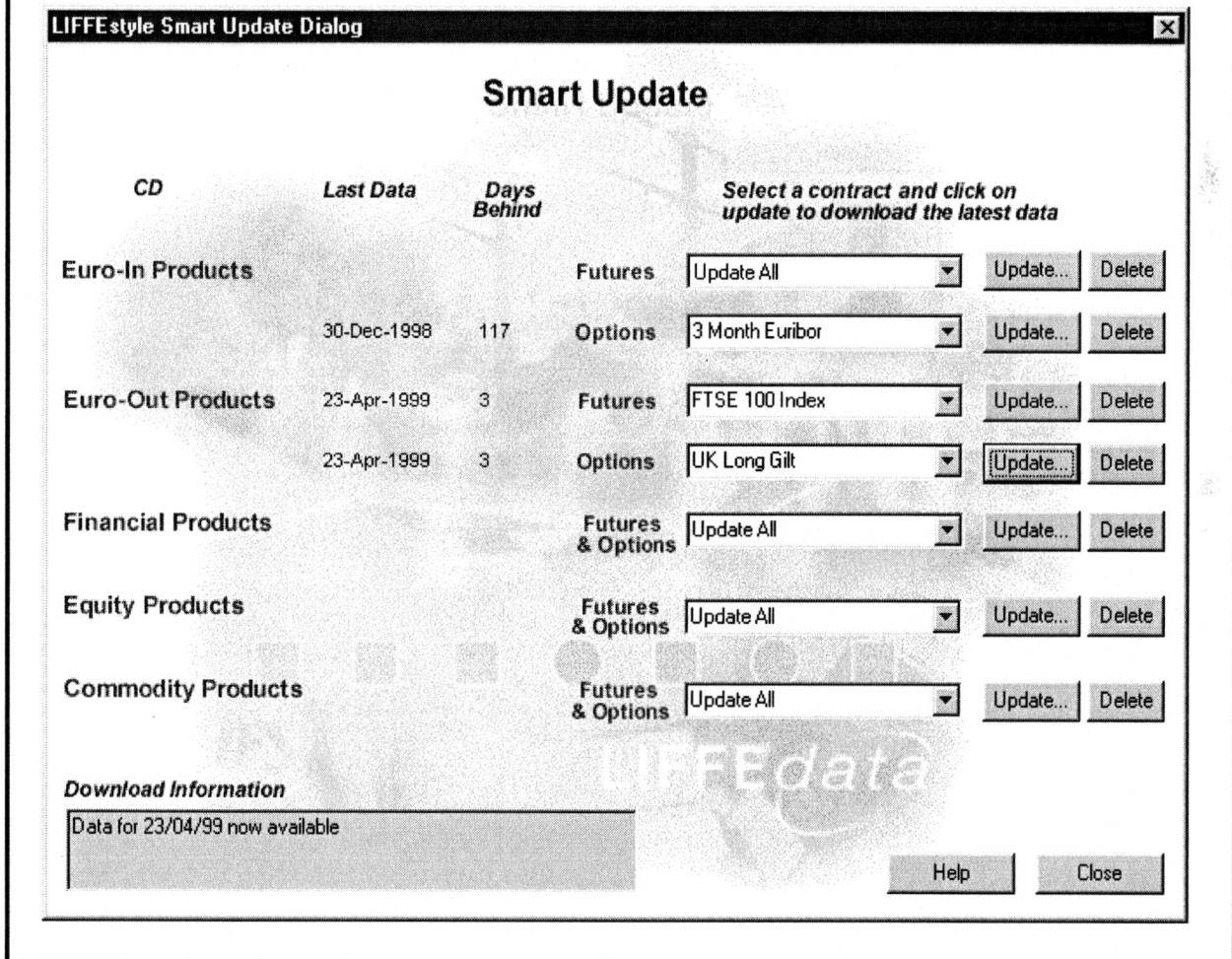

the NYSE, the American Stock Exchange (Amex), Nasdaq and regional exchanges. It is generally not possible to identify from this type of database whether a trade was directly routed to the downstairs market or was upstairs facilitated (Cheng and Madhavan, 1994). However, it is possible to make this distinction with the Consolidated Audit Trail Data (CAUD) files maintained by the NYSE, although these files are generally not publicly released.

Specialist data providers

There are a number of specialist organisations that prepare and supply off-the-shelf or customised high-frequency data products. We will discuss some of the leading providers in this section.

Olsen & Associates

Olsen & Associates (O&A), a research institute based in Zurich, Switzerland, is a major provider of time series of high-frequency historical data. The company offers a potential set of over 7,900 instruments, including computed yield curves. Typical instruments include foreign exchange spot rates, implied volatilities of foreign exchange spot rates and Eurodeposit cash interest rates. Most aspects of the O&A service can be customised, with user-defined market coverage, historical start–end dates and delivery formats. Particular attention is paid to the development of filtering algorithms in order to ensure the quality and integrity of the database (see Chapter 3).

A major contribution by O&A has been the collection and analysis of a large continuous database of foreign exchange spot quotes. Using software developed in-house, O&A collects (predominantly through Reuters), validates and stores price quotes for future use. This database of foreign exchange rates consists of time-stamped (to the nearest second) bid–ask quotes. Each quote record includes the name and location of the originating bank or institution submitting the quote. Outliers or errors in the bid–ask quotes are identified with filter flags.

O&A can also provide real-time forecasts, historical analyses and trading advice for various instruments. Based on their foreign exchange data, a set of real-time intra-day trading models has been developed (Pictet *et al*, 1992). These trading models have predominantly used Reuters data, but other high-frequency data suppliers provide similar information in their foreign exchange quotes. The models give explicit trading recommendations and have been shown to be successful in practice, running in real time over a number of years. More detail on the data is given in Müller *et al* (1990) and Dacorogna *et al* (1993).

Berkeley Options Data Base

The Berkeley Options Data Base (BODB) offers a reprocessed version of the CBOE's Market Data Reports. The database contains every bid–ask quote and every trade recorded on the floor of that exchange, time-stamped to the nearest second. The database extends back to August 1976 and is updated annually. BODB screens the exchange data for bad or duplicate observations and alters certain fields to facilitate interpretation. The database contains quoted and traded prices, volumes, different types of trade, and matching values of the underlying asset.

Other suppliers

Other specialist data providers include The Futures Industry Institute (FII), Tick Data Inc, and Francis Emory Fitch. The FII is based in

Washington DC and supplies ASCII-format high-frequency data on CD-ROM for a wide range of futures and options contracts traded in North America and elsewhere.

Real-time data providers

Although archived historical data is vital for a vast range of applications, including the back testing of proposed trading models, real-time data is essential for day-to-day risk management and control, and for early identification of trading opportunities. Real-time information providers send out millions of data items over their electronic pages every day. Their services are focused on current information rather than the storage of historical databases. Market participants can thus keep abreast of developments in continuous time during trading hours.

Exchanges use various means for distributing price information, including quote vendors, information services and Web sites. For example, Liffe sells real-time data to around 100,000 users via over 80 vendors and sub-vendors worldwide. The London Stock Exchange provides market data via its London Market Information Link (LMIL) services. This datafeed is available in real time, via extractions throughout the day, or by means of a download at the market close. Customers may then choose to take all the information or to select a user-defined portion. A number of stock exchanges around the world follow a similar approach. The data typically includes trades, quotes and volumes.

In addition to direct feeds from an exchange, there is the alternative of using a specialist information service such as Bridge-CRB or Bloomberg. For example, Bridge-CRB provides a trading platform called Market Center Plus that delivers data via the Internet. This includes price data, news and charts in real time, together with historical formats. This type of service typically collates data from a wide range of different exchanges and other sources.

Real-time data services (eg Reuters, Telerate) are an excellent source for foreign exchange market data. Bid–ask price quotes are displayed continuously, while other pages offer single price series constructed from the sequence of newly updated quotes. The information shown on Reuters' FXFX (dollar exchange rates) and WXWX (major cross rates) pages, provided by Reuters' contributors (mainly large banks and brokers), represents an indication of the current trading price of the market participant. However, using Reuters' data as opposed to brokers' trading data introduces several additional sources of noise (see earlier).

Summary

This chapter briefly illustrates the major sources of high-frequency financial market data. Key issues arise in considering the types, quality and timeliness of the data. It is vital to recognise the variety in coverage and scope between different sources. The user must ensure that any data being purchased is adequately comprehensive and reliable for its purpose, because the quality and relevance of any research or analysis is heavily dependent on the underlying data. Chapters 4–10 discuss applications of high-frequency data and provide further detail on the types and sources of data available.

An issue that is not addressed in detail here is that of the purchase costs of high-frequency datasets. It is difficult to make sensible comparisons, since costs vary significantly, depending on the source and type of data. For example, a real-time feed will obviously be far more costly than a set of historical data. The condition of the data when supplied will also be a key determinant of cost, as will the existence of any front-end software and the level of filtering or cleaning which has been applied to the data (see Chapter 3).

3 Managing and exploiting high-frequency data

This chapter aims to describe the multitude of issues which arise in managing high-frequency data and in its exploitation in trading and research applications. Many additional issues arise when using intra-day data rather than lower-frequency data. Several microstructural effects, for example bid–ask bounce, discreteness and clustering, can be ignored on, say, a daily basis, but become vital with high-frequency data. The statistical characteristics of high-frequency data also present problems since standard time-series methodologies are not well suited to irregular data arrival, distributions with unusually heavy tails and the non-synchronicity of information arrival across different markets.

With most applications of high-frequency financial market data, after any kind of data purchase there is a need for cleaning, filtering and checking before proceeding with data manipulation. Together with the typically extensive size of high-frequency datasets, these issues imply that data management and warehousing are important considerations.

There are also a number of associated variables that can be constructed from the raw series when adequate data is available, eg returns, price volatility, the spread between bid and offered prices, and the elapsed time between trades or quotes. Different problems arise depending on the use of trade data, quote data, or both. Another issue involves incorporation of new data into existing models as and when it becomes available: in many cases, models will be set up based on historical data and then updated using real-time data feeds to facilitate detection of trading opportunities.

The treatment of time is important in several respects. Some time intervals witness no trades, implying a problem in measuring returns. The timing of trades can also be regarded as an information signal. Decisions on whether to work in clock time or activity time are central to any application. A related scaling issue involves selecting an economically meaningful time interval, eg sampling data on a five-minute, 15-minute, or hourly basis (if working in clock time). The latter is partly driven by the frequency of trading and the liquidity of the asset under analysis. Such problems do not arise with low-frequency regularly spaced data. A further consideration involves the different investment horizons that are relevant for different market participants, ranging from a few minutes for local traders on a futures exchange to the long-term perspective of pension fund trustees. This becomes especially important when modelling short-run and long-run volatility.

The data in Panel 3.1 illustrates some of the key issues encountered in dealing with high-frequency data, namely unequal time spacing of data, the need to deal with quotes versus trades, multiple simultaneous bid, ask or traded prices, and overnight market closures. This chapter highlights how coping with such issues makes modelling of high-frequency data challenging.

> **Panel 3.1: Illustrative high-frequency data for the first minute of trading in the FTSE100 futures contract on August 1, 1997**
>
> 08:35:10, SEP97, 49300, T
> 08:35:10, SEP97, 49300, T
> 08:35:10, SEP97, 49300, T
> 08:35:10, SEP97, 49300, T
> 08:35:11, SEP97, 49290, T
> 08:35:11, SEP97, 49290, T
> 08:35:12, SEP97, 49290, T
> 08:35:12, SEP97, 49290, T
> 08:35:13, SEP97, 49300, T
> 08:35:13, SEP97, 49300, T
> 08:35:14, SEP97, 49320, T
> 08:35:14, SEP97, 49320, T
> 08:35:15, SEP97, 49310, T
> 08:35:18, SEP97, 49340, T
> 08:35:18, SEP97, 49340, T
> 08:35:19, SEP97, 49310, T
> 08:35:24, SEP97, 49320, T
> 08:35:33, SEP97, 49340, T
> 08:35:33, SEP97, 49340, T
> 08:35:38, SEP97, 49340, T
> 08:35:38, SEP97, 49340, T
> 08:35:39, SEP97, 49330, T
> 08:35:39, SEP97, 49350, T
> 08:35:39, SEP97, 49350, T
> 08:35:43, SEP97, 49340, A
> 08:35:44, SEP97, 49330, A
> 08:35:45, SEP97, 49320, B
> 08:35:46, SEP97, 49320, T
> 08:35:50, SEP97, 49320, T
> 08:35:53, SEP97, 49340, T
>
> This sub-sample of the data includes the time stamp, expiry month, futures price, and bid/ask/trade indicator.

Data storage, filtering and cleaning

Size of datasets

One of the major issues with the analysis of high-frequency data, whether on a real-time basis or as an archived historical database, is the sheer quantity of data points. A dataset of monthly price observations contains hundreds of observations at most. A typical dataset of daily observations spanning a number of years contains a couple of thousand observations. In contrast, using intra-day data potentially involves hundreds of thousands or millions of observations.

Archiving data on actively quoted assets implies that the datasets will contain millions of records even over a relatively short time period. For instance, in 1988 the ISSM database of trades and quotes for US equities held 52 million observations, and such databases can grow by millions of observations per year. It is often easier to describe such datasets in terms of the amount of computer disc storage space required rather than in terms of the number of observations. For example, Lequeux (1997) indicates that one year of tick data for the US$/DM spot exchange rate represents approximately 1.5 million quotes or an ASCII file of approximately 60 megabytes. The Berkeley Options Database (BODB) contains 35 gigabytes of options price history over 20 years (see Chapter 2).

Table 3.1 presents the Huber taxonomy (cited by Wegman, 1995) of dataset sizes. According to this classification, many high-frequency datasets would be defined as large (around 100 megabytes) and some would be huge (around 10 gigabytes). Wegman (1995) discusses some of the computational issues in dealing with datasets of this size.

With such large datasets, there is obviously a need to identify and summarise empirical regularities in trading patterns and returns (see later in this chapter). High-frequency data is useful for identifying short-term effects that may be repeated each day, or many times per day. Therefore only a short time period, a few months for example, is necessary to obtain sufficient data for a meaningful statistical analysis. In contrast, researchers looking for, say, a "January" effect must employ many years of data.

Data filtering and cleaning

After the establishment of a real-time data feed or an archived database, there is an important further step required before data analysis. This involves ensuring the integrity of the data by designing appropriate filtering algorithms to identify rogue or corrupted observations or outliers. Chung (1991) reports severely corrupted data for futures on the Major Market Index (MMI), with 0.25% of quotes outside the reported daily high and low, while Dacorogna *et al* (1995) estimated the error rates on forex quote data to be between 0.11% and 0.81%.

Such incorrect data often remains despite the quality controls imposed by suppliers. It may arise due to human errors, such as mistyped prices, or through technical problems, for example with data transmission. Incorrect data items have serious implications because new techniques and methodologies tend to be more sensitive to minor price variations. The existence of outliers presents a serious problem for

Table 3.1: The Huber taxonomy of dataset sizes

Descriptor	Dataset size (bytes)	Storage mode
Tiny	10^2	Piece of paper
Small	10^4	A few pieces of paper
Medium	10^6	A floppy disk
Large	10^8	Hard disk
Huge	10^{10}	Multiple hard disks
Ridiculous	10^{12}	Magnetic tape

modelling and can distort the performance of risk management or trading strategies.

MacGregor (1999) describes the procedures for correcting erroneous data entries under an open outcry trading environment at Liffe. Data is collected by price reporters during the trading process, and is filtered at the end of the day using an algorithm that matches deleted quotes with their previous erroneous entries. All deleted quotes are flagged, so that users of Liffe's tick data products are aware of them and exclude them from any data analysis. MacGregor points out that users of tick data may want to see deleted quotes in the database in order to check that erroneous quoted or traded prices have indeed been deleted from the record.

Whatever the source of data corruption, it creates the need to filter and clean data, as these observations will adversely affect the results obtained during statistical analysis. Lequeux (1997) notes that data filtering and cleaning can be a difficult and tedious task, with the need to be able to differentiate between a market crash and incorrect data entry. The solution to this issue involves setting up filtering algorithms that are informed by the researcher's expertise and understanding of the underlying market.

Some data suppliers offer pre-filtered historical datasets. For example, through a contractual arrangement with the Chicago Board Options Exchange (CBOE), the BODB offers a reprocessed version of the CBOE's Market Data Reports (MDR), whereby the MDR records have been screened for corrupt or duplicate observations. Bolland *et al* (1998) indicate that Reuters pages are subject to some pre-filtering involving an automated procedure to remove any extreme observations, and they also note that the pages are '"throttled" so that prices are not updated at such a rate they become unreadable.

Dunis *et al* (1998) describe the data-filtering process within a specific bank. The methodology has the primary goal of suppressing individual outliers, and uses the median of the last three ticks as a basis for the cleaning procedure. They highlight that cleaning and filtering of an archived database will typically be far more rigorous than what can feasibly be achieved for incoming real-time data.

The filtering method used and supplied by Olsen & Associates is described further in Panel 3.2.

The treatment of time

The timescales used in the time-series analysis of financial data have shortened in two respects over recent years: firstly, in terms of the observation frequency, or differencing interval, ie the period of clock time for which price changes or returns are computed; and, secondly, the data-sample period, ie the clock time between the first and last observations in the dataset. Traditionally, researchers studied data with a differencing interval of one month for a data-sample period covering several decades. As more data became available, there was a move towards studying daily data collected over a number of years. The focus nowadays is on the use of high-frequency data for a sample period that is often as short as a few days.

Thus both the differencing interval and the data-sample period have decreased in length. For a given data-sample period, the relationship

---

Panel 3.2: Olsen Filtering System

Olsen & Associates is a data supplier with particular expertise in the filtering and cleansing of real-time and archived high-frequency datasets, for both single-source and merged feeds. Its data service employs adaptive filters that can deal with changing market conditions and new instruments.

The design of robust filtering algorithms must address the following issues:

✦ market structures and data structures differ;

✦ different data sources have different quality controls and reliability;

✦ there are many different types of erroneous data entries;

✦ filters must have a high degree of adaptability to cope with time-varying statistical properties; and

✦ filters must be able to handle irregularly spaced data.

Filtering of foreign exchange data is more problematic due to round-the-clock global trading, where average market volatility varies by a factor of three during any 24-hour period. Also, foreign exchange trading is an over-the-counter market that is active in different time zones, and hence there is no centralised source of information for collecting all quotes.

The Olsen Filtering System consists of a series of hierarchical, modular filters that are flexible enough to adapt to the properties of high-frequency data. The filters draw upon a database of past filtering results, applying knowledge of past price behaviour to current data. The filtering system has the following features:

✦ multiple filtering criteria, with each quote component validated by its own adaptive filter;

✦ quantitative measurements of credibility applied to each quote;

✦ tested price changes that are related to statistical measures of seasonal and recent volatility; and

✦ composite time series originating from multiple sources can be filtered.

---

between the differencing interval and sample size is a rectangular hyperbola. This relationship is highly non-linear, with the sample size increasing at a faster and faster rate as the differencing interval is reduced. Therefore, while the length of the data-sample period has also tended to fall as the differencing interval has been reduced, the net effect has been towards much larger sample sizes.

The shortening of the data sample period is usually justified by the potential problem of non-stationarity of the data. Since high-frequency data is now available for data-sample periods similar to those for daily data, this raises the question of whether increasing the observation frequency, ie chopping up a given data period into, for example, minutes rather than days, improves the resulting estimation. Increasing observation frequency with a fixed length observation interval does not necessarily improve parameter estimation, and hence having more data does not always improve matters. As a consequence, Zhou (1998) introduced the concept of *f-consistency*, which is the consistency of an estimator as the observation frequency increases while the data period is held constant. For example, for a stationary process, increasing the observation frequency has no effect on estimates of the mean but it does improve estimates of the variance (Merton, 1980).

Figure 3.1 Time and high-frequency data

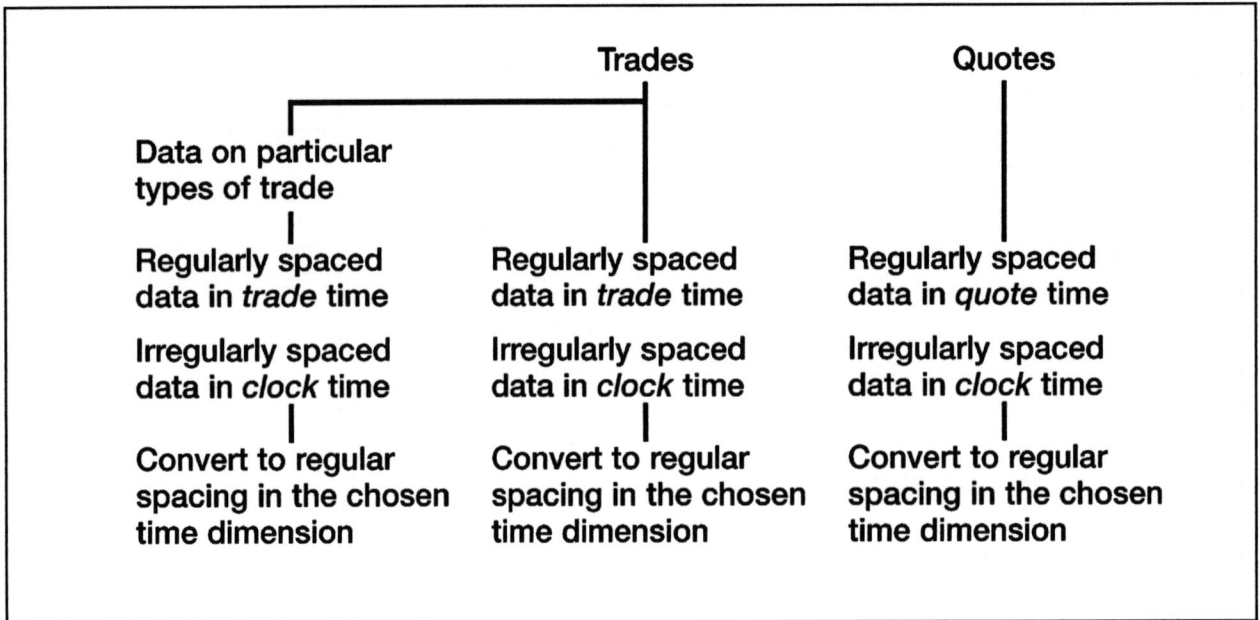

Trades		Quotes

Data on particular
types of trade

Regularly spaced
data in *trade* time

Regularly spaced
data in *trade* time

Regularly spaced
data in *quote* time

Irregularly spaced
data in *clock* time

Irregularly spaced
data in *clock* time

Irregularly spaced
data in *clock* time

Convert to regular
spacing in the chosen
time dimension

Convert to regular
spacing in the chosen
time dimension

Convert to regular
spacing in the chosen
time dimension

Irregular versus regular spacing in clock time

There are essentially two types of analysis that can be conducted with high-frequency data. First, analysis where the information concerning each trade or quote is processed independently, eg the distribution of trade sizes by time of day. Second, analysis of the time series of trades, returns, quotes, etc, in which the time sequence is crucial (for example, the autocorrelation of returns). The latter case is complicated by the fact that, in contrast to daily, weekly or monthly data, high-frequency data using trades or quotes are randomly spaced in time. This characteristic results in intra-day seasonalities in key market variables such as price volatility, traded volume, and bid–ask spreads (Chapter 5). Such sporadic trading makes measuring volatility problematic and this dictates a need to view volatility as a process rather than a number (Goodhart and O'Hara, 1997).

The distinction between trade and quote data, and between regularly and irregularly spaced time series is illustrated in Figure 3.1, along with the independent analysis of particular types of trade data. Initially, trade data is regularly spaced in trade time, while quote data is regularly spaced in quote time, and both are irregularly spaced in clock time. This data can then be converted into a format that is regularly spaced in the chosen dimension, eg clock time, by discarding observations.

Some studies are concerned with trades of a particular type, assuming the relevant identifiers are part of the dataset. For example, the data may identify arbitrage trades, inter-market-maker trades, programme trades, basket trades, worked principal trades, block trades, etc. The analysis may deal with time-independent features of such trades, eg the size distribution of block trades. However, the analysis may involve an event study of each selected trade, the price impact of block trades, for example, in which case the analysis becomes a time-series problem and a time dimension must be chosen.

Although the empirical literature does not offer any universally accepted approach to the problem of irregularly spaced high-frequency data, the most commonly adopted approaches involve either working in tick time or adopting regular spacing in clock time. These alternatives assume different underlying mechanics of price evolution. Using tick time assumes that the price evolves along a univariate time index relating to the dynamics of price observations. Using clock time assumes that the price process evolves on the timescale of the chosen interval.

Tick time

Various interpretations of "tick by tick" appear in the literature, variously involving quote-by-quote data, trade-by-trade data, and combined trade and quote data. Essentially, tick time assigns one time unit per tick. Conducting the analysis in tick time implies investigation on a trade-to-trade or quote-to-quote basis, which results in irregular spacing in clock time. It is also possible to study a time series containing both trades and quote revisions, and to analyse this in terms of "activity time", ie event to event (Goodhart and Payne, 1996). Such definitions of time tend to give more weight to periods with high activity levels. Further discussion of timescaling appears below.

Regular spacing in clock time

This involves converting the irregular timings of quotes or trades to regularly spaced intervals in clock time (sometimes referred to as "binning" the data). Various possibilities have been employed for constructing a regularly spaced time series from tick-by-tick data. A frequently used method is to sample intra-daily data at regular intervals of physical time. Any resulting gaps in the data must either be resolved by interpolation or treated as missing observations. The time-series methodology applied to such data must therefore be able to cope with these issues.

The choice of a given fixed time span, such as five or 10 minutes, is necessarily somewhat arbitrary. Bolland et al (1998) noted that the choice of time interval can have serious implications for the quality of the final model produced. Dacco' and Satchell (1998) discussed the importance of such issues of temporal aggregation in high-frequency data analysis. The aggregation of transactions data into a short fixed time interval is likely to result in some intervals with no new information and conditional heteroscedasticity of a particular form will be introduced into the data. If a long fixed time interval is chosen, some interesting features of the data will inevitably be lost.

The choice between trade-to-trade (or quote-to-quote) data, and data that is regularly spaced in time is important because the differently spaced data means that the hypothesis being tested is different. There may be substantial differences in the clock time between different trades (or quotes), for example trades (or quotes) may be clustered in clock time. Since the price-generating process may be hypothesised to evolve in trade time, quote time or calendar time, the appropriate version of time must be used in the analysis. Thus a study of return autocorrelations using trade-to-trade returns uses trade time, and the time intervals between trades are treated as equivalent, even if one interval is 10 seconds and another is 10 minutes. A study of return autocorrelations, using minute-to-minute returns, ignores the fact that between some trades used in computing these returns there were perhaps 20 trades, while for other trades there may have been no intervening trades. Thus, autocorrelation in trade-to-trade returns is a different concept from autocorrelation in minute-to-minute returns.

A common method when using clock time is to take the last (or first) price in each time interval for use in computing a returns series. Previous trade information must be maintained for any intervals with no data. It should be noted that using the average value for each time interval would distort the data by introducing positive serial correlation and reducing the variance. The use of linear interpolation to impute prices to the chosen times necessarily introduces distortions into the data series, as it is effectively averaging the data over time. Further discussion of the above issues appears in the next main section.

Mucklow (1994) analysed three alternative ways of dealing with non-trading periods when converting trade or quote data into fixed-length time intervals. Suppose that 10-minute time periods are being used, and that there was a trade at one minute past the hour at a price of 100 pence, and the next trade was another 28 minutes later at 29 minutes past the hour for a price of 110 pence. The returns for the two 10-minute periods of 11–20 minutes past the hour (period-2) and 21-30 minutes past the hour (period-3) may be computed using any of the following:

✦ *Realisation method*. Period-2 return is 0%, with no trade implying no equilibrium price change. The period-3 return is 110/100 = 10%.

✦ *Quasi-accrual method*. Allocate the price increase evenly over the period of the price movement. Since the price increase of 10p occurred over a 28-minute period, or 0.36p per minute, the period-2 return is 3.6%, while the period-3 return is 3.24% plus any price change over the last minute of this period. This approach gives returns with a lower variance than the other two methods because it is averaging over time.

✦ *Consecutive-returns method*. The returns for periods 2 and 3 are undefined and become missing values.

While returns computed using trade prices are subject to non-trading periods and bid–ask bounce (see below), returns computed using quotes are not (Mucklow, 1994).

Barclay and Litzenberger (1988) discuss three methods of converting trade data into intra-day returns over fixed time intervals for the purpose of measuring the price response to announcements. The *continuous-time approach* uses maximum likelihood to estimate expected returns over fixed-length intra-day intervals using irregularly spaced transaction data. If a return accrues over more than one interval, this technique assigns a fraction of the return to each interval in a way that maximises the overall likelihood of the sample. This approach is broadly similar to the quasi-accrual method described above. The *cumulative-return technique* is based on the last transaction prices within each interval. If there is no trade in consecutive intervals, the return for the current interval is undefined and will thus cause a problem with missing returns observations. This is the same as the consecutive-return method described above. The *transaction-return technique* measures returns over a fixed number of transactions, rather than over intervals of fixed length. This is based on the implicit assumption that the speed of response to new information is measured more accurately in transaction time rather than clock time.

Further, the data-generating process may evolve in some other version of time, such as volume, volatility, news arrivals, etc. For example, the justification for the mixture of distributions hypothesis uses news-arrival time. Also, it is possible to convert the data into observations that are regularly spaced in some dimension other than clock time – volume, for example – with an observation for every 100 contracts traded.

Heteroscedasticity and time deformation

If short-interval returns are independently and identically distributed, there is a simple relationship between the differencing interval and return variance. The variance of returns over long periods (comprising T short periods) is equal to T times the variance over a single short period. However, when using high-frequency data, returns are unlikely to be independently and identically distributed, therefore this relationship will not hold. For example, Müller *et al* (1995) showed that the volatility of foreign exchange returns does not increase in the predicted manner as the differencing interval is lengthened, and concluded that forex data are not self-similar fractals, ie the distribution of exchange rates is not invariant to changes in the differencing interval. The notion of timescaling has been proposed to deal with this problem (Müller *et al*, 1990, Dacorogna *et al*, 1993, and Schnidrig, 1998).

An empirical relationship between the length of the differencing interval and mean absolute price change (which is similar to the variance of returns) has been obtained for forex markets (Müller *et al*, 1990). Piccinato *et al* (1998) have shown that this timescaling law also applies to interest rate futures. This law has been used to remove heteroscedasticity from returns data by converting returns to a new form of time. Time is expanded at volatility peaks and contracted during inactive periods, so that the resulting returns series is homoscedastic.

Müller *et al* (1995) applied timescaling to remove two different forms of heteroscedasticity. First, they used timescaling to remove daily and weekly seasonalities in volatility – in which case the resulting time is termed υ-time, or business time. They have also used timescaling to remove Arch (autoregressive conditional heteroscedasticity) effects from the data – when the resulting time is called τ-time, or intrinsic time. Müller *et al* (1995) subjected both 20-minute returns and one-day returns for US$/DM exchange rates to timescaling so as to convert them to υ-time. They found that the resulting autocorrelation functions for the absolute values (or volatility) of these timescaled returns were the same, ie they exhibited a fractal property. Despite daily and weekly seasonalities having been removed from the volatility of returns, Arch effects may still remain. Therefore, Müller *et al* (1995) proposed a transformation of υ-time to τ-time in order to remove these Arch effects. Thus the use of τ-time is an alternative to Arch models.

Such timescaling is designed for adjusting a univariate time series. It is not applicable to a multivariate analysis, such as when studying links between different markets, as two observations may have the same deformed time and therefore be paired, but their clock times may be markedly different.

The problem of dealing with heteroscedastic data by scaling the returns has been discussed by many other researchers, including Clark (1973), Tauchen and Pitts (1983), Müller *et al* (1990), Ghysels *et al* (1998), and Engle and Russell (1998). The approach adopted by Clark (1973) of using volume to scale the data is not usually a feasible option for forex markets.

Zhou (1996, 1998) identifies heteroscedasticity as one of the most significant characteristics of financial time series. The problem tends to be more severe as the sampling frequency is increased, and is thus a source of particular difficulty when modelling high-frequency data. Zhou discusses two approaches to reduce heteroscedasticity in high-frequency data, namely de-volatilisation and normalisation, which are similar in spirit to the timescaling proposals discussed above.

De-volatilisation involves analysing observations at unequally spaced time periods. By taking more observations in a volatile market and fewer observations in a steady market, it becomes possible to reduce or eliminate heteroscedasticity. Essentially, this involves shortening the differencing interval in clock time when volatility is high, and increasing the interval when volatility is low.

Normalisation is an alternative to de-volatilisation, and is designed for applications requiring observations that are equally spaced in clock time. To normalise an equally spaced time series, it is necessary to estimate the volatility of two consecutive prices and then rescale the return by its standard deviation. Zhou (1998) illustrates this point by means of the following example: "When daily prices are required in an empirical analysis, we can use high-frequency data in every 24-hour period to estimate daily volatility. We then normalise daily returns by the square root of the estimated volatility." Since normalisation does not require the estimation of volatility every tick, computational time is not a major concern.

Many financial models assume homoscedasticity, and therefore employing de-volatilisation or normalisation can increase the power of such models. It is important to recognise that the two approaches are not equivalent and a choice should be made dependent on the application. De-volatilisation lengthens volatile periods and so tends to place more weight on volatile periods. Normalisation involves a re-scaling of returns, essentially equalising returns from volatile and stable periods, and so does not place particular importance upon the market conditions from which the data is generated.

Duration

In the conventional analysis, the price (or return) of the security is regarded as the random variable. A different approach is to treat time as the random variable (Zumbach, 1998). The time elapsed between trades or quotes is termed "duration", and is viewed as extremely useful in analysing the trading process. Such gaps may be perceived as a signal, just as the trade size itself is perceived as informative. This perspective leads to questions such as "how long will it take for returns to reach a specified level for the first time?" (the "first hitting time"), or "how long will it take for returns to exit from a specified band around the current price for the first time?" (the "first exit time"). Gaviridis (1998) noted that the use of high-frequency data is essential for investigating the extent to which timing is important in financial time series. Dacorogna *et al* (1993) showed how the time dimension of trading can be responsible for the trading patterns observed in high-frequency foreign exchange data.

When analysing a time series of trades, a common approach is to discard the clock times of the trades and retain only the time sequence. Thus, whether there is a one-second or a one-hour gap between successive trades is of no interest. However, the clock time between trades represents valuable information. For example, an absence of trading may be because bad news has arrived, and those in possession of this private information do not own the asset and are unable to short sell (Diamond and Verrecchia, 1987). Alternatively, an absence of trading may be because no news has arrived. Recent microstructure models (eg Easley and O'Hara, 1992) use the length of time elapsed between consecutive transactions as a signal revealing information known to market participants. Easley *et al* (1997b) proposed analysing quote revisions by market-makers as an extensive form game. They showed how the parameters of the decision tree can be estimated using signed trade data to give the implied probabilities that: (a) information has arrived before the start of trading; (b) any news is bad news; (c) an uninformed trader chooses to trade; and (d) a trader is informed. They also showed how trade size can be incorporated into this flexible model. Despite being based on trades, this model relies on clock time.

One of the earliest studies to model the time gaps between trades was Garbade and Lieber (1977), who found that, over short intervals, trades in IBM and Potlatch shares tended to cluster in time and be on a particular side of the market. Dufour and Engle (1997) incorporated the elapsed time between trades into a VAR regression model of quote changes and trade volume and direction for 18 US stocks during 1990–91. They found for their sample that shorter time gaps were associated with both faster and larger quote changes. Hausman *et al* (1992) made allowance for clock-time effects in order to examine whether trade-to-trade prices are stable in transaction time versus clock time.

Engle and Russell (1997) proposed a new way of modelling the time gaps between irregularly spaced events such as trades or quote revisions, termed the Autoregressive Conditional Duration (ACD) model. Engle and Russell (1998) found evidence of duration clustering for trades in IBM shares during 1990–91, ie short time gaps between trades tend to cluster together. Engle (1996) examined the same data and concluded that shorter time gaps between trades are associated with higher volatility.

Future developments are likely to involve the refinement of econometric techniques that incorporate the information in the clock time between trades into an analysis of trade-to-trade data. In addition to the separate analysis of time series of trades or quotes, future research is likely to address the modelling of the interaction between trades and quotes in a way that incorporates the time elapsed between trades and quotes (Engle and Lunde, 1998).

Heterogeneous markets

Müller *et al* (1997) argued that there is a fundamental asymmetry between short- and long-term volatility in forex markets. Foreign exchange traders are heterogeneous and can be divided into short- and long-term traders. Short-term traders react not only to changes in short-term volatility but also to changes in long-term volatility (ie volatility measured over longer differencing intervals), while long-term traders react only to changes in long-term volatility. The consequence of this behaviour is that long-run volatility affects subsequent short-run volatility, but the reverse is not the case. There is an asymmetry in the lagged correlations of volatility, with long-term volatility leading short-term volatility. This effect is not present in a simple Garch (generalised Arch) model.

To address this, Müller *et al* (1997) and Dacorogna *et al* (1996, 1998) developed a modified form of the Arch model, termed Harch (heterogeneous-interval Arch), where the conditional variance equation contained squares of lagged *aggregate* returns, ie the previous volatility over longer and longer time intervals. Therefore, the signs of price changes matter, and price changes in the same direction have a bigger effect than changes that are offsetting. Using quotes from 1987–94 for US\$/DM spot foreign-exchange rates for 30-minute periods in υ-time, they have found that the Harch(7) model fits this data better than does Garch(1,1). Because estimating Harch models is computationally demanding, Dacorogna *et al* (1998) developed a new form of Harch model – an exponential moving average Harch (or EMA-Harch) – which is easier to fit than Harch and performs well in forecasting short-term volatility.

Constructing continuous series

A primary task in dealing with high-frequency data is the construction of continuous series from the raw tick data. Sampling will be on the basis of either tick time or clock time (see earlier in this chapter). Choice of a time-deformation method will naturally produce a continuous series in some version of activity time. Researchers occasionally choose to sample from such a series, eg every *n* ticks. If clock time is chosen in order to work in fixed time intervals, a decision must be taken on an appropriate interval frequency and the question of interpolating any resultant missing data points must be addressed.

Whenever the nature of the differencing interval is changed, a different hypothesis is effectively being tested. Furthermore, choosing one differencing interval rather than another again involves choosing to test a different hypothesis. For example, while one-minute returns may have negative autocorrelation, 60-minute returns may not. Therefore, in order to test a given hypothesis, researchers may have little choice of differencing interval in practice.

Differencing intervals in clock time

To the extent that there is a choice of differencing interval in clock time, this involves a balance between the problems incurred by making the interval longer and those incurred when the interval is made shorter. Converting data for individual trades or quotes into a time series of high-frequency data that is regularly spaced in clock time precludes some forms of analysis, eg testing hypotheses in trade or quote time.

With regard to relatively long differencing intervals, much of the available data is discarded, and thus there is a risk that valuable information is lost. This loss of information takes two forms. First, any intervening observations within the interval are discarded. Second, regularly spaced observations usually have a value for price, and possibly a value for traded volume, during each time interval. However, much of the remaining information, such as individual trade or quote size, trade or quote time, trade type, and the identity of the quoter or the trade counterparties, is lost.

When using relatively short differencing intervals, numerous different problems are faced, as follows:

✦ missing values;

✦ inaccurate time recordings;

✦ lack of normality;

✦ stale prices; and

✦ non-synchronous prices.

Each of these problem areas is discussed further below.

Missing values

There are likely to be time intervals with no trades or quotes, leading to the "missing observation" problem. De Jong and Nijman (1997) and Lundin et al (1999) have proposed methods for computing correlation coefficients between two time series that in each case avoids this non-trading bias by imputing values for the intervals with missing values. An analysis of a time series of trades or quotes, with irregular intervals in clock time, has the advantage that, by definition, there cannot be any missing observations, provided that no trades have been omitted from the dataset (a characteristic very hard to detect).

Lequeux (1997) has indicated that whatever method of interpolation is used to deal with missing values (ie linear, weighted or exponential), the artificial smoothing will create fictitious autocorrelations and will impact upon data analysis. The shorter the differencing interval, the more data points that must be interpolated. Lengthening of the differencing interval will always reduce the unwanted effect of interpolated data points.

Inaccurate time recordings

Users of high-frequency data should be aware of the implications of potential recording lags when constructing continuous series. In the case of an electronically traded market, time recording of quotes and trades should be reliable as they are created by the system's audit trail. However, in some markets the times recorded for trades are inaccurate. The time stamps may be subject to a systematic delay, for example 20 seconds, and some researchers have adjusted the times by subtracting such a delay period from the recorded times. In other cases the time stamps may be subject to random inaccuracy, which is sometimes well outside the tolerance set by the exchange rules and claimed for the dataset. For example, in some open outcry markets, quotes and trades may not be time stamped until the trader's transaction card is entered in the computer system. For high-frequency data, these inaccuracies become more important because as the time interval shortens, either more trades or quotes are assigned to the wrong interval, or the time sequence of trades or quotes is incorrect.

Lack of normality

It has been argued that returns in financial markets will have a normal distribution because of the central-limit theorem. This states that the sum of a large number of independently and identically distributed variables has a normal distribution. For log returns, the return over a month is the sum of all the one-minute returns over the month, and so monthly returns tend to normality. However, as the time period over which returns are measured becomes shorter, this argument for normality loses its force. The empirical evidence from high-frequency data tends to support this prediction, and the distribution of returns becomes less normal as the differencing interval is shortened. Therefore, the non-normality of returns is a more substantial problem for analysts using high-frequency data than for those using less-frequent observations. Non-normality is important, not only because it invalidates the standard statistical tests, but also because the assumption of normality underlies models such as the Black–Scholes option pricing model and is important for value-at-risk analysis where the densities in the lower tail of the distribution are of paramount importance.

Following Harry Markowitz, the usual measure of volatility is the variance. However, when using high-frequency data Guillaume *et al* (1997) argued, in connection with foreign exchange markets, that the average absolute return is a superior measure because the fourth moment of the returns distribution does not exist, as found by Dacorogna *et al* (1995) and Müller, Dacorogna and Pictet (1998).

Stale prices

A price is "stale" when it refers to the price of a trade that took place some time ago. If trade data is converted into price data that is regularly spaced in clock time, such as 15-minute returns, stale prices will be present to some degree. This is because if the 15-minute returns are based on the last price in each 15-minute interval, the price could be current or it could be up to 15 minutes old. In consequence, returns may be for trades that were apart by anywhere from 0 minutes (if the first price was right at the end of the previous 15-minute period, while the second price was right at the start of the current 15-minute period) to 30 minutes (for the opposite extremes). Treating such returns as if they were based on an equivalent time interval can introduce bias. Using trade data in trade time (or quote data in quote time) avoids the stale-price problem. Any data that is regularly spaced in clock time is vulnerable to stale prices.

The choice of time interval impacts upon the stale-price effect in two ways. First, using shorter time intervals implies that the maximum possible staleness of prices is reduced (assuming that the non-trading or missing-value problem is not solved by using the most recent price, even though it was from many time intervals ago). Second, using shorter time intervals also means that the magnitude of changes in price between intervals is smaller, and so the size of the stale-price effect, relative to the effect being studied, may increase. On balance, stale prices are a more serious problem for shorter time periods.

Non-synchronous prices

When prices subject to the stale-price effect are combined in any way (eg in multivariate analysis), this gives rise to the non-synchronous trading problem. For instance, reporting of daily closing prices in the financial press implies that they are all equally spaced observations at 24-hour intervals. Campbell *et al* (1997) noted that "such an assumption can create a false impression of predictability in price changes and returns even if true price changes or returns are statistically independent". Several explicit models of non-trading have been developed, for example Lo and MacKinlay (1988, 1990). The common theme of these and other such models is the modelling of the behaviour of asset returns that are mistakenly assumed to be measured at evenly spaced time intervals.

A good illustration of the non-synchronous trading problem involves the computation of indexes. Stock market indexes are usually calculated using the most recent transaction price of each share. Since shares in the market index do not trade continuously, it is highly likely that some of the prices used in computing the index occurred a few minutes – or even a few hours – previously. This means that, implicitly, an index computed using such non-synchronised prices measures an average value of the "true" index over the period to which the constituent prices relate.

As an example, suppose the "true" value of the market index has been rising steadily throughout the day because the "true" prices of the constituent shares have been rising. Since share prices are trending upwards, an index computed using transactions that took place at different times throughout the day will be lower than the current "true" value of the index. In effect, it will be a weighted average of the "true" values of the index during the day, where the weights depend on the times of the actual trades used in constructing the index. This averaging will introduce (or increase) positive serial correlation into changes in the index, and will also lower the variance and mean of the stock market index; although not its covariance with individual shares.

Many studies using high-frequency time series have employed data on a market index, eg the S&P500. The non-synchronicity bias implicit in the index increases in importance as the time interval used in the analysis becomes shorter, and as the magnitude of the effects being studied decreases in size. Thus, non-synchronicity bias is at its most troublesome when using data sampled at high frequency. Various techniques for purging the effects of non-synchronicity from index data have been used by many of the empirical studies discussed in Chapter 6.

Continuous series for futures or options contracts

Each derivative contract has a fixed expiry date with a life that is typically about nine months. At any point in time there are a number of outstanding contracts – such as the near contract, the next-near contract, the far contract, etc – meaning that there are always a number of different futures or options prices available at any time. Empirical researchers can choose either to analyse the data on a contract-by-contract basis, or to create a single continuous time series by joining together the data on the various contracts. Creating a continuous series from the various derivative contract maturities traded at any given time is an important issue whatever frequency of data is under consideration. The purpose is usually to create a single time series, using data on the most liquid contract. Most trading in stock index futures tends to remain in the near contract right up to delivery, while other futures tend to exhibit a switch some days or weeks before delivery. For instance, rollover in government bond futures will be partly determined by the "first notice day", which is the point from which contract holders may become obliged to deliver an underlying bond.

There are four obvious occasions on which the data series can switch from using the near to the second nearest contract:

✦ The switch may occur at the point of volume crossover, ie on the day when traded volume in the second-nearest contract exceeds traded volume in the nearest maturity (front month) contract. This is a commonly used method applied in a very large number of empirical studies.

✦ The switch may occur at the point of open interest crossover, ie when open interest in the second-nearest contract exceeds that in the nearest maturity contract.

✦ Under the volume threshold method, the switch into the next contract occurs when its volume exceeds a predetermined threshold.

✦ The switch may occur at a pre-determined date, ie a fixed number of days from the expiry of the nearest maturity contract.

In each case, if overnight returns are ignored, there will be no danger of calculating returns based on two different maturity contracts at any time.

A different approach to selecting a way of joining contracts together is to a specify a set of desirable axioms that any such rule should meet, and then to discover which rules satisfy the axioms. This has led to the development of rules that involve a gradual shift from the prices of the near contract to those of the second-nearest contract, rather than a single discrete switch. Geiss (1995) set out six criteria to be met by a price index that links the price series of different futures contracts. Only one class of price index meets these conditions – a weighted average of the prices of the outstanding contracts, where the weights are a function of time. While many possible patterns of weights are possible, Geiss considered only a two-price index, where the weight on any one price level is tent-shaped. Thus, the initial weight on the price of a particular contract is zero. It increases over time in a linear manner to 100%, and then declines to zero as the next contract is included in the price index. In this way the price of each contract gradually enters and then leaves the price index before the contract expires, and so there is a smooth seamless splice.

Rougier (1996) adopted a similar approach, and derived a set of weights for the prices of outstanding contracts, where the weights are a function of time. For two outstanding contracts, the weighted average price has a fixed maturity equal to the time between contract maturities (v), the weight on the near contract is m/v, and that on the far contract is (v–m)/v, where m is the maturity of the near contract. Thus, as for Geiss (1995), the weights on a particular contract are tent-shaped. For three outstanding contracts, three alternative sets of weights are permissible, with fixed maturities varying from v to (4/3)v.

This section of the chapter considers some of the main complications encountered in manipulating high-frequency data. We begin with a discussion of how some such issues may be specific to trade or quote data, while others apply to both.

Key considerations in manipulating high-frequency data

Trade data versus quote data

There are typically three prices in existence for most financial assets at any given point in time, based on the bid, the ask and the latest trade. The trade price is often not equal to the bid or the ask, nor need it be bounded by these two prices (though it normally will be). The use of trade data clearly results in a single price series. In contrast, when using quote data, it is often necessary to construct a single price series on the basis of midpoint prices. This involves reducing the dual bid and ask price series to a single price series by computing the average of the bid and ask prices or the log(bid) and log(ask) prices. However, Ghysels *et al* (1998) have suggested that using the midpoint prices averages the outcomes of the distinct trading strategies of buyers and sellers, and high-frequency data reveals several differences in the properties of bid and ask price series. Andersen and Bollerslev (1997b) employed the average of bid and ask quotes to define exchange rates at any given time using a linear interpolation formula that uses two quotations immediately preceding and following the required sampling time.

The use of trade data to measure the current market price is subject to the problem that buy trades tend to be at the ask price, and sell trades tend to be at the bid price. It could be argued that the presence of a bid–ask spread will just introduce noise into price measurement and, given a large sample, tend to cancel out. However, using trade and quote data on US share options for 1976 and 1985, Vijh (1988) shows that there are about 30% more trades at the ask than at the bid. For US stocks the difference was only about 4%. For UK stocks over a two-year period, Board and Sutcliffe (1995b) found that 61.5% of trades were sells, while only 38.5% were buyer initiated. Therefore, the trade price can be a biased estimator of the midpoint price, although the direction of this bias may vary from market to market. Porter (1992) found that for US stocks, there are more buy trades at the open and close, while in Canada there are more sells at the open and more buys at the close. He argues that this may explain some intraday patterns in returns, and partly explain the weekend effect.

Trade data and quote data (including limit orders) are likely to have some types of information in common, for instance price data, volume or size, direction (buy or sell), timing (of a trade or the posting of a quote), and identity (of a quoter, or the buy and sell sides of a trade). However, there are important differences between quote and trade data, and some items of information that seem similar incorporate important differences. These are discussed below.

Sampling the price process

Trade prices are non-random samples of the underlying price process because they tend to occur just after new information has arrived. Therefore, for trade data the variance of the observed price series varies over time and will tend to overstate the variance of prices (Goodhart and

O'Hara, 1997). These biases may well be smaller for quotes because only one person is required to update a quote, while two people are needed to generate a trade.

Bid–ask spreads

In quote-driven markets, quotes reveal the quoted bid–ask spread at each point in time, and at any one time there is a unique touch or inside spread (the lowest ask less the highest bid). Trades must be either buyer- or seller-motivated, and so are likely to be at either the buy price or the sell price. Therefore at any point in time, unless there are simultaneous buy and sell trades, the traded spread (the price of a buy trade less the price of a sell trade) is not defined. A further possibility is that at some moments there are several buy (or sell) trades at different prices. In such situations there is not a well defined traded spread. Thus it is easier to measure the quoted spread than the traded spread. Further discussion of spread estimation appears below.

Volume of quote/trade

For trades, the size of each trade is the actual volume traded, while for quotes it represents the maximum volume up to which the quote is valid. The volume of trades can be summed to give total trading volume for the interval, although by the foregoing definition it is not possible to estimate traded volume by summing the quote volumes. Thus volume is only available from trade data. It should be noted that some high-frequency datasets from open-outcry markets contain estimated, rather than actual, values for volume.

Direction of quote/trade

Whether the quote is an ask or a bid is an intrinsic part of the data. For many purposes, trades must also be identified as a buy or a sell. Some datasets give the trade direction, eg trades on quote-driven markets where market-makers are presumed to be passive counterparties. However, for trades on order-driven markets the trade direction may not be apparent (see below).

Time of quote/trade

Since a trade is an event, it has a unique time. A quote has a start time and an end time. The length of time for which quotes are valid differs considerably between markets. For example, there is an important difference between quotes on stock markets and those on futures markets: on futures markets quotes are typically valid only as long as the breath is warm, while quotes posted by dealers on quote-driven stock markets are valid until withdrawn. Similarly, limit orders on order-driven stock markets are valid until filled or withdrawn.

Identity of counterparties

The identity of a trader making a quote is usually public, while the identity of the parties to a trade is generally confidential. In consequence, in quoting a particular price, traders know they are revealing information about their trading strategy (eg their current inventory), while the information content of trade prices is different because the identity of the traders is usually unknown – sometimes even to each other.

There are various levels of information on the identity of the counterparties involved in a trade. One level is the identity of the floor traders or brokers involved in a trade, and this may be observable by other floor traders. A deeper level of information is the identity of the principals involved in the trade, and this information may not be readily available to the exchange. Many high-frequency datasets do not contain information on trader or quoter identities, even if this is known to the exchange, and this can sometimes be due to regulatory constraints.

Depth of actual or potential trades

The maximum quantities that traders are prepared to buy or sell at stated prices are revealed from the quote information for all traders. In the absence of multiple quotes for each trader, specifying their entire demand–supply function, data on the most competitive quotes for each trader is still very useful in quantifying market depth at each point in time. Hausman *et al* (1992) gained insights into the market microstructure from the price impact per unit of volume traded, which they measured in terms of how the conditional distribution of price changes shifts in response to a trade of a given volume.

Number of quotes or trades

Quote data permits the computation of the number of quote changes, while trade data allows the calculation of the number of trades within a given time period. In empirical studies, considerable use has been made of the number-of-trades variable, while much less use has been made of the number-of-quotes variable. Indeed, it has been argued that the number of trades is a better proxy for information arrival than is total volume.

In addition to using trade or quote data for a time series analysis, it can also be used to analyse trades or quotes where the time of the observation is irrelevant, eg studies of price clustering or the distribution of prices. Such analyses can be performed using regularly or irregularly spaced trade or quote data, and the results are comparable with those for studies that have made a different choice, as they are both testing the same basic hypothesis. However, the full set of trade or quote data provides a larger dataset than one that has been compressed by discarding intervening observations.

Trade data represents the most fundamental level of data on the trading process. However, researchers may seek data on additional variables related to the trading process, eg the internal aggregation of orders into one large trade, the internal crossing of trades, the process of deciding when to trade (the trading strategy), the portfolio positions of traders at the time they decide to trade, the motives for trading, etc. Additional issues are considered below.

Bid–ask bounce and reversals

In addition to being a transaction cost that introduces noise into arbitrage-based pricing relationships, the bid–ask spread also influences the dynamics of a time series of prices. If no new information arrives to the market, the fundamental value of a financial asset remains constant; yet observed variation may be caused by the difference between bid and

Figure 3.2: Illustration of the bid–ask bounce effect

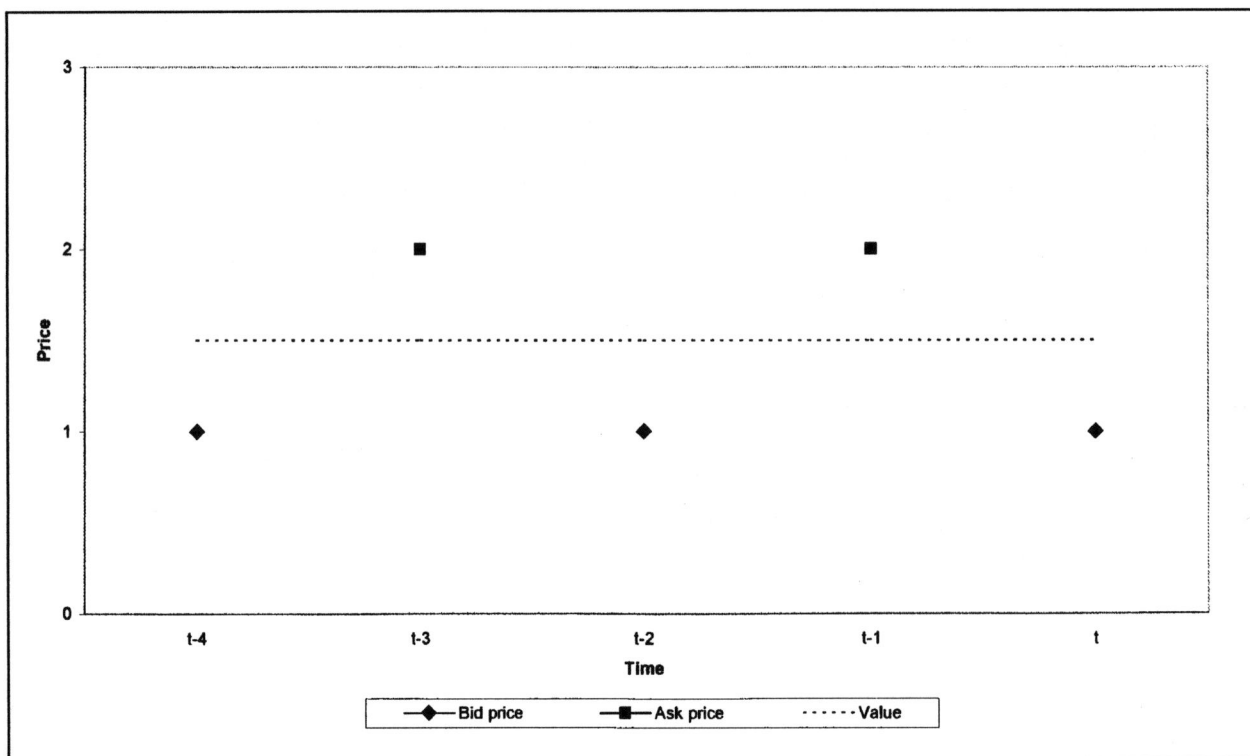

ask prices. Clearly, any bouncing between bid and ask prices gives rise to strong negative autocorrelation.

A price "reversal" is defined as a price change that is in the opposite direction to the previous price change. A price change in the same direction as the previous price change is termed a "continuation". Reversals have been used empirically as a proxy for returns autocorrelation. One reason for this is that the data from US futures exchanges such as the Chicago Mercantile Exchange (CME) only contain trades that involve a price change; hence the true returns autocorrelation is not recoverable.

Reversals are generally a consequence of the random arrival of buy and sell orders that are executed at stationary bid and ask prices. The price change transaction series will then display a sequence of up and down movements between the bid and ask prices. Continuations, on the other hand, are usually associated with information arriving into the market. Traders then revise their view of the value of the security and if this new value lies outside the current bid–ask spread, the spread will change to capture the new security value. Thus, a low level of reversals (ie a high level of continuations) is typically a consequence of new information arriving into the market.

Since many price changes do not involve movement in the equilibrium price but are merely reversals between bid and ask prices, it is desirable to control for such effects. Hausman *et al* (1992) noted that if, for example, in a sequence of three trades the first and third were buyer-initiated and the second was seller-initiated, the sequence would exhibit reversals due solely to the bid–ask "bounce" (Figure 3.2).

Inferring trade direction

For many high-frequency datasets (such as those for the London Stock Exchange), the trade direction for at least some types of trade (agent to market-maker, for example) can be clearly identified. Nevertheless, for many order-driven markets the trade direction may not be apparent. Clearly every trade has a buyer and a seller, but researchers often need to know which of these is more anxious to conduct the trade and is therefore willing to pay in the form of the bid–ask spread. A number of different methods have been developed for estimating trade direction; some use quote data in addition to the trade data, while others use just trade data.

Trade and quote data

If the trade occurs at the bid price, it is most likely to be a "sell", and if it occurs at the ask, it is most likely a "buy". This is the simplest approach to classification of trade direction, but may result in a large proportion of trades with indeterminate direction, ie trades that were not at either the bid or the ask price.

Hasbrouck (1987, 1988) and Blume *et al* (1989) have suggested classifying a transaction as a buy if the transaction price is higher than the mean of the prevailing bid–ask quote, and classifying it as a sell if the price is lower. If the traded price equals the mean of the prevailing quoted bid–ask spread, the trade is classified as "indeterminate". This quote-based method results in far fewer indeterminate trades than if classifying according to transactions at the bid or at the ask. In this context Hausman *et al* (1992) defined a variable whose purpose was to indicate whether a transaction was buyer-initiated or seller-initiated. The variable takes the value 1 if the transaction price is greater than the average of the quoted bid and ask prices at a given time, the value -1 if the transaction price is less than the average of the quoted bid and ask prices at a given time, and 0 otherwise. If the transaction price is at the midpoint of the quoted bid and ask prices, the indicator is indeterminate. Note that these methods rely on the use of the midpoint, and therefore both quote and trade data must be available.

Trade data

The tick test, widely used by researchers without access to quote data, classifies a transaction as a buy, a sell or indeterminate if its price is greater than, less than, or equal to the previous transaction's price, respectively. Lee and Ready (1991) and Wood and McCorry (1994) tested the classificatory accuracy of the tick test. The former suggest 90% accuracy based on NYSE data, while the latter suggest 80–82% accuracy using Nasdaq data. However, using cleaner intra-day data from the Australian Stock Exchange, Aitken and Frino (1996) cast some doubt on the wider applicability of the tick test, since they found only 74% accuracy.

Hasbrouck (1998) proposed an estimation method (Markov chain Monte Carlo) that uses only trade data and that jointly estimates both the trade direction and the parameters of the model.

Comparison of the two approaches

A direct comparison of the tick test with the bid–ask mean rule was made by Robinson (1988), who examined a sample of 196 block trades initiated by two major Canadian life assurance companies and concluded that the bid–ask mean rule is considerably more accurate than the tick test.

Estimating various measures of the bid–ask spread

In quote-driven markets, dealers are typically obliged to continuously quote bid and ask prices, and thus an individual dealer's quoted spread is directly observed. The quoted market inside spread can then be inferred from the best bid and offer (BBO) prices – ie the highest bid and lowest offer. Effective spreads, as defined in (3.1) below, can then be computed by combining this information with transactions data. In contrast, order-driven markets place no obligation upon market-makers to post two-way quotes.

For markets where quote data is available, some researchers choose to split the trading day into discrete intervals and sample the first or last bid and ask prices in each time interval – Shyy and Lee (1995) did this using one-minute intervals, and Abhyankar *et al* (1995) using five-minute intervals. A more comprehensive method can be used (see ap Gwilym and Thomas, 1998; Board and Sutcliffe, 1995b), whereby the first bid and first ask of each day is taken as the opening spread, and a new spread is calculated whenever a new bid or ask is posted. In most futures markets, since quotes are usually valid only as long as the breath is warm, this method may be biased if the time that elapses between the bid and ask quotes is lengthy. It may then become necessary to restrict the sample to cases where the bids and asks are posted within very short periods of each other. Any locked or crossed quotes, ie where the bid is greater than or equal to the ask, must be discarded.

The quoted spread may overstate trading costs since trades can occur at prices within this spread, and this motivates calculation of the effective spread where transactions data is available. Petersen and Fialkowski (1994) calculated the effective spread for stocks based on the notion of "price improvement", which is the reduction in trading costs compared with the posted quotes. The price improvement is calculated as follows:

Ask price – Transaction price = Price improvement for buy orders
Transaction price – Bid price = Price improvement for sell orders.

Petersen and Fialkowski (1994) noted that a trader may receive price improvement by both buying and selling, and thus:

Effective spread = Quoted spread – 2 x (Price improvement)   (3.1)

Intuitively, the effective spread is the expected purchase price minus the expected sales price. The above equation assumes that the same price improvement is received on both the buy and the sell side. If this is not true, the estimated effective spread will be incorrect for individual observations. However, Petersen and Fialkowski (1994) have shown that the average estimated effective spread will still be correct. The evidence they presented indicated that quoted and effective spreads are significantly different in US equity markets. This implies that the quoted prices are not always representative of the best prices at which investors can transact.

Estimating effective spreads from trade data

A number of methods have been employed to estimate effective spreads from price change transactions data. This has been largely motivated by the fact that studies of US futures markets are unable to employ direct measures of the effective spread due to non-recording of quoted prices and zero price change transactions. The most prevalent methods in the literature at present are those proposed by Thompson and Waller (1988), Smith and Whaley (1994), Bhattacharya (1983) and Roll (1984).

Thompson and Waller (1988) estimated the bid–ask spread as the average absolute tick-to-tick price change over a time interval. If there are n price changes during an interval, the estimated spread over the interval is

$$S_{TW} = \frac{\sum_{i=1}^{n} |P_i - P_{i-1}|}{n} \tag{3.2}$$

where P is the price and i indexes the sequence of prices. The primary limitation of this measure is that transactions price changes may also be due to changes in the equilibrium price, rather than only to movements between the bid and ask prices.

Smith and Whaley (1994) showed how the magnitude of the bias in the above method depends on the variance of true price changes and they derived a measure based on the moments of the absolute price change distribution, which is shown to be robust to varying degrees of price change correlation and volatility. Assuming that the true price change over a given interval is distributed normally with mean zero and variance σ^2, the first two moments of the distribution of absolute price changes ($|\Delta Pt|$) are defined by:

$$E(|\Delta P_t|) = \sqrt{\frac{2}{\pi}} \, \sigma \, e^{-S_{SW}^2/2\sigma^2} - S_{SW} \, [1 - 2 \, N(S_{SW}/\sigma)] \tag{3.3}$$

$$E(|\Delta P_t|^2) = \sigma^2 + S_{SW}^2 \tag{3.4}$$

where S_{SW} is the estimated bid–ask spread, and $N(d)$ is the cumulative unit normal distribution function with upper integral limit d. To estimate the spread (and the variance of true price changes), $E(|\Delta Pt|)$ and $E(|\Delta Pt|^2)$ are replaced with the mean absolute price change and the mean squared price change from the observed futures price change distribution, and the equations are solved iteratively. Smith and Whaley (1994) empirically tested this method using daily data on the S&P500 futures contract, thus implicitly assuming that the effective spread is constant throughout any given day. For empirical examination of the estimator on an intra-day basis, see ap Gwilym and Thomas (1998).

The Bhattacharya (1983) method of calculating the spread is based on price reversals (see above). Therefore, this method only considers data consisting of non-overlapping consecutively reverting sets of three or more price records, to constitute a valid bid–ask–bid or ask–bid–ask sequence. It then assumes that an up-tick (down-tick) transaction price surrounded by down-tick (up-tick) prices represents an ask (bid) price.

Ma *et al* (1992) noted some of the shortcomings of this method. First, any positive serial correlation will result in dropping prices from the sample. Second, ignoring any large price changes that are not followed by a reversal may result in understating large quoted spreads. Followill and Rodriguez (1991) noted the potential difficulties with this method if applied to thinly traded securities with lengthy intervals between price changes.

Ma *et al* (1992) suggested that the Bhattacharya (1983) and Thompson and Waller (1988) measures may provide upper and lower bounds on the effective spread. They also showed that the use of these measures on US futures markets data (containing price change transactions only) tends to result in upwardly biased spreads at certain times of day (eg around lunchtime) when trades are relatively more likely to occur at unchanged prices. Both measures will also be affected by the degree of price clustering in the market.

The most commonly used spread measure in the literature is that of Roll (1984). With random arrival of buy and sell orders, a spread induces negative serial correlation in price changes as trades "bounce" between the bid and ask prices. Under the assumptions of efficient markets, a stationary underlying distribution of price changes and equal probability of arrival of buy and sell orders, Roll (1984) uses the first-order serial covariance of price changes to estimate the effective bid–ask spread as

$$S_{ROLL} = 2 \sqrt{-cov(\Delta P_i, \Delta P_{i-1})} \qquad (3.5)$$

where $\Delta P_i = P_i - P_{i-1}$. If the covariance is positive, possibly due to changes in the equilibrium price, the spread is undefined. This estimator only reflects order-processing costs, ignoring the adverse selection and inventory risk components of the bid–ask spread. Laux and Senchack (1992) argue that this is less of a problem in futures markets, where order-processing costs are the main component of the spread.

Seasonality

Analysis of high-frequency data has to cope with strong seasonal patterns, particularly on an intra-day basis. Empirical studies have highlighted a number of regularities in various market settings. As an example, the data represented in Figures 3.3 and 3.4 highlight the intra-day variability of returns volatility and traded volume for the Short Sterling futures contract over the period November 1992 to October 1993.

The key point to highlight is the U-shape in intra-day trading volume and volatility, patterns that are partly driven by the overnight closure of the markets. The case of the foreign exchange market is more complex due to its operating on a 24-hour basis. A second factor to note is the peaks in both volume and volatility at the times of public information release (UK macroeconomic announcements). Major news events are

Figure 3.3: Intraday standard deviation of five-minute returns for Short Sterling futures contract

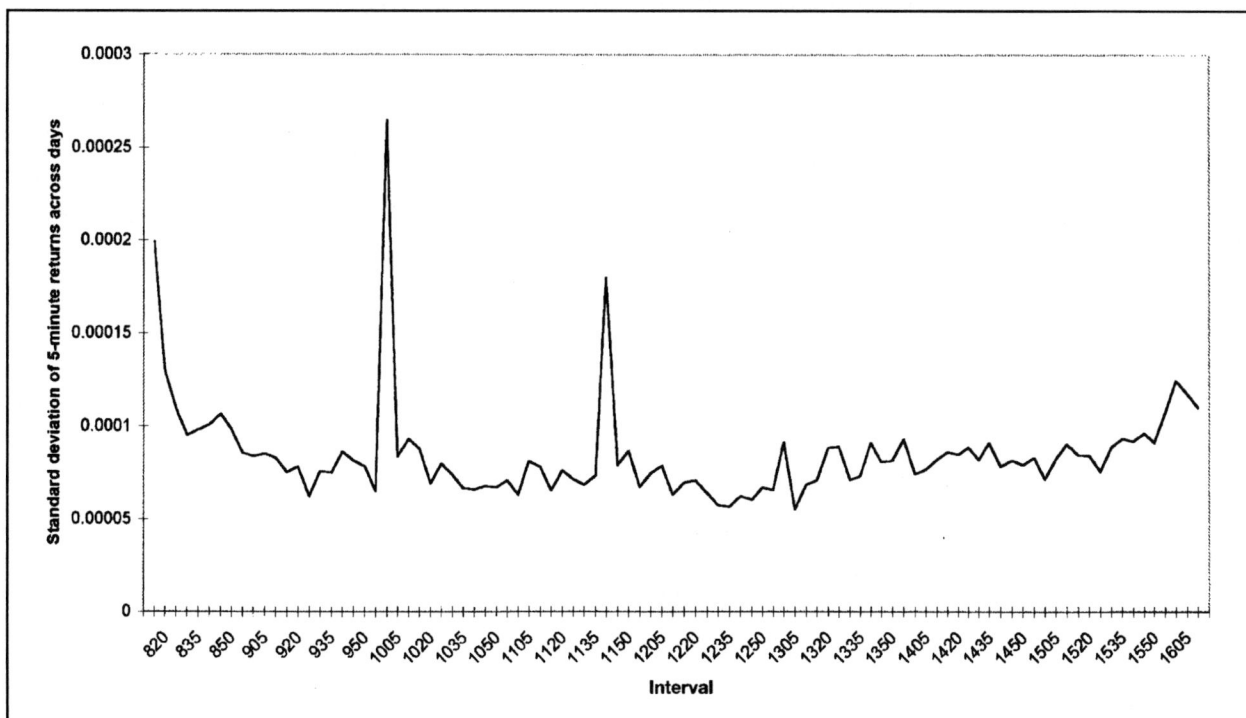

Figure 3.4: Intraday five-minute mean traded volume for Short Sterling futures contract

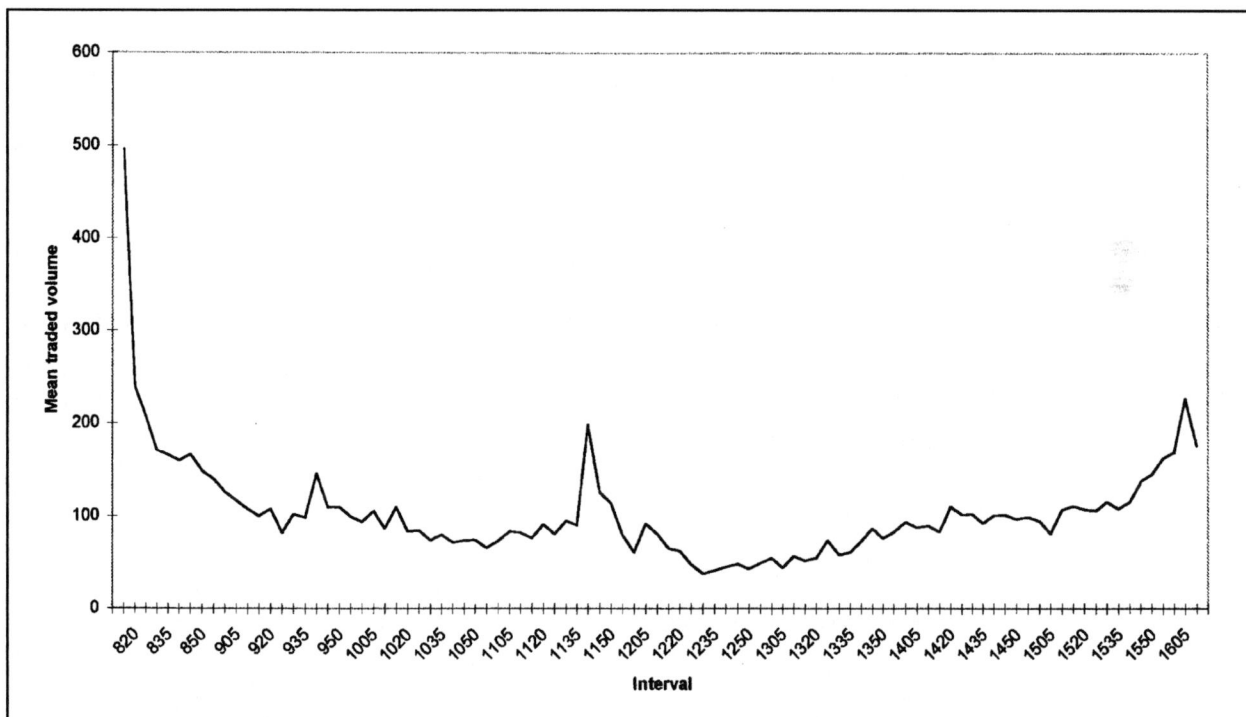

crucial since they typically result in some of the largest price movements and volumes on a given day. In the context of examining the impact of a given information arrival or news event on an asset or market, daily data would be of limited value since there may be multiple relevant news events. High-frequency datasets enable the study of price and volumes evolving over time, in the context of the interaction between differently informed traders. The extensive literature on the intra-day behaviour of financial time series is considered in detail in Chapter 5.

Discreteness

Security prices are generally quoted in discrete units or ticks. While there are no theoretical reasons to rule out continuous prices, the transactions costs associated with quoting and processing such prices makes them highly impractical. However, an unresolved issue is the optimal degree of discreteness. Price discreteness is less of a problem for less frequently sampled data that takes a wide range of values, which can be well approximated by a continuous-state process. However, discreteness is vitally important for intra-day price movements, as they may take only five or six possible values. Campbell *et al* (1997) noted that the empirical relevance of discreteness for returns depends on the holding period and the price level.

Prices might intuitively be assumed to be uniformly distributed across the possible values implied by the tick size, but in practice, prices are frequently rounded to "popular" values. Price clustering usually involves the occurrence of significantly greater than 50% of prices at even price fractions, or at certain integers. See Chapter 5 for further discussion of the impact of tick sizes and price clustering.

As an example of price discreteness, Table 3.2 shows how transaction-by-transaction price changes in FTSE100 index futures tend to cluster at a limited number of values. Price changes of 0 or 1 index point (2 ticks) account for the vast majority (93%). The lack of price changes at odd tick values in the FTSE100 futures contract results from severe price clustering at even ticks, which is analysed in detail by ap Gwilym *et al* (1998b). Price changes of 0, +/–2, and +/–4 account for 97.5% of all price changes. This lack of continuity suggests that modelling with continuous state spaces will not represent the data very well.

Table 3.2 also illustrates how discreteness becomes less severe as a differencing interval (five minutes in this case) is introduced. Within a short sample period, since prices vary over a relatively small range, discreteness will also be apparent in the returns series. The issue becomes less of a problem as the differencing interval increases, ie when lower frequency data are used.

Trade prices are subject to both discreteness and the bid–ask bounce effect, and they thus deviate from the equilibrium price that would be observed in the absence of these effects. Mucklow (1994) argues that there is an upward bias in both arithmetic returns and the variance of returns when prices are measured with noise, such as that induced by bid–ask bounce and discreteness. While the size of this bias is small for returns computed over periods such as a day, as the differencing interval shortens, the importance of this bias increases. Consequently, this bias can be important when using high-frequency data.

Modelling issues

Chapters 4–10 consider modelling and applications in detail. Here, we discuss some of the broader modelling issues. The nature of the data and the purpose of the modelling impact upon the type of model being

Table 3.2: Values taken by price changes in FTSE100 stock index futures (sample period from January 1992 to June 1995)

Price change (in ticks)	Trade-by-trade		At 5-minute intervals	
	Number of observations	% of sample	Number of observations	% of sample
less than − 6	651	0.07	5266	6.84
− 6	2324	0.27	4246	5.52
− 5	49	0.01	129	0.17
− 4	20305	2.33	7600	9.87
− 3	607	0.07	274	0.36
− 2	196523	22.54	11983	15.57
− 1	7447	0.85	476	0.62
0	416805	47.80	16772	21.79
+ 1	7285	0.84	497	0.65
+ 2	196289	22.51	12310	15.99
+ 3	544	0.06	256	0.33
+ 4	20128	2.31	7610	9.88
+ 5	45	0.01	109	0.14
+ 6	2335	0.27	4344	5.64
more than + 6	698	0.08	5114	6.64
Total	872035	100	76986	100

developed. While some models aim to assist with the timing of market transactions, others predict volatility for hedging, and so on.

Zhou (1998) notes that increasing the observation frequency does not necessarily make the task of modelling and forecasting financial markets any easier, since increasing noise levels and heteroscedasticity remain significant obstacles. Estimators developed for low-frequency data are not always applicable to high-frequency data, with observation noise being the key problem. This noise involves the deviation of the price from an assumed underlying continuous process, and typically includes microstructural effects that are not relevant to a particular application.

Zhou (1998) suggests that for low-frequency observations, observation noise is overwhelmed by the signal change, so that short-term price effects such as the bid–ask bounce have little effect. For high-frequency observations, however, the signal change becomes smaller while the size of the noise component remains the same; therefore the noise may eventually dominate the price signal in high-frequency data.

Short-run and long-run volatility

Dacorogna *et al* (1998) have suggested that a key challenge posed by the study of high-frequency data is to model the empirical behaviour of the data at any frequency from minutes to months. A good example involves volatility clustering for financial assets. The most popular model is Garch, which was originally developed to study data measured at daily or lower frequencies (Engle, 1982; Bollerslev, 1986).

Modelling and forecasting volatility is important for pricing financial instruments (eg options), and Arch models are a well established way of estimating volatility persistence. However, Dacorogna *et al* (1998) noted that "the volatility memory seems quite short-lived when measured with high-frequency data, while it seems long-lived when measured with daily or lower frequency data". Andersen and Bollerslev (1997b) attributed this to the presence of many independent volatility components in the data. Müller *et al* (1997), on the other hand, identified these components as heterogeneous market agents following various investment strategies depending on their institutional constraints, geographical location and risk profile.

The evidence is that data sampled at a daily or lower frequency exhibits persistent volatility that decays at a hyperbolic rate. However, problems arise when Arch models are fitted to high-frequency data. Such models work well for data at a daily or lower frequency, but are less effective at the intra-day level. Using five-minute returns for US$/DM spot exchange rates for 1992–93, Andersen and Bollerslev (1998a) showed that when the differencing interval is shortened to 90 minutes, the volatility persistence estimated by a Garch(1,1) model collapses. Similarly, when fitting Arch models to one-minute returns on S&P500 futures, Locke and Sayers (1993) concluded that the models contained a mis-specification for high-frequency data.

Andersen and Bollerslev (1997b) prove that under specified conditions the rate of volatility decay is independent of the length of the differencing interval. Therefore, the volatility persistence of high-frequency data should be the same as for lower-frequency data; which conflicts with the empirical findings of very short volatility persistence for models using high-frequency data.

Andersen and Bollerslev (1997b, 1998a) have suggested that the lack of volatility persistence for high-frequency data models is due to the failure of the Arch model to account for the predictable intra-day seasonalities in volatility (see earlier). To overcome this problem, they have proposed a model with both the standard Arch effect and also a predictable volatility component. They have proposed using a flexible Fourier framework (FFF) to remove the predictable intra-day seasonality, and then estimate the Garch model. Using foreign exchange data at five-minute intervals, they found that the resulting volatility persistence looks much more plausible. Andersen and Bollerslev (1998b) found that, after controlling for intra-day patterns in volatility, the volatility of US$/DM five-minute returns exhibits hyperbolic decay, which accords with the inter-day results and with the theory that both high-frequency and daily data should have the same rate of long-term volatility decay. This result opens up a new avenue of research on long-term volatility persistence: provided high-frequency data is purged of the intra-day patterns in volatility, it can be used to examine long term volatility decay. Given the very large size of high-frequency datasets, this could be a fruitful approach (Andersen and Bollerslev, 1997b, 1998a).

This section summarises the main problems encountered in managing high-frequency data, which have been discussed in greater detail within this chapter.

Summary

+ The size of effects being investigated is usually much smaller than in studies using daily data, and so measurement problems that were unimportant at the macro level become important at the micro level. Effects such as bid–ask bounce or stale prices can induce non-zero autocorrelation in returns and need to be explicitly modelled in the data analysis. In addition, the estimation techniques need to allow for price discreteness (the tick) and price clustering.

+ Because high-frequency data is usually pooled across different times of day, intra-day seasonals in the data need to be allowed for – for example in volatility, volume, bid–ask spread.

+ If the dataset contains only *changes* in price, it may tend to induce significant levels of negative serial correlation in returns.

+ The time stamps for high-frequency data may be inaccurate.

+ The large sample sizes associated with high-frequency datasets imply that almost any difference between numbers is very likely to be highly statistically significant, eg with extremely large t-statistics. With enormous numbers of degrees of freedom, almost any difference between two numbers is statistically significant at the conventional levels of 95% or 99%, and so the null hypothesis is rejected. Granger (1998) has suggested that the traditional concept of statistical significance will be replaced by economic significance. The large sample sizes mean that data mining is less of a problem with high-frequency data, while the use of this data opens up the possibility of fitting non-linear models. Also, while high-frequency data can greatly increase the sample size for routine events, it cannot increase the sample size for rare events, eg stock market crashes (Granger, 1998).

+ High-frequency data tends to be non-normal, so the usual significance tests are inappropriate.

+ Given the much larger size of the dataset (some empirical studies have used over 12 million observations), the additional complexity of handling trades of different types, etc, the data analysis is more demanding.

+ Results from a time-series analysis using high-frequency data in a particular time dimension and differencing interval are not directly comparable with those obtained using a different time dimension and differencing interval.

+ Missing values may be a problem for high-frequency data that has been converted to short time intervals.

+ In a multivariate context, taking into account the fact that most financial markets do not move independently of each other, the non-synchronicity of high-frequency data arrival poses major practical problems.

Dealing with many of these problems has been greatly eased by advances in computing technology. Many of the issues have motivated the development of new and innovative statistical and econometric techniques. Despite the difficulties encountered, analysis of high-frequency data is extremely rewarding and has allowed researchers to investigate many angles of financial market behaviour, as will be discussed in the remaining chapters.

4 Arbitrage opportunities in equity markets

The presence or absence of arbitrage opportunities is important for traders in financial markets for a number of reasons. Arbitrage opportunities allow traders to make large riskless profits, and high-frequency data is necessary to identify such opportunities and how long they may last. In addition to arbitrage trades, if a trade must be made for other reasons, it is often possible to use high-frequency data to identify which of two related securities (eg index futures and the index basket of shares) is relatively underpriced, and to buy the underpriced asset or sell the overpriced asset. If the prices of two financial markets are locked together by an arbitrage relationship, there will be a high correlation in returns, and one asset will make an excellent hedging instrument for positions in the other asset. Thus, knowledge of the extent to which the arbitrage relationship between related financial markets is violated is of interest to hedgers. For hedges over short periods of time, high-frequency data is needed to quantify this relationship.

What is arbitrage?

In finance, arbitrage is viewed as the simultaneous purchase of one asset against the sale of the same or equivalent asset from zero initial wealth to create a riskless profit due to price discrepancies. Thus arbitrage is riskless, requiring zero wealth, and so can be of arbitrary scale. Hence, only a few rational traders are required to remove arbitrage opportunities.

The absence of arbitrage opportunities in financial markets is a fundamental prediction of financial economics, and the theorems of Modigliani and Miller on the cost of capital and dividends can be viewed as an application of arbitrage, as can the Black–Scholes option pricing model, and the arbitrage pricing theory of Ross. If there are two identical products, the possibility of arbitrage requires them to have an identical price. If not, arbitrageurs will buy the cheap product and sell it as the expensive product. Such action will raise the price of the cheap product and lower the price of the expensive product, so equalising prices and eliminating the arbitrage opportunity.

Arbitrage has proved useful for valuing complicated new financial instruments because, if such an instrument can be replicated by combining existing instruments whose individual values are known, the value of the new instrument must be equal to that of the replicating strategy. If not, an arbitrage opportunity exists. Replicating strategies can be used to generate pricing equations for financial instruments. The extent to which actual prices differ from these no-arbitrage prices can then be investigated empirically. Deviations from the no-arbitrage price, called "mispricings", become arbitrage opportunities when the mispricing is sufficiently large to cover transactions costs and execution risk. Thus prices are free to fluctuate around the no-arbitrage price within the upper and lower bounds set by the transactions costs (which vary between markets). Such fluctuation between upper and lower barriers tends to introduce mean reversion into mispricings.

The presence of deviations from the no-arbitrage price that exceed the transactions costs can indicate one or more of the following:

✦ the existence of an arbitrage opportunity;

✦ the omission of some relevant factor from the pricing model (eg price limits or short sales restrictions);

✦ an error in the pricing model; or

✦ some flaw in the empirical procedures, for instance the use of non-synchronous observations.

Empirical studies of arbitrage opportunities

A large number of studies have looked for arbitrage opportunities across a wide range of markets (equity and equity futures, equity and equity options, etc). The early arbitrage studies used closing prices for the markets concerned, and these were often at slightly different times. In consequence, the prices in the two markets were non-synchronous, and so not linked by a no-arbitrage relationship. The use of high-frequency data has permitted the use of synchronous prices from two related markets in computing mispricings and arbitrage opportunities.

In addition to quantifying the size and distribution of mispricings using synchronous data, the use of high-frequency data has also enabled the time pattern of mispricings and arbitrage opportunities to be studied. The questions addressed using high-frequency data include the following.

✦ Do arbitrage opportunities persist long enough to permit traders to lock in arbitrage positions?

✦ Are mispricings and arbitrage opportunities mean-reverting?

✦ How long is the time lag between an arbitrage opportunity appearing and the initiation of arbitrage trades to exploit the opportunity?

✦ How long is it before the mispricing is eliminated?

✦ Is the mispricing eliminated by movements in the spot price or the futures price?

Almost all the arbitrage studies conducted to date have used observations that are evenly spaced in calendar time. This is often achieved by using trade data and selecting those prices that are closest to the chosen times. Studies have used a wide range of time periods, ranging from one second to one hour. Because they are concerned with relative prices in two (or more) markets, the use of high-frequency data requires that such data be available for both markets, and an important constraint on the choice of time interval is the frequency of price observations in both markets. For example, if a trade in an index futures contract occurs only about once every 10 minutes, while the index changes every 10 seconds, use of a five-minute time period would be inappropriate because there would be many periods where either the same futures price was repeated or the observation was classified as missing.

Arbitrage in financial markets has been found to take a variety of forms, including:

✦ equity and equity futures;

✦ equity and equity options;

◆ equity options and futures;

◆ fixed interest and fixed interest futures;

◆ fixed interest and fixed interest options;

◆ fixed interest options and futures;

◆ foreign exchange and foreign exchange futures;

◆ foreign exchange and foreign exchange options; and

◆ foreign exchange options and futures.

For illustrative purposes, we focus in this chapter on equity-market-based arbitrage.

Arbitrage in equity markets

High-frequency data has been available for both the spot and index futures markets in the US, the UK, Japan, Germany, Hong Kong and Australia, permitting studies of equity market arbitrage. Using high-frequency data to study mispricings involving the stock market has the advantage that, within the course of a day, the entitlement to dividends and interest payments is unchanged and so there is no need to collect data on these variables when studying intra-day movements in the mispricing. This feature of high-frequency data was used by Dwyer *et al* (1996) and Miller *et al* (1994).

In order to discover arbitrage possibilities in the FTSE100 index, it is necessary to keep track of the prices of the 100 shares in the index, as well as the present value of the expected dividends before delivery for each of these 100 shares for each of three outstanding derivatives delivery dates. In addition, the price of the futures contract for the three delivery dates, the cost of borrowing funds (r) for the three periods, and the transactions costs must also be considered. Since the analysis of this data must be performed in real time, traders use real time feeds of the requisite data.

As well as arbitrage between the spot and futures markets, an arbitrage relationship also exists between the futures and options markets on the same underlying asset. While such arbitrage tests require prices from three markets – put index options, call index options, and the index futures – they have the substantial advantage of not requiring any dividend data, because the spot market is not directly involved.

Firstly, the empirical evidence on the size and frequency of arbitrage opportunities using high-frequency data is presented below. This is followed by information from those studies that have used high-frequency data to look at the dynamics of arbitrage and mispricings, which is useful because potential arbitrageurs need to know how quickly they must trade before any one arbitrage opportunity disappears.

Do arbitrage opportunities exist in equity markets?

The details of those studies that have looked for equity-market-based arbitrage opportunities using high-frequency data are summarised in Table 4.1. These studies have generally found that arbitrage opportunities exist in all the countries studied, that the size of these opportunities is small and decreasing over time, that over and underpricings are equally common, and that allowance for trading lags decreases arbitrage profits. Thus, small arbitrage opportunities may arise

Table 4.1 Empirical studies of arbitrage opportunities using high-frequency data

Study	Year	Spot	Data period	Time interval (minutes)	Features
Index futures and index					
MacKinlay and Ramaswamy	1988	S&P500	1982–87	15	–
Dwyer, Locke and Yu	1996	S&P500	1982–90	1	–
Klemkosky and Lee	1991	S&P500	1983–87	10	Trading lags
Daigler	1993a pp 195–8, 1993b pp 110–14	S&P500 NYSE Comp. MMI	1987–88	5	Trading lags
Finnerty and Park	1988a	MMI	1984–86	Futures trades	–
Chung	1991	MMI	1984–86	1 second	Trading lags
Lim	1992a, 1992b	Nikkei	1988–89	5	–
Arai, Akamatsu and Yoshioka	1993	Nikkei	1991	1	–
Lim and Muthuswamy	1993	Nikkei	1988–91	5	Trading lags
Chung, Kang and Rhee	1994b	Nikkei	1988–91	1	Trading lags
Ho, Fang and Woo	1992	Hang Seng	1991	1	–
Hodgson, Kendig and Tahir	1993	All Ord	1992	15	Trading lags
Brailsford and Cusack	1997	Australian Shares	1994–95	Futures trades	–
Yadav and Pope	1994	FTSE100	1986–90	60	–
Strickland and Xu	1993	FTSE100	1988–90	60	Stock exchange accounts
Grünbichler and Callahan	1994	DAX 30	1990–91	5	–
Bamberg and Röder	1994a, 1994b	DAX 30	1991–92	1	Trading lags
Bühler and Kempf	1995	DAX 30	1990–92	1	Trading lags
Index futures and options					
Sternberg	1994	S&P500	1983	Trades	Arbitrage opportunities
Lee and Nayar	1993	S&P500	1989–91	Trades	No arbitrage opportunities
Fung and Fung	1997	Hang Seng	1993–95	Trades	No arbitrage opportunities
Fung, Cheng and Chan	1997	Hang Seng	1993–94	Trades	No arbitrage opportunities
Bae, Chan and Cheung	1998	Hang Seng	1993–94	Trades and quotes	Few arbitrage opportunities

from time to time, and traders need to use high-frequency data to spot such opportunities in real time.

Apart from one early study, the empirical results for index options and futures arbitrage summarised in Table 4.1 indicate a lack of profitable arbitrage opportunities. However, only two countries have been studied using high-frequency data.

The dynamics of the arbitrage response

If futures are mispriced by an amount exceeding the transactions costs, this will lead to arbitrage transactions, and these will tend to remove the initial mispricing by pushing the spot and futures prices back into line. This suggests that mispricings can be used to predict subsequent spot and futures price movements. Since these effects occur within a few minutes, high-frequency data is needed to investigate such effects.

The dynamics of arbitrage have been examined in a number of different ways: movements in the mispricing over time, the volume of arbitrage trading in the stock market, the effect of arbitrage trades on the mispricing, and whether the mispricing is removed by changes in the spot or futures price. These aspects are described further below.

Autocorrelation in mispricings

An obvious first step in investigating the time-series properties of the arbitrage response is to examine the time series of mispricings. Table 4.2 summarises studies that have used high-frequency data to quantify the autocorrelations in mispricings and the changes in mispricings. As can be seen from the table, there is a marked tendency for mispricings to persist over periods of 5 to 15 minutes with first-order serial correlations of over 0.8. However, there is also a tendency for these mispricings to diminish in size, as indicated by the negative first-order serial correlation coefficient of changes in mispricings.

The studies reported in Table 4.2 looked for linear relationships in the time series of mispricings. However, a few studies have looked for more complicated relationships. Vaidyanathan and Krehbiel (1992) used the data from the MacKinlay and Ramaswamy (1988) study to look for non-linear dependence over time in the percentage mispricings of the S&P500. Using analytical techniques from chaos theory, they found evidence of non-linear dependence, although the form of this dependence is not known.

Yadav and Pope (1992c) considered two datasets: 15-minute observations on the S&P500 from June 1983 to June 1987 (the data used by MacKinlay and Ramaswamy in their 1988 study), and hourly data on the FTSE100 between April 1986 and March 1990. Yadav and Pope found that, for both the UK and the US, the change in the mispricing depended on the level of the mispricing in the previous period. If the previous mispricing was positive (the future was overpriced), then the change in the mispricing tended to be negative (the overpricing declined), and vice versa. Thus, mispricings are a mean-reverting process. Yadav and Pope then divided the mispricings by size into one of five categories and found that the mean-reversion effect was strongest in the USA and UK when the absolute value of the mispricing in the previous period was largest. This supports the results of Pope and Yadav

Table 4.2 Empirical studies of autocorrelation in mispricings using high-frequency data

Study	Year	Spot	Data period	Time interval (minutes)	Autocorrelation
Index futures and index					
MacKinlay and Ramaswamy	1988	S&P500	1982–87	15	$r_a = 0.93$ $r_b = -0.23$
Miller, Muthuswamy and Whaley	1994	S&P500 VLCI	1982–91 1982–88	15 15	$r_b = -0.37$ $r_b = -0.18$
Lim	1992a, 1992b	Nikkei	1988–89	5	$r_a = 0.80$
Lim and Muthuswamy	1993	Nikkei	1988–91	5	$r_b = -0.2$ to -0.5
Ho, Fang and Woo	1992	Hang Seng	1991	1	$r_a = 0.8$
Grünbichler and Callahan	1994	DAX 30	1990–91	5	$r_a = 0.9$ $r_b = -0.2$
Kempf and Korn	1998	DAX 30	1995–96	1	Mean reversion

r_a = First-order serial correlation coefficient of mispricings
r_b = First-order serial correlation coefficient of changes in mispricings

(1992) that there are a number of groups of arbitrageurs, each facing different transactions costs. Kempf (1998), who analysed five-minute data periods for the DAX30 from 1990 to 1992, also found evidence of mean reversion in mispricings.

Arbitrage transactions

If an arbitrage opportunity exists, theory predicts that this will quickly trigger arbitrage trades (usually involving programme trades on the stock market). High-frequency data can be used to investigate this matter. In the US, traders must specify their motivation for initiating a programme trade, and so every programme trade that takes place for index arbitrage purposes can be identified. Furbush (1989) used the volume of such trading in the US during the crash of 1987 to investigate the relationship between arbitrage trading and mispricings. Using a five-minute time interval, he found that the primary response to an arbitrage opportunity for the S&P500 occurred within five minutes of the opportunity arising, and that these trades tended to reduce the mispricing.

Neal (1993b) studied programme trades during the first three months of 1989 on the NYSE. He found that for five-minute periods where one or more index arbitrage trades occurred, the average period contained 1.84 index arbitrage trades. He also found that the first-order serial correlation of the signed volume of index arbitrage trading in each five-minute period was 0.31. These results suggest that arbitrage trades occur in clusters, and that these clusters last for longer than five minutes.

Harris *et al* (1994) found that index arbitrage programme trades are clustered in time. Using data from the NYSE for 1989 and 1990, the average number of such trades in each cluster was 2.5, while the average duration of a cluster was 2.3 minutes. This indicates that the typical arbitrage response involved two or three arbitrageurs, and that they all submitted their orders at approximately the same time.

Removal of mispricings

The next question relates to how long it takes before an arbitrage opportunity is removed. Sofianos (1993) found, using one-minute spot and futures prices for the S&P500 during the first six months of 1990, that arbitrage opportunities lasted for just 3–5 minutes, while in a study of mispricings every five minutes for the MMI, Chan and Chung (1993) found that from August 1984 to June 1985, absolute mispricings persisted for about 10 minutes.

Eagle and Nelson (1991) used minute-by-minute observations on the S&P500 from 1985 to 1989 to compute mispricings. They found evidence of a small reduction in the mispricing after one minute, with larger and larger reductions as the response time was extended to 20 minutes. Pope and Yadav (1992) used hourly data for the FTSE100 from 1986 to 1988 to investigate the speed with which a mispricing was reversed. They found that the main response occurred within the first hour.

A study by Harris *et al* (1994) of programme trading on the NYSE in 1989 and 1990 found evidence that index arbitrage programme trading occurred when the basis (the difference between the futures and spot prices) is wide, and that the basis closed to its usual level within about 10 minutes of the submission of the programme trades. Neal (1996) analysed 837 S&P500 arbitrage trades on the NYSE in the three-month period of January to March 1989. He plotted the average mispricing for the 10 minutes before and after the submission of an arbitrage trade. For both over and underpricings, there was evidence that the submission of an arbitrage trade was associated with a statistically significant reversion of the mispricing towards zero.

Arbitrage and changes in futures and spot prices

If arbitrage trades tend to remove mispricings, the question arises as to whether this is accomplished by an adjustment in the spot price, in the futures price, or in both.

Dwyer *et al* (1996) studied minute-by-minute mispricings for the S&P500 from April 1982 to December 1990. They found evidence that mispricings tended to persist over time, and that arbitrage opportunities led to a reduction in the size of the mispricing that was twice as fast as when the mispricing was inside the transaction-cost threshold. The reduction in the mispricing was achieved primarily by movements in the spot price; although there was also some adjustment in the futures price.

Harris *et al* (1994) found for both over and underpricings that, because all the arbitrage trades in response to a particular mispricing are submitted more or less concurrently, the spot and futures price response to index arbitrage was of equal and opposite size. Thus, prices in both markets were found to adjust equally to remove the mispricing. They also discovered little difference in the price response between the first and subsequent arbitrage programme trades in each cluster.

Swinnerton *et al* (1988) used minute-to-minute data on the S&P500 for 1986, and found that the mispricing was a modest predictor of movements in the spot price over the following five minutes, particularly when futures were overpriced. This suggests that the spot price responds to the trades triggered by arbitrage opportunities.

Using one-minute data on 37 S&P500 stocks from November 1990 to January 1991, Hasbrouck (1996a) investigated the effect of index arbitrage programme trades on stock prices. He found that index arbitrage trades had a significantly smaller effect on the S&P500 index than did other trades (0.019 index points rather than 0.024). This lower price impact is consistent with these trades being viewed as informationless, which makes them less effective than other trades in moving share prices back to their no-arbitrage level.

General conclusions

The studies of the dynamics of arbitrage response using high-frequency data have brought to light a number of facts, as set out below.

+ Mispricings tend to persist for 5–15 minutes.

+ Mispricings tend to be mean-reverting, in other words they tend towards zero over time.

+ Arbitrage trades occur within a couple of minutes of the arbitrage opportunity, and typically involve two arbitrageurs.

+ Arbitrage trades lead to movements in both the spot and futures prices towards each other, with some evidence that movements in the spot price are larger.

Closing out an arbitrage position in an equity market

The standard equity-market-based arbitrage is one where the position is held to the derivative's expiry date and then liquidated. However, there some alternative strategies (early unwinding and rollover) which can lead to additional certain profits. The profitability of these strategies has been investigated using high-frequency data. The empirical evidence is that early unwinding and rollover are very important phenomena, and should be incorporated in the initial arbitrage decision. High-frequency data is needed both to quantify the value of the early unwinding and rollover options, and to decide when to exercise these options.

These two strategies can be viewed as an American-style option that is embedded in the initial arbitrage trade, which may itself be exercised if it is in-the-money. Using high-frequency data to evaluate these embedded options is important because the presence of these options increases the attractiveness of the initial arbitrage position. In consequence, a trader might decide to open an arbitrage position, even though the initial mispricing was not quite large enough to cover the transactions costs. The result is "risky arbitrage", with the trader hoping – but not being certain – to exercise one of the embedded options at a profit that will more than offset the initial loss.

The two "risky arbitrage" strategies are described further below.

Early unwinding

If at any time during the life of the arbitrage position the no-arbitrage condition is met, there is no need to wait until delivery to close out the arbitrage transactions. Early unwinding raises the possibility of making a profit from an arbitrage position over and above the riskless arbitrage profit that was locked in initially. At any time before delivery, the initial mispricing (which led to the creation of the arbitrage position) may be reversed, leading to a mispricing in the opposite direction. If this situation arises, early unwinding of the arbitrage position amounts to arbitraging this reverse mispricing and will lead to an additional riskless profit. This is particularly attractive because the additional transactions costs of this reverse arbitrage are very low as no additional trades in the spot position are required.

There have been a number of studies that have used high-frequency data to investigate the profitability of early unwinding, and these are summarised in Table 4.3. Since arbitrageurs look for early-unwinding opportunities on a continuous basis, high-frequency data is needed to properly examine this topic – an early-unwinding opportunity could arise around 2pm on a particular day, and could have disappeared by the market close, and so be entirely missed by daily data.

These empirical studies have shown that early unwinding can be very valuable, suggesting that it should be an important market phenomenon. This is confirmed by Sofianos (1991, 1993) who reported that, for the first half of 1990, two-thirds of the arbitrage transactions in S&P500 futures were unwound early.

Rollover, or delayed unwinding

Instead of liquidating the share position at the maturity of the derivatives contract, it may be beneficial to use this situation to create an arbitrage position in a more distant maturity (or far) contract. If at any time during the life of an arbitrage trade the far contract is (a) mispriced in the same direction as the initial arbitrage (in the nearest maturity contract), and (b) either the initial mispricing is reversed, or the current mispricing in the nearest maturity contract is smaller than that for the far contract, then a new arbitrage position can be established by closing out the initial

Table 4.3 Empirical studies of early unwinding using high-frequency data

Study	Year	Spot	Data period	Time interval (minutes)	Outcome
Index futures and index					
Brennan and Schwartz	1990	S&P500	1983–87	15	Profitable
Finnerty and Park	1988	MMI	1984–86	Futures trades	Profitable
Habeeb, Hill and Rzad	1991	S&P500	1987–90	5	Profitable
Sofianos	1993	S&P500	1990	1	Profitable
Neal	1996	S&P500	1989	1	Liquidated 99% early
Yadav and Pope	1994	FTSE100	1986–90	60	Profitable
Strickland and Xu	1993	FTSE100	1988–89	60	Profitable

futures position and replacing it with a position of similar size and direction in the far contract. Since there is no need to trade shares, the only transaction costs involved in this new arbitrage position are those for trading the futures.

Both Yadav and Pope (1994) and Strickland and Xu (1993) used hourly data for the FTSE100 to show that rollover can be profitable. They found that the additional profits from rollover can be substantial, and were sometimes more than double the profit from the initial arbitrage.

Individual arbitrage trades

As well as looking for arbitrage opportunities, it is also possible to use high-frequency data, in conjunction with information that particular trades were arbitrage trades, to study the nature of actual arbitrage trading. The questions that have been addressed include:

✦ the average profit per arbitrage trade;

✦ the number of different stocks traded for buy, sell and short sell arbitrage; and

✦ the dollar value of arbitrage trades.

Of course, data on individual trades does not have to come from a set of high-frequency data, but often the desired data has been collected as part of a dataset on all trades, from which the trades of interest can be extracted. This situation has the advantage that the chosen trades can be studied "in context".

Neal (1996) analysed 837 S&P500 arbitrage trades on the NYSE in the three-month period of January–March 1989. The average gross profit per trade (ignoring the time value of money, and assuming no trading lag and that the position was held to delivery) was 0.31% for overpricings and 0.32% for underpricings. For these arbitrage trades to have been profitable implies that transaction costs were very low. During this period, the average bid–ask spread for the S&P500 index basket was 0.64%, and so the gross arbitrage profit was just half the bid–ask spread. Thus the expected profits that triggered these arbitrage trades were very small.

Neal further found (in the same study) that for the arbitrage of overpricings the average number of stocks traded was 412 (out of 457). The arbitrage of underpricings was split into situations where the arbitrageur sold shares already held (direct-sell arbitrage), and those where short selling was required. Neal found that 28% of the arbitrage of underpricings did not involve short selling, because the arbitrageurs simply sold stocks they already held and so were not constrained by the uptick rule. Direct-sell arbitrage (which was conducted almost entirely by institutional investors) involved the sale of 441 stocks, while for arbitrage involving short selling (which was carried out almost entirely by NYSE member firms) only 184 stocks were sold short.

Sofianos (1993) studied the establishment of 1,442 arbitrage positions in the S&P500 during the first six months of 1990. He found that for arbitrage involving a long position in shares (overpricings), approximately 400 of the 500 S&P500 stocks were traded. For an arbitrage involving a short position in shares (underpricings), only 140 stocks were traded. The much smaller number of stocks for short positions is probably due to difficulties with short selling (the uptick rule and higher transactions costs).

Harris *et al* (1994) found that for the 29,186 index arbitrage programme trades on the NYSE during the years 1989–90, the average trade was valued at US$5.9 million and involved shares in 201 stocks for buy trades, and 154 stocks for sell trades. Sofianos (1993) found that, for the first six months of 1990, the average S&P500 index arbitrage position involved 280 stocks and was valued at US$7 million. In Neal's 1996 study of 837 arbitrage trades on the NYSE in the first three months of 1989, he found that the average value per trade was about US$9 million.

Arbitrage and market direction

Yadav and Pope (1994) considered the suggestion that, when the index is rising, market-makers run down their holdings of the shares in which they make a market, and when the index is falling they increase their holdings of such shares. Arbitrageurs, who are also market-makers in many of the index stocks, tend to buy and sell shares "in-house". When the market-making arm of the company has run down its holdings, in-house arbitrage of overpricings (which involves "buying" shares from a market-maker) will be possible only to a limited extent. Conversely, when the market-making arm has increased its holdings, in-house arbitrage of underpricings (which involves "selling" shares to the market-maker) may be unattractive.

Similar difficulties will be faced by arbitrageurs who are not also market-makers. This implies that futures will tend to be overpriced in a rising market and underpriced in a falling market. Yadav and Pope (1994) used hourly data for the FTSE100 index from April 1986 to March 1990 to examine whether there was a connection in the UK between index returns and mispricings. They found a significant positive relationship, as predicted, but concluded that it was not of economic significance.

Summary

The empirical studies using high-frequency data have found, in relation to arbitrage opportunities in equity markets, that:

✦ arbitrage trades are triggered by very small mispricings;

✦ arbitrage that requires short selling uses only about 30–40% of the shares in the index basket, and so is risky; and

✦ in 1990, the average US index futures arbitrage trade was valued at about US$7–9 million.

The use of high-frequency data is essential if intra-day patterns in financial markets are to be discovered. Such patterns can be helpful in a number of ways: traders who have some discretion over when they trade can choose the most advantageous time of day; financial market supervisors can become aware of consistent patterns in behaviour, which may have regulatory implications; and the presence of such patterns provides a good area for testing theories of market microstructure. In addition, when analysing high-frequency data, it is important to control for intra-day patterns in the data if the results are to be reliable.

Using high-frequency data, researchers have found various intra-day patterns for financial assets, and a wide range of daily seasonals have been investigated: returns, volume, number of trades, trade size, volume of limit orders, volatility, high and low times, market depth, number of traders in the pit, hedge and spread ratios, bid–ask spreads, traded spreads, autocorrelation of returns, mispricings, price reversals, and volatility ratios. Each of these is explored further within this chapter.

While some empirical studies of intra-day patterns have used transactions data, most have used equally spaced observations. This is probably because the seasonalities are time-of-day related, and so it is natural to use data that relates to specific time periods.

Intra-day patterns in returns

There are well-known seasonals in stock and equity futures returns: the "January" effect and the "weekend" effect, as well as lesser known monthly and quarterly patterns in returns. This has led to the investigation of intra-day patterns in returns, and the results from using high-frequency data are summarised in Table 5.1. The information represented in the table shows that there do not appear to be strong daily patterns in returns. There is some support for a day-end effect in equity markets, with high returns just before the daily close. A few studies also report a U-shaped pattern in returns. Such a pattern could be explained by the U-shaped pattern in volatility, with higher returns compensating for higher (systematic) risk.

Intra-day patterns in volume

The clear result from the empirical studies of equity and interest-rate markets that have used high-frequency data is that volume (or the number of trades) is U-shaped within each day. These empirical results are summarised in Table 5.2.

The patterns are much less clear for forex markets because forex is a global 24-hour market, and the patterns of higher volume, volatility and spreads seen in other markets at the open and close do not apply – although there is evidence of daily waves of activity as the three major forex markets open and close. There is also the problem for spot forex markets that, except for a few short periods when data has been specifically collected, only indicative quote data is available; volume cannot therefore be studied.

Table 5.1 Empirical studies of intra-day returns using high-frequency data

Study	Year	Spot	Data period	Time interval (minutes)	Findings
Index futures					
Lauterbach and Monroe	1989	S&P500	1988	1	Rose on Mondays during the first 30 minutes
Ekman	1992	S&P500	1983–88	15	Negative on Monday mornings
Chang, Jain and Locke	1995	S&P500	1982–90	1	High in the last 5 minutes (except Fridays)
Andersen and Bollerslev	1997a	S&P500	1986–89	5	No pattern
Ho and Lee	1998	Hang Seng	1993–97	1	U-shapes in the morning, afternoon, and after stock market closes, ie triple U
Yadav and Pope	1992a	FTSE100	1986–90	60	Decline throughout the day
Abhyankar, Copeland and Wong	1995	FTSE100	1991–93	5	No pattern
Buckle, ap Gwilym, Thomas and Woodhams	1998	FTSE100	1992–93	5	No pattern
Lequeux	1999b	FTSE100	1987–97	15	No pattern
Aitken, Frino and Jarnecic	1997	All Ord	1992–94	10	No pattern
Interest futures					
ap Gwilym, Buckle, Foord and Thomas	1996	Bund, BTP and Long Gilt	1992–93	5	No pattern
Buckle, ap Gwilym, Thomas and Woodhams	1998	Short Sterling	1992–93	5	No pattern
Lequeux	1999b	Long Gilt	1987–97	15	No pattern
Forex futures					
Cornett, Schwartz and Szakmary	1995	US$, DM, £, Sfr, ¥,C$	1977–91	60	U-shaped pattern

Table 5.1 – continued

Study	Year	Spot	Data period	Time interval (minutes)	Findings
Equity options					
ap Gwilym, Buckle and Thomas	1997	FTSE100	1993–94	60	No pattern
Sheikh and Ronn	1994	US options	1986–87	60	Positive call returns for 2pm–close
Equities spot					
Wood, McInish and Ord	1985	Index of US equities	1971–72, 1982	1	U-shaped pattern
Harris	1986	Index of US equities	1981–83	15	U-shaped pattern
Harris	1989b	NYSE	1981–83	Trades	Day-end effect, with a large price increase for the last trade
McInish and Wood	1990b	Toronto SE	1987	1	U-shaped pattern
Ho and Cheung	1991	Hang Seng	1986–89	15	A day-end effect
Cheung	1995	Hang Seng	1986–90	15	A day-end effect
Chang, Fukuda, Rhee and Takano	1993	Topix	1987–91	1	High returns at the open and close, with negative returns just before and just after lunch time break
Niemeyer and Sandås	1995	OMX	1990–91	1	No pattern
Forex spot					
Lyons and Rose	1995	DM/L and DM/Ffr	1979–92	1.15pm and 5pm	Currencies under speculative attack *appreciate* during each day
Andersen and Bollerslev	1997a	US$/DM	1992–93	5	No pattern

There are two theoretical explanations for intra-day patterns in volume in equity and interest-rate markets, although they differ in their predictions concerning the daily patterns in the bid–ask spread and volatility. The first explanation is that if both liquidity and informed traders have discretion over when they trade, they will choose to trade at the same time as each other so that their trades have the minimum price impact (Admati and Pfleiderer, 1988). Volatility will also increase at the times when informed traders choose to trade. These periods of high volume (and volatility) are likely to be at the open and close because non-discretionary traders will tend to increase volume at these times, and so there will be U-shaped patterns in volume and volatility. However, this

Table 5.2 Empirical studies of the volume or number of intra-day trades using high-frequency data

Study	Year	Spot	Data period	Time interval (minutes)	Findings
Index futures					
Ekman	1992	S&P500	1983–88	15	U-shaped number of trades
Vila and Sandmann	1995	Nikkei	1993	1	U-shaped number of trades
Ho and Lee	1998	Hang Seng	1993–97	1	U-shapes in the morning, afternoon, and after stock market closes, ie triple U
Gannon	1994	All Ord.	1992	15	U-shaped volume
Abhyankar, Copeland and Wong	1995	FTSE100	1991–93	5	U-shaped volume
Buckle, ap Gwilym, Thomas and Woodhams	1998	FTSE100	1992–93	5	U-shaped volume
Tse	1999	FTSE100	1995–96	5	U-shaped volume and number of trades, with a 1.30pm spike
De Jong and Donders	1998	AEX	1992–93	5	U-shaped number of trades
Interest futures					
Franses, Ieperen, Kofman, Martens and Menkveld	1994	Bund (Liffe and DTB)	1992	5	U-shaped volume
ap Gwilym, Buckle, Foord and Thomas	1996	Bund, BTP and Long Gilt	1992–93	5	U-shaped volume
ap Gwilym, Buckle and Thomas	1999	Long Gilt	1992–93	5	U-shaped volume
Buckle, ap Gwilym, Thomas and Woodhams	1998	Short Sterling	1992–93	5	U-shaped volume
Piccinato, Ballocchi and Dacorogna	1998	Eurodollar, EuroSwiss, Euromark, Short Sterling, Eurolira, three-month ECU	1996–97	Trades quotes	U-shaped number of trades and quotes
Piccinato, Ballocchi, Dacorogna and Gençay	1998	Eurodollar, EuroSwiss, Euromark, Short Sterling, three-month ECU	1994–97	Trades quotes	U-shaped number of trades and quotes

Table 5.2 – continued

Study	Year	Spot	Data period	Time interval (minutes)	Findings
Equity options					
Stephan and Whaley	1990	US stocks	1986	5	U-shaped call volume
Chan, Chung and Johnson	1995	US stocks	1986	15	U-shaped volume
ap Gwilym, Buckle and Thomas	1997	FTSE100	1993–94	Trades and quotes	U-shaped number of trades and quotes
Equity spot					
Stephan and Whaley	1990	US stocks	1986	5	U-shaped volume
McInish and Wood	1990b	Toronto SE	1987	1	U-shaped volume
Jain and Joh	1988	NYSE	1979–83	60	U-shaped volume
Gerety and Mulherin	1992	NYSE	1933–88	60	U-shaped volume
Lee, Mucklow and Ready	1993	209 US stocks	1988	30	U-shaped volume
Foster and Viswanathan	1993	NYSE	1988	Trades	U-shaped volume
Atkins and Basu	1995	NYSE	1984	Trades	U-shaped volume
Chan, Chung and Johnson	1995	NYSE	1986	15	U-shaped volume
Chan, Christie and Schultz	1995	Nasdaq	1991–92	5	U-shaped volume and number of trades
Madhavan, Richardson and Roomans	1997	274 NYSE stocks	1990	Trades	U-shaped volume and number of trades
Lehmann and Modest	1994	Tokyo SE	1991–92	30	U-shaped volume, but no pattern in the number of trades
Niemeyer and Sandås	1995	30 Swedish stocks	1990–91	10	U-shaped volume and number of trades, and volume and number of limit orders
Benos and Rockinger	1998	120 French stocks	1995–97	60	U-shaped volume
Werner and Kleidon	1996	UK and US stocks	1991	15	U-shaped volume in both countries
Abhyankar, Ghosh, Levin and Limmack	1997	UK stocks	1991	15	M-shaped volume and number of trades

theory has difficulty in explaining why informed traders choose to trade at times when the empirical evidence is that bid–ask spreads are highest, which is also at the open and close of each day (see Table 5.4 on page 73).

The second explanation is that the optimal portfolio to be held over a non-trading period is different from that which is optimal for an open market period. Thus, there is an increase in volume at the open and close due to portfolio-rebalancing trades (Brock and Kleidon, 1992), yielding daily U-shaped patterns in both the volume and the number of trades. For a monopolistic market-maker this will lead to a widening of the bid–ask spread at the open and close of each trading day due to a shortage of liquidity (ie U-shaped patterns in the bid–ask spread), although in markets with competing market-makers (eg futures markets) this may not happen. Since the number of informed traders is constant over time, there is no reason why volatility should vary over the day.

As volatility and the bid–ask spread are highest at the open and close, discretionary traders may wish to avoid these times, although the volume evidence is that they do the opposite. Such traders may be drawn to these times because they are uninformed traders who are rebalancing their portfolios (Brock and Kleidon, 1992) or because they are informed traders who seek to hide their trades in a period of thick trading (Admati and Pfleiderer, 1988). In each case the benefits of portfolio rebalancing or informed trading must outweigh the costs of a higher bid–ask spread and volatility. These explanations are complementary in that the portfolio rebalancing occurs at the open and close, which then creates thick trading in which the informed traders seek to hide.

Intra-day patterns in volatility

Admati and Pfleiderer (1988) predicted that volatility increases when informed traders choose to trade, while the Brock and Kleidon (1992) model does not include informed traders and so does not predict intra-day patterns in volatility. The overwhelming result from the high-frequency data studies of equity and interest rate markets is that the unconditional variance of returns is U-shaped within each day. However, there is some evidence that when attempts are made to control for other factors (such as volume), the variance may no longer follow a U-shaped pattern. A summary of the empirical studies is given in Table 5.3.

The spot forex markets operate globally for 24 hours per day with three main trading zones: Europe, Asia and North America. Because the global market never opens or closes, there is not a simple U-shaped pattern but instead a complicated composite pattern with a 24-hour cycle.

A related question is the distribution of the daily high–low prices. If futures prices are assumed to follow a random walk, the daily high and low prices are about four times more likely to occur at the beginning and end of the day than in the middle of the day. In an analysis of trade prices for FTSE100 futures from July 1992 to September 1995, Acar et al (1996) found that the proportion of daily highs and lows occurring at the beginning of the day was about 50% higher than expected. This finding is consistent with higher volatility at the start of the day.

Herbst and Maberly (1992) examined the variance of S&P500 futures returns between 4 pm (when the NYSE closes) and 4.15pm (when futures trading ceases). They found highly significant differences between the days of the week, with the largest variance on Fridays and the smallest on Wednesdays. They concluded that the flow of information is a function of the day of the week.

Table 5.3 Empirical studies of the volatility of intra-day returns using high-frequency data

Study	Year	Spot	Data period	Time interval (minutes)	Intra-day variances
Index futures					
Kawaller, Koch and Koch	1990	S&P500	1984–86	30	U-shaped pattern
Froot, Gammill and Perold	1990	S&P500	1988–89	15	U-shaped pattern
Cheung and Ng	1990	S&P500	1983–87	15	U-shaped pattern
Chan, Chan and Karolyi	1991	S&P500	1984–89	5	U-shaped pattern
Ekman	1992	S&P500	1983–88	15	U-shaped pattern
Daigler	1997	S&P500, MMI	1988–89	1	U-shaped pattern
Lee and Linn	1994	S&P500	1983–87	10	U-shaped pattern
Wang, Michalski, Jordan and Moriarty	1994	S&P500	1987–88	30	U-shaped pattern
Kawaller, Koch and Peterson	1994	S&P500	1988	1	U-shaped pattern for historic volatility, but no pattern for implied volatility
Chang, Jain and Locke	1995	S&P500	1982–90	1	U-shaped pattern while the spot market is open
Andersen and Bollerslev	1997a	S&P500	1986–89	5	U-shaped pattern while the spot market is open and after it closes, ie W
Kofman and Martens	1997	S&P500 FTSE100	1993	1	U-shaped pattern U-shaped pattern
Park	1993	MMI	1984–86	30	U-shaped pattern
Hiraki, Maberly and Takezawa	1995	Nikkei	1988–91	10	High for the last 10 minutes
Ho and Lee	1998	Hang Seng	1993–97	1	U-shapes in the morning, afternoon, and after stock market closes, ie triple U
Gannon	1994	All Ord.	1992	15	U-shaped pattern
Yadav and Pope	1992a	FTSE100	1986–90	60	U-shaped pattern
Abhyankar, Copeland and Wong	1995	FTSE100	1991–93	5	U-shaped pattern with a 1.30pm spike
Buckle, ap Gwilym, Thomas and Woodhams	1998	FTSE100	1992–93	5	U-shaped pattern
Lequeux	1999b	FTSE100	1987–97	15	U-shaped pattern, with an inverted V for kurtosis

Table 5.3 – continued

Study	Year	Spot	Data period	Time interval (minutes)	Intra-day variances
Tse	1999	FTSE100	1995–96	5	U-shaped pattern with a 1.30pm spike

Interest futures

Study	Year	Spot	Data period	Time interval (minutes)	Intra-day variances
Franses, Ieperen, Kofman, Martens and Menkveld	1994	Bund (Liffe and DTB)	1992	5	U-shaped pattern
ap Gwilym, Buckle, Foord and Thomas	1996	Bund, BTP and Long Gilt	1992–93	5	L-shaped pattern
Buckle, ap Gwilym, Thomas and Woodhams	1998	Short Sterling	1992–93	5	U-shaped pattern, with spikes at macroeconomic news announcements
Lequeux	1999	Long Gilt	1987–97	15	U-shaped pattern, with an inverted V for kurtosis
ap Gwilym, Buckle and Thomas	1999	Long Gilt	1992–93	5	U-shaped pattern
Becker, Finnerty and Kopecky	1993	Long Gilt, Treasury bonds, Eurodollar	1986–90	15	U-shaped pattern, with spikes at macroeconomic news announcements
Piccinato, Ballocchi and Dacorogna	1998	Eurodollar, EuroSwiss, Euromark, Short Sterling, Eurolira three-month ECU	1996–97	Trades and quotes	No clear patterns
Piccinato, Ballocchi, Dacorogna and Gençay	1998	Eurodollar, EuroSwiss, Euromark, Short Sterling, three-month ECU	1994–97	Trades and quotes	U-shaped pattern for trades and quote prices
Daigler	1997	Treasury bonds	1988–89	1	U-shaped pattern
Lequeux and Acar	1996	Bund, BTP	1992–95	60	U-shaped pattern
Kawaller, Koch and Peterson	1994	Eurodollars	1988	1	U-shaped pattern for historic volatility, but no pattern for implied volatility
Docking, Kawaller and Koch	1999	Eurodollars	1988–95	1	Declines during the day, with a mid-day spike

Forex futures

Study	Year	Spot	Data period	Time interval (minutes)	Intra-day variances
Harvey and Huang	1991	US$ and £, DM, ¥, Sfr, C$	1980–88	60	Inverse U-shaped pattern for Monday to Wednesday

Table 5.3 – continued

Study	Year	Spot	Data period	Time interval (minutes)	Intra-day variances
Equity options					
ap Gwilym, Buckle and Thomas	1997	FTSE100	1993–94	60	U-shaped pattern
Chan, Chung and Johnson	1995	NYSE	1986	15	U-shaped pattern
Sheikh and Ronn	1994	US equities	1986–87	60	U-shaped pattern
Forex options					
Hilliard and Tucker	1992	US$ and £, ¥, DM	1982–88	120	U-shaped pattern
Equity spot					
McInish and Wood	1990a	1,400 US equities	1980–84	1	U-shaped pattern
Chan, Chung and Johnson	1995	NYSE	1986	15	U-shaped pattern
Wood, McInish and Ord	1985	Index of US equities	1971–72, 1982	1	U-shaped pattern
Lehmann and Modest	1994	Tokyo SE	1991–92	30	U-shaped pattern
Chang, Fukuda, Rhee and Takano	1993	Topix	1987–91	1	U-shaped patterns in both the morning and afternoon sessions
Gerety and Mulherin	1992	Dow Jones	1933–88	60	U-shaped pattern
Ito and Lin	1992	S&P500 Nikkei225	1985–89	60	U-shaped pattern
Foster and Viswanathan	1993	NYSE	1988	60	Adverse selection cost (price response to unexpected volume) is U-shaped
Chan, Christie and Schultz	1995	Nasdaq	1991–92	5	U-shaped pattern
Niemeyer and Sandås	1995	OMX	1990–91	1	High at the open
Benos and Rockinger	1998	120 French stocks	1995–97	60	U-shaped volume
Werner and Kleidon	1996	UK and US stocks	1991	15	U-shaped pattern in both countries
Abhyankar, Ghosh, Levin and Limmack	1997	UK stocks	1991	15	U-shaped pattern
Forex spot					
Baillie and Bollerslev	1990	US$ and £, DM, ¥ and Sfr	1986	60	Volatility increases at the opening of the London and New York markets

Table 5.3 – continued

Study	Year	Spot	Data period	Time interval (minutes)	Intra-day variances
Goodhart and Giugale	1993	US$ and £, DM, ¥ and Sfr	1986	60	Higher on Monday mornings. Higher between 15.00 and 19.00 GMT
Low and Muthuswamy	1996	US$/DM US$/¥ DM/¥	1992–93	Quotes	Spikes when markets open and close
Hsieh and Kleidon	1996	US$/DM	1989	1	U-shaped pattern for London, and U-shaped for New York
Andersen and Bollerslev	1997a 1998b	US$/DM	1992–93	5	High for 12.00–17.00 GMT. Very low for 3.00–4.00 GMT / Tokyo lunch
Docking, Kawaller and Koch	1999	US$/DM	1988–95	1	Declines during the day, with a mid-day spike

Intra-day patterns in the bid–ask spread

Brock and Kleidon (1992) predicted a U-shaped daily pattern in the bid–ask spread because the increased order flow at the open and close exhausts the available liquidity. The evidence from the studies using high-frequency data, summarised in Table 5.4, is for a U-shaped daily pattern in the bid–ask spread for equity, interest rate and forex markets. These studies have used both regularly and irregularly spaced data. Since the costs of trading are highest at the open and close, traders will have lower costs if they avoid these times.

Intra-day patterns in the autocorrelation of returns

Autocorrelation in returns can be induced by the market microstructure, where bid–ask bounce will generate negative autocorrelation, while stale prices lead to positive autocorrelation in indexes. If the degree of bid–ask bounce or stale prices varies over the day, this could induce daily patterns in autocorrelation. Table 5.5 summarises the high-frequency data evidence for equity markets and shows that short-run autocorrelation is negative and may follow intra-day patterns. However, there is not enough evidence to identify specific patterns.

Intra-day patterns in hedge ratios

The risk-minimising hedge (or spread) ratio between two securities depends on the ratio of their standard deviations of prices, multiplied by the correlation of their prices, all at the end of the hedge. Therefore intra-day seasonalities in volatility and correlation may produce intra-day patterns in the hedge ratio.

Table 5.4 Empirical studies of the bid-ask spread using high-frequency data

Study	Year	Spot	Data period	Time interval (minutes)	Findings
Index futures					
Wang, Moriarty, Michalski and Jordan	1990	S&P500	1987–88	Trades	U-shaped pattern
Wang, Michalski, Jordan and Moriarty	1994	S&P500	1987–88	Trades	U-shaped pattern
Abhyankar, Copeland and Wong	1995	FTSE100	1991–93	5	U-shaped pattern
Tse	1999	FTSE100	1995–96	5	Inverted U-shape
Henker	1998	FTSE100	1994–96	10	Flat
Interest futures					
Ma, Peterson and Sears	1992	Treasury bonds	1980–83	Quotes	U-shaped pattern
Franses, Ieperen, Kofman, Martens and Menkveld	1994	Bund (Liffe)	1992	5	Flat
Forex futures					
Ding	1999	US$/DM US$/¥	1990	Trades	U-shaped pattern
Equity options					
Chan, Chung and Johnson	1995	NYSE	1986	15	High at the open and low at the close
ap Gwilym, Buckle and Thomas	1997	FTSE100	1993–94	Trades and quotes	Decline during the day
Berkman	1992	22 Dutch options	1989	60	V-shaped pattern
Equities spot					
Abhyankar, Ghosh, Levin and Limmack	1997	UK stocks	1991	15	U-shaped pattern
Lee, Mucklow and Ready	1993	209 US stocks	1988	30	U-shaped pattern in quoted and effective spreads and a reverse U-shape in depth
Chan, Chung and Johnson	1995	NYSE	1986	15	U-shaped pattern
McInish and Wood	1992	NYSE	1989	Quotes	Reverse J-shape that declines during the day, with an upturn towards the close
Lehmann and Modest	1994	Tokyo SE	1991–92	30	U-shaped pattern

Table 5.4 – continued

Study	Year	Spot	Data period	Time interval (minutes)	Findings
Chan, Christie and Schultz	1995	Nasdaq	1991–92	5	The average market maker spread is flat, while the inside spread (touch) declines during the day
Madhavan, Richardson and Roomans	1997	274 NYSE stocks	1990	5	U-shaped pattern
Werner and Kleidon	1996	UK and US stocks	1991	15	U-shaped pattern in both countries
Brockman and Chung	1998	Hong Kong SE	1996–97	5	U-shaped pattern
Niemeyer and Sandås	1995	OMX	1990–91	1	High at the open
Levin and Wright	1999	100 UK stocks	1994–95	1	U-shaped pattern in the touch. The average bid-ask spread for individual market makers is largely flat
Forex spot					
Hsieh and Kleidon	1996	US$/DM	1989	Quotes	U-shaped pattern for London, and U-shaped pattern for New York

In a study of Bund and BTP futures using 60-minute data from the period 1992–95, Lequeux and Acar (1996) found that the spread ratio falls during the day. Gavridis *et al* (1999) discovered that the correlations between 30-minute quote changes for 13 spot currencies varied with the time of day, again suggesting that hedge ratios depend on the time of day.

The Epps effect

This effect is only revealed when using high-frequency data, and concerns the relationship between the differencing interval and the correlation between the returns on two financial securities. As the differencing interval is reduced, there is only a modest reduction in the correlation between returns for forex and stocks. However, when the differencing interval is reduced below about 60 minutes, there is a dramatic decrease in the correlation coefficient. (Epps, 1979, who studied 10-minute returns on the shares of four US car manufacturers in 1971; Lundin *et al*, 1999; Low and Muthuswamy, 1996). Thus there is no

Table 5.5 Empirical studies of the autocorrelation of returns using high-frequency data

Study	Year	Spot	Data period	Time interval	Findings
Index futures					
Ekman	1992	S&P500	1983–88	15	Negative, with an S-shaped pattern
Yadav and Pope	1992b	S&P500 FTSE100	1983–87	15 60	Negative, with a U-shaped pattern
Equity spot					
Chang, Fukuda, Rhee and Takano	1993	Topix	1987–91	1	1st order return autocorrelations show a U-shaped pattern in both the morning and afternoon sessions
McInish and Wood	1991	23 US indexes	1984	15	Tends to rise during the day, with a U-shaped pattern

unique correlation between the returns of two financial instruments; rather, there is a range of correlations, depending on the differencing interval.

The Epps effect has important implications for short-term risk estimation, because the usual correlations are gross overestimates, and the risk of a portfolio of foreign currencies is much less over a few minutes than over a few days. The Epps effect implies that hedge ratios are much lower for intra-day hedging than for hedging over longer periods. Indeed, such hedging may be of little value in reducing risks.

Other intra-day patterns

There have been studies using high-frequency data of trade size, mispricings, and the number of traders in the pit, and all these studies yielded U-shaped patterns within the day, while the number of price reversals was lower at the open. However, there have been very few studies of these intra-day seasonalities.

Effects of news announcements on intra-day patterns

The pattern of intra-day prices and volumes may be affected by news announcements. Some announcements are made at set times, for example the latest macroeconomic statistics, and so can induce regular intra-day patterns. To the extent that the content of announcements is unexpected, the arrival of news is likely to change market prices and will usually be associated with a rise in volume as traders impound this information into prices. Therefore, if news tends to arrive at certain times of day, on those days when such news arrives the usual daily patterns will be altered by "spikes" in price volatility and volume.

Table 5.6 Empirical studies of macroeconomic announcements using high-frequency data

Study	Year	Spot	Data period	Time interval (minutes)	Findings
Index futures					
Becker, Finnerty and Friedman	1995	FTSE100	1986–90	30	Returns responded to US and UK macroeconomic news
ap Gwilym, Buckle, Clare and Thomas	1998	FTSE100	1992–95	Trades	Volatility increases for about 1½ minutes after a macroeconomic announcement
Buckle, ap Gwilym, Thomas and Woodhams	1998	FTSE100	1992–93	5	Returns and volatility are increased by macroeconomic news
Interest futures					
Becker, Finnerty and Kopecky	1993	Long Gilt, Treasury bonds, Eurodollar	1986–90	15	Volatility spikes at macroeconomic news
Smith and Webb	1993	Eurodollar	1987–90	5	Volatility increases during "Fed time" (10am–12 noon)
Becker, Finnerty and Kopecky	1996	Eurodollars Treasury bonds	1986–90	15 and 60	US macroeconomic news is not instantly impounded into prices in an unbiased manner
Buckle, ap Gwilym, Thomas and Woodhams	1998	Short Sterling	1992–93	5	Returns and volatility are increased by macroeconomic news
Crain and Lee	1995	Eurodollars	1990–93	60	Volatility is increased by macroeconomic news
Ederington and Lee	1993	Eurodollars	1988–91 T-bonds	5	Volatility is increased by macroeconomic news
ap Gwilym, Buckle, Clare and Thomas	1998	Short Sterling	1992–95	Trades	Volatility increases for about two minutes after a macroeconomic announcement
Forex futures					
Ederington and Lee	1994	US$/¥	1988–93	10 seconds	Volatility increase for about 50 seconds after US macroeconomic announcements

Table 5.6 – continued

Study	Year	Spot	Data period	Time interval (minutes)	Findings
Crain and Lee	1995	US$/DM	1990–93	60	Volatility is increased by macroeconomic news
Leng	1996	US$/DM US$/¥	1988–93	5	Volatility rises when there is a macroeconomic announcement
Interest spot					
Crain and Lee	1995	Eurodollars	1990–93	60	Volatility is little changed by macroeconomic news
Forex spot					
Ederington and Lee	1993	US$/DM	1988–91	5	Volatility is increased by macroeconomic news
Payne	1997	US$/DM	1992–93	5	Volatility of returns increases for the following hour
Almeida, Goodhart and Payne	1998	US$/DM	1992–94	5	Returns respond to unexpected macroeconomic announcements
Andersen and Bollerslev	1998a 1998b	US$/DM	1992–93	5	Volatility spike at 8.30 EST due to US macroeconomic announcements
Tanner	1997	US$/DM	1987–91	60	Returns respond to unexpected trade deficit and CPI announcements
Crain and Lee	1995	US$/DM	1990–93	60	Volatility is increased by macroeconomic news

These effects have been investigated empirically using high-frequency data, and the studies are summarised in Table 5.6. This shows clearly that regular macroeconomic announcements lead to spikes in volume and volatility, and discretionary traders need to allow for this when devising a trading strategy. It is also important to allow for such factors when modelling relevant markets.

Table 5.7 Empirical studies of the turn-of-the-year effect using high-frequency data

Study	Year	Spot	Data period	Time interval (minutes)	Findings
Equities spot					
Keim	1989	Nasdaq	1983–88	Last trade	December closing prices are at the bid, while January closing prices are at the ask, leading to a turn-of-the-year effect
Griffiths and White	1993	Toronto SE	1977–89	Trades and quotes	The turn of the year effect is due to small sell trades before the tax year end, followed by small repurchase trades – a bid–ask effect coupled with a price pressure effect

The turn-of-the-year effect and high-frequency data

As well as studying intra-day seasonalities, high-frequency data has also been used to investigate annual seasonalities. There have been many empirical studies of the turn-of-the-year effect using monthly, weekly or daily data, and it may be thought that high-frequency data is of little relevance to understanding this anomaly. However, high-frequency data enables the direction of trades around the end of the tax year to be determined, revealing selling just before the year end, which pushes the price down. In the new year, these shares are repurchased, which pushes the price back up. This price-pressure effect is amplified by a bid–ask bounce effect.

Table 5.7 summarises two studies that relate to turn-of-the-year effects.

Conclusions

The use of high-frequency data has revealed the presence of some powerful intra-day seasonalities in financial markets. There are clear U-shaped daily patterns in volume, volatility and the bid–ask spread in equity and interest rate markets (although the patterns in forex markets are more complicated because they are 24-hour markets). There are also spikes in volume and volatility when macroeconomic information is released. These findings have important consequences for traders. Unless they have a good reason, they should avoid trading at the open or close as they will encounter higher volatility and bid–ask spreads.

These intra-day seasonalities also have major implications for models employing high-frequency data. The models must take account of predictable intra-day seasonalities if the analysis of other features of the market is not to be biased by the failure to exclude these time-of-day effects. The potential importance of allowing for such effects is illustrated by the disappearance of the weekend effect when the flexible Fourier framework was used to allow for intra-day seasonalities in forex high-frequency data (Andersen and Bollerslev, 1997a). Payne (1997) found that failure to adjust for intra-day seasonalities led to the overstatement of the effect of news on the volatility of forex returns. Goodhart *et al* (1993) showed that if intra-day news is not included as an explanatory variable in a model of US$/DM quote changes, the conclusions are radically altered.

Some ways in which intra-day seasonalities can be allowed for include:

✦ the incorporation of time-of-day dummy variables;

✦ the flexible Fourier framework (FFF) of Andersen and Bollerslev (1998b);

✦ time-deformation models, eg ν-time;

✦ the inclusion of trigonometric terms, eg Payne (1997);

✦ the use of cubic splines (Engle and Lunde, 1998; Engle and Russell, 1998); and

✦ a comparison of news days with no-news days (Ederington and Lee, 1993).

6 Links between markets

An important trading issue involves the degree to which related markets move together, and the extent to which one market leads or lags another. This question can be examined from a number of angles:

✦ the prices or volatility of a spot market and its associated derivative markets;

✦ the prices or volatility of geographically separated markets trading the same or very similar financial assets;

✦ the volume of trading in a spot market and its associated derivative markets; or

✦ the volume of trading in geographically separated markets trading the same or very similar financial assets.

The prices and level of trading in strongly related products are likely to be influenced by the same economic news and forces – for example, the markets in S&P500 and FTSE100 index futures, and therefore markets in such products are generally expected to be closely linked. A number of researchers have used high-frequency data to analyse these linkages on a minute-by-minute basis for markets that have at least some trading hours in common.

If a lead–lag relationship in prices exists, this may present a trading opportunity because knowledge of the current value of the leading market enables forecasting of movements in the lagging market. Many lead–lag relationships are short-lived, and so their detection is only possible with high-frequency data. Empirical investigation of lead–lag relationships using high-frequency data requires that such data be available for both the leading and the lagging variables, and this may not always be the case.

Leads and lags in prices between different types of market based on the same asset

Inter-market linkages are of considerable interest to regulators, practitioners and academics. With no market frictions, the prices of securities and their derivatives must simultaneously reflect new information. If this were not the case, arbitrage profits would be possible. However, there are numerous market frictions cited in the literature, each of which can cause prices in one market to lead or lag another market. For example, the lower trading costs in the derivative markets may induce informed traders to transact there first, and therefore these markets may lead the spot market, while screen-based trading systems arguably allow prices to react to information more quickly than in floor-based markets.

Many studies have used high-frequency data to examine the lead–lag relationships between the prices of equity products (mainly index futures and the underlying spot index), as well as a few studies of interest rates. These studies are summarised in Table 6.1 and cover the USA, Japan, Australia, Hong Kong, Malaysia, the UK, Germany, France, the Netherlands and Sweden.

Investigation of leads and lags requires synchronous observations on the two markets so that matched values are available. Data analysis is

Table 6.1 Empirical studies of leads and lags in returns using high-frequency data

Study	Year	Spot	Data period	Time interval (minutes)	Findings
Index futures and index					
Kawaller, Koch and Koch	1987, 1988	S&P500	1984–85	1	Futures lead by 20–45 minutes
Kawaller, Koch and Koch	1993	S&P500	1986	1	Futures lead
Herbst, McCormack and West	1987	S&P500 VLCI	1982	10 seconds	Futures lead by 42 seconds Futures lead by 54 seconds
Furbush	1989	S&P500	1987	5	Futures lead by 5 minutes
Kutner and Sweeney	1991	S&P500	1987	1	Futures lead by 20 minutes
Stoll and Whaley	1990b, 1993	S&P500 MMI	1982–87	5	Futures lead by 5 minutes
Cheung and Ng	1990	S&P500	1983–87	15	Futures lead by 15 minutes
Chan, Chan and Karolyi	1991	S&P500	1984–89	5	Futures lead by 5 minutes
Fleming, Ostdiek and Whaley	1996	S&P500	1988–91	5	Futures lead by 20 minutes
Ghosh	1993a	S&P500	1988	15	Futures lead by 15 minutes
Mercer	1997	S&P500	1987–88	1	No leads or lags
de Jong and Nijman	1997	S&P500	1993	1	Futures lead by 10 minutes, spot leads by 2 minutes
Pizzi, Economopoulos and O'Neil	1998	S&P500	1987	1	Futures lead by 20 minutes, spot leads by 3–4 minutes
Finnerty and Park	1987	MMI	1984–86	1	Futures lead by 1 minute
Laatsch and Schwarz	1988	MMI	1984–86	1	Futures lead by 1 minute
Swinnerton, Curcio and Bennett	1988	MMI	1986	1	Futures lead by 5 minutes
Chan	1992	MMI	1984–87	5	Futures lead by 15 minutes
Lim	1992a, 1992b	Nikkei	1988–89	5	No leads or lags
Hiraki, Maberly and Takezawa	1995	Nikkei	1988–91	10	Futures lead by 2 days

Table 6.1 – continued

Study	Year	Spot	Data period	Time interval (minutes)	Findings
Iihara, Kato and Tokunaga	1996	Nikkei	1989–91	5	Futures lead by 20 minutes, spot leads by 5 minutes
Chung, Kang and Rhee	1994a	Nikkei	1988–91	5	Futures lead by 20 minutes, spot leads by 15 minutes
Sim and Zurbreugg	1999	Nikkei 300	1997	10	Futures leads spot by 10 minutes and spot leads futures by 10 min
Fung and Jiang	1999	Hang Seng	1993–96	1	Futures lead by 25 minutes, spot leads by 20 minutes
Min and Najand	1999	Kospi200	1996	10	Futures lead by 30 minutes
Hodgson, Kendig and Tahir	1993	All Ord.	1992	15	Futures lead by 30 minutes, spot leads by 15 minutes
Sim and Zurbreugg	1999	All Ord.	1997	10	Spot leads futures by 10 minutes
Abhyankar	1998	FTSE100	1992	5	Bi-directional nonlinear leads and lags
Grünbichler, Longstaff and Schwartz	1994	DAX30	1990–91	5	Futures lead by 15 minutes
Kempf and Korn	1998	DAX30	1995–96	1	Futures lead by a few minutes
Shyy, Vijayraghavan and Scott-Quinn	1996	CAC30	1994	1	Spot leads by 3 minutes
Niemeyer	1994	OMX	1991–93	5	Spot leads by 60 minutes, futures lead by 60 minutes
de Jong and Donders	1998	AEX	1992–93	5	Futures lead by 15 minutes
Index futures and options					
de Jong and Donders	1998	AEX	1992–93	5	Futures lead by 10 minutes
Equity options and equities					
Bhattacharya	1987	US stocks	1977–78	15	Options lead spot, but this does not create arbitrage opportunities

Table 6.1 – continued

Study	Year	Spot	Data period	Time interval (minutes)	Findings
Stephan and Whaley	1990	US stocks	1986	15	Stocks returns lead options by 15 minutes. Stock volume leads options by 30 minutes
Kumar, Sarin and Shastri	1992	US stocks	1983	15	Options lead spot by 15 minutes
Chan, Chung and Johnson	1993	US stocks	1986	5	Stocks lead over options is due to the larger tick size of options
Fleming, Ostdiek and Whaley	1996	S&P100	1988–91	5	Futures leads options, and options leads spot
Finucane	1999	10 US stocks	1990	5 quotes	Bi-directional leads and lags of 5 minutes, stocks lead options by a few minutes.
Interest futures and spot					
Holland	1999	Gilt, OAT, BTP and Bund	1996	5	Futures lead spot

normally based on regularly spaced observations, as it is difficult to match individual trades. The need to obtain matched data also means that the shortest time interval that can be used in the analysis is set by the less heavily traded market. Finucane (1999) is an exception as he analysed non-synchronous quote changes in different markets in quote time.

The studies given in Table 6.1 have found that when high-frequency data is used, small market-microstructure problems with the data become relatively more important and can therefore no longer be ignored as insignificant. In this case the relevant microstructure effects are bid–ask bounce and stale prices (see Chapter 3). Many of the studies have tried to remove from the data the effects of stale prices (which give futures a lead over spot) and bid–ask bounce (which tends to generate movements in the futures price that are not replicated by the spot price). The overall results of the studies in Table 6.1 tend to show that the futures market leads the spot market by a few minutes, while the results for equity options are mixed.

Although not reported in Table 6.1, the quoted studies also found evidence for a strong contemporaneous relationship between the spot and futures markets. Sometimes bi-directional leads and lags are found; this also supports the view that lead and lag relationships change over time as traders change the market in which they choose to exploit information.

It is possible that the degree to which one market leads another is affected by variables such as the volume in each market, macroeconomic announcements, screen versus floor trading systems, the arrival of bad news, price volatility, changes in futures margin levels and changes in transactions costs. Some high-frequency data studies have attempted to control for these factors, and have found some evidence that lead–lag relationships vary as circumstances change.

The 1987 stock market crash

During the 1987 stock market crash, the price of S&P500 futures plunged much faster than did the S&P500 index. This led to charges that index futures caused the 1987 crash. Subsequently, a range of empirical studies

Table 6.2 Empirical studies of leads and lags during the 1987 crash using high-frequency data

Study	Year	Spot	Time interval (minutes)	Findings
Index futures and index				
Harris	1989a	S&P500	5	Strong stale price effect. After adjustment, futures led spot by a few minutes
Moriarty, Gordon, Kuserk and Wang	1990	S&P500	5	Strong stale price effect. After adjustment, futures led spot by a few minutes
Kleidon and Whaley Kleidon	1992 1992	S&P500	5	Initially a non-trading stale price effect, followed by an out-of-date information stale price effect
Arshanapalli and Doukas	1994	S&P500	5	Spot and futures returns followed different Arch processes
Wang and Yau	1994	S&P500	5	Spot and futures returns were not cointegrated during the height of the crash (October 19–21)
Bassett, France and Pliska	1989	MMI	1	Strong stale price effect. After adjustment, futures led spot by 5 minutes
Antoniou and Garrett	1993	FTSE100	1	After adjusting for stale prices, spot led futures by 1 minute, and futures led spot by 10 minutes
Equities spot				
Blume, MacKinlay and Terker	1989	S&P500	15	S&P500 prices were more volatile during the Crash than non-S&P500 prices
Jones, Nachtmann and Phillips-Patrick	1993	S&P500	1	S&P500 and non-S&P500 returns remained co-integrated during the 1987 and 1989 crashes

Table 6.3 Empirical studies of leads and lags in return volatilities using high-frequency data

Study	Year	Spot	Data period	Time interval (minutes)	Findings
Index futures and index					
Kawaller, Koch and Koch	1990	S&P500	1984–86	1	No leads or lags
Cheung and Ng	1990	S&P500	1982–87	15	Futures lead by 15 minutes. Spot leads by 15 minutes
Chan, Chan and Karolyi	1991	S&P500	1984–89	5	Futures lead by 15 minutes. Spot leads by 15 minutes
Lee and Linn	1994	S&P500	1983–87	10	Clear evidence of a futures lead by up to 60 minutes. Weaker evidence that spot leads by up to 60 minutes
Iihara, Kato and Tokunaga	1996	Nikkei	1989–91	5	Futures lead by 5 minutes
Min and Najand	1999	Kospi200	1996	10	Bi-directional
Abhyankar	1995a	FTSE100	1986–90	60	No leads or lags
Grünbichler, Longstaff and Schwartz	1994	DAX30	1990–91	5	Futures lead by 20 minutes
Interest futures and spot					
Crain and Lee	1995	Eurodollars	1990–93	60	Futures lead by 2 hours
Forex futures and spot					
Crain and Lee	1995	US$/DM	1990–93	60	Futures lead by 5 hours
Index futures and options					
So, Booth and Loistl	1997	DAX30 futures and options	1992–94	5	Common volatility process for 30 minute returns, but not for 15 minute and 5 minute returns

Table 6.4 Empirical studies of links between geographically separated markets using high-frequency data

Study	Year	Spot	Data period	Time interval (minutes)	Findings
Index futures					
Hodgson	1994	All Ord. S&P500	1992–93	15	All Ord. returns responded to the preceding S&P500 return
Kofman and Martens	1997	FTSE100 S&P500	1993	1	The S&P500 returns and volatility leads by a few minutes
Gannon	1995	FTSE100 S&P500	1992–93	15	Conflicting results on volatility linkages
Kim, Szakmary and Schwarz	1999	S&P500 NYSE Comp and MMI	1986–91	5	S&P500 leads by 10 minutes
Sim and Zurbreugg	1999	Nikkei 300 All Ord.	1997	10	Nikkei spot and futures lead All Ord. spot and futures
Index and interest futures					
Lequeux	1999b	FTSE100 Long Gilt	1987–97	15	Long Gilt returns lead by 15–45 minutes
Index options and equities spot					
Board and Sutcliffe	1998	23 UK stocks	1992–94	30	No link between non-transparent equity trades and options volume
Interest futures					
Ballocchi, Dacorogna, Hopman, Müller and Olsen	1998	Eurodollars, Euromark, Short Sterling, Euroyen	1992–97	Trades and quotes	Some leads and lags of 30–60 minutes in the implied forward rates between futures
Equities spot					
Goodhart	1986	FT Ord Dow Jones	1986	60	US price movements after the UK closes are impounded in the subsequent UK opening price
King and Wadhwani	1990	UK and US indexes	1987–88	15	Support for contagion between markets, ie pricing mistakes in one market are transmitted to another

Table 6.4 – continued

Study	Year	Spot	Data period	Time interval (minutes)	Findings
Becker, Finnerty and Tucker	1992	S&P500 Nikkei	1985–89	60	Open–close return in one country has a positive correlation with the subsequent 60 minute return for the first hour in the other country
Susmel and Engle	1994	Dow Jones FT 30	1987–89	60	Little evidence for volatility spillovers (or meteor showers) between the US and UK
Kim, Szakmary and Schwarz	1999	S&P500 NYSE Comp MMI	1986–91	5	MMI leads by 5 minutes
Forex spot					
Low and Muthuswamy	1996	U$/DM, U$/¥ DM/¥	1992–93	Quotes	Bi-directional leads and lags in returns of up to 20 minutes

used high-frequency data to investigate the extent of leads and lags between these two markets during the 1987 crash. The results of these investigations have important implications, not only for market regulators, but also for traders involved in strategies such as portfolio insurance using the dynamic replication of a bought put option. If the futures market tends to crash first, then such traders should use shares rather than futures in their dynamic replication strategies, and hope to trade out of the stock positions before the crash hits the stock market (or vice versa).

Table 6.2 summarises a number of high-frequency data studies of the relationship between the futures and spot markets during the 1987 crash. With the exception of one UK study, all of these consider US markets. After adjusting the data for market-microstructure effects, it has been found that the futures market led the spot market by a few minutes at the time of the 1987 crash, which is the same result as for non-crash periods.

These findings provide no support for the view that the index futures market "caused" the 1987 crash. The lag of a few minutes between the futures and spot markets indicates that creating synthetic portfolio insurance by trading equities and hoping to trade out of these equities just before a crash by closely monitoring the futures market is unlikely to be successful. There is also the issue that, while a lead or lag may be just statistically significant, the size of the effect may be small and a trading strategy based on this relationship may only make small amounts

Table 6.5 Empirical studies of dual listed securities using high-frequency data

Study	Year	Spot	Data period	Time interval (minutes)	Findings
Index futures					
Shyy and Shen	1997	Nikkei (Osaka and Simex)	1993	1	Bi-directional leads and lags of a few minutes between price changes in the two markets
Vila and Sandmann	1995	Nikkei (Osaka and Simex)	1993	1	Wider bid–ask spread in Osaka, Simex returns led Osaka returns by 4–6 minutes
Interest futures					
Franses, Ieperen, Kofman, Martens and Menkveld	1994	Bund (Liffe and DTB)	1992	1	No leads and leads in volatility for 5 minute returns, but bi-directional leads and lags in volatility for 1 minute returns
Kofman, Bouwman and Moser	1994	Bund (Liffe and DTB)	1992	1, Trades	Liffe has the wider bid–ask spread using the Roll estimator but, when corrected for changes in expected returns, Liffe has the narrower spread. Volatility on Liffe leads that on the DTB
Franke and Hess	1995	Bund (Liffe and DTB)	1991–93	3	Bi-directional leads and lags in price changes
Shyy and Lee	1995	Bund (Liffe and DTB)	1993	1, Quotes	No arbitrage opportunities, DTB leads Liffe by 1 minute, and Liffe has a narrower bid–ask spread, although the information asymmetry is smaller for the DTB
Pirrong	1996	Bund (Liffe and DTB)	1992–93	15	DTB has a narrower bid–ask spread and greater depth, ie increases in volume have a smaller price effect

Table 6.5 – continued

Study	Year	Spot	Data period	Time interval (minutes)	Findings
Kofman and Moser	1997	Bund (Liffe and DTB)	1992	1, Trades and quotes	Liffe has a narrower bid–ask spread. There are bidirectional leads and lags of a few minutes
Breedon and Holland	1998	Bund (Liffe and DTB)	1995	1, Trades and quotes	Liffe has wider effective spreads and narrower quoted spreads, and there is bi-directional causality
Martens	1998	Bund (Liffe and DTB)	1995	1	Liffe dominates price discovery when volatility is high, and the DTB dominates when volatility is low
Frino, McInish and Toner	1998	Bund (Liffe and DTB)	1997	1	DTB has a narrower bid–ask spread
Shyy and Shen	1997	JGB (Osaka and Simex)	1993	1	Bidirectional leads and lags of a few minutes between price changes in the two markets
Equities spot					
Blume and Goldstein	1997	US stocks	1990–91	Trades and quotes	Non-NYSE markets in the US attract a significant part of their volume when not offering the best quotes
Schmidt and Iversen	1992	30 stocks in DAX	1991	Trades and quotes	Spreads for the same stock differ as between trading systems (IBIS, MATIS and SEAQ-I)
Interest rates spot					
Umlauf	1991	US treasury notes and bonds	1987	Trades and quotes	Primary dealers lead secondary dealers by 2–4 minutes, and the primary dealers' bid–ask spread is narrower

of money occasionally. In consequence, after allowing for transactions costs and risk, it may not be an attractive trading rule.

Leads and lags in price volatility

As well as leads and lags in the level of prices in different types of market for the same underlying asset, there may also be leads and lags in price volatility between these markets. Again, such a situation could prove useful to traders as volatility in the lagging market is thereby predictable.

The studies of equity markets suggest that futures volatility may lead spot volatility, and Table 6.3 indicates that such a lead is several hours long in interest rate and forex markets.

Links between geographically separated markets

Markets trading similar products in different locations should be linked by the arrival of information that affects both markets simultaneously. While riskless arbitrage may not be possible between such markets because the underlying assets are slightly different, strong positive relationships between price movements (eg returns and returns volatility) are still expected.

Empirical studies using high-frequency data have investigated this question for equity and interest futures and for the equity and forex spot markets, and the results are summarised in Table 6.4. These show that, in some cases, there are leads and lags in returns and volatility of somewhere between five and 60 minutes.

Rival markets

As well as using high-frequency data to study the links between markets that are trading different products, it has also been used to compare the performance of markets trading essentially the same product.

If traders have a choice over where to execute trades, they may wish to use high-frequency data to investigate the relative characteristics of the available markets. For example, the spread measures one component of transactions costs, and traders may choose to trade where such costs are lowest. Traders may also be interested in market depth, ie the price impact of trades, as well as how quickly they can trade for a given price impact, etc. Empirical studies have compared a number of markets, with many looking at the "battle of the Bund futures contract" between Liffe and the DTB (see Table 6.5). The papers quoted in Table 6.5 are also studies of the battle between the trading floor (Liffe) and screens (DTB, the German stock exchange).

While the studies of the links between markets, as listed in Tables 6.1–4 earlier in this chapter, have used time-matched observations to investigate leads and lags, etc, studies of rival markets do not necessarily need time-matched observations. This is because comparisons of various measures of market quality, such as liquidity, depth and bid–ask spread can be performed without using matched observations. However, matched observations are required for some performance measures, such as price discovery, opportunities for arbitrage between the rival products, and volatility spillovers. The high-frequency data studies of rival markets generally show that such markets move contemporaneously, although there may sometimes be lags of a few minutes in prices and volatility. The studies of the size of the bid–ask spread for the Bund on Liffe and the DTB are mixed, with the conclusions influenced by how the spread is measured.

Conclusions

High-frequency studies of the relationship between related pairs of markets have generally found that such markets are strongly integrated. They have very strong contemporaneous linkages, with simultaneous responses in both markets to the arrival of information. However, there is also evidence of leads and lags lasting for a few minutes. These leads and lags may be due to market-microstructure effects (eg bid–ask spread, stale prices, or tick size) and so do not represent profitable opportunities, particularly when transactions costs are taken into account.

High-frequency data has also been used to compare the quality of rival markets (eg the Bund futures market in London and Frankfurt) along a number of dimensions, and this information may prove useful to traders who are choosing where they wish to trade.

7 Destabilisation of markets

One aspect of linkages between markets is the theoretical possibility that trading in one market could destabilise trading in a related market – an empirical issue that cannot be resolved theoretically.

Since the crash of 1987 the potential problem of destabilisation has assumed particular importance in equity markets, and almost all of the studies using high-frequency data to look at destabilisation have considered equity markets. The stock market crash of October 1987 led to considerable concern about a connection between the recent creation of markets in index futures and options and the extreme volatility that the spot market exhibited during October 1987. This question is of interest to regulators, financial exchanges and participants in financial markets. Specifically, four issues are of interest when considering the relationship between derivative markets and share price volatility:

1 the relative volatility of derivative prices and the price of the underlying asset;

2 the effect on the price volatility of the underlying asset of creating a derivatives market;

3 the influence of programme trading (much of which is due to the existence of a derivatives market) on the price volatility of the underlying asset; and

4 the effect of a derivative market on the systematic risk of the shares in the index.

The first and third issues have been investigated using high-frequency data, while the studies of the second and fourth issues have generally not used high-frequency data (apart from one study of the second question). As well as examining the effect of the existence of a derivatives market on the level of volatility of the underlying market, some studies using high-frequency data have looked for occasional effects on spot volatility – that is, the volatility effects of the simultaneous expiration of several derivatives (eg the "triple witching hour").

Relative volatility

If the derivatives market is more volatile than the spot market, there are implications for traders – for example with risk-minimising hedge ratios, which depend on the ratio of the standard deviations of the spot and futures prices. Higher derivatives volatility also means that derivatives markets have the potential to transmit extra volatility to the spot market.

The relative volatility of the spot and futures markets depends, in part, on the time intervals used to measure volatility. For returns, if the condition is met for an absence of arbitrage opportunities (the "no-arbitrage condition"), and interest rates and dividends are certain, then the variance of returns on the index computed using an input frequency (namely the time interval over which the returns are computed) of a day or shorter should be the same as the futures variance. As the input frequency lengthens, the volatility of futures returns tends to be less than the spot volatility, but only by a very small amount. For example, the variance of futures returns measured with an input frequency of one year

Table 7.1 Empirical studies of the extra volatility of index futures using high-frequency data: (a) prices changes and (b) returns

Study	Index	Input frequency	Output frequency	Extra volatility (%)
(a) Price changes				
Kawaller, Koch and Koch (1990)	S&P500	1 minute	30 minutes	732
Kawaller, Koch and Koch (1990)	S&P500	1 minute	Day	630
Miller, Muthuswamy and Whaley (1994)	S&P500	15 minutes	9 years	83
Miller, Muthuswamy and Whaley (1994)	S&P500	30 minutes	9 years	58
Miller, Muthuswamy and Whaley (1994)	S&P500	60 minutes	9 years	45
Miller, Muthuswamy and Whaley (1994)	VLCI	15 minutes	9 years	659
Miller, Muthuswamy and Whaley (1994)	VLCI	30 minutes	9 years	431
Miller, Muthuswamy and Whaley (1994)	VLCI	60 minutes	9 years	269
(b) Returns				
Harris, Sofianos and Shapiro (1994)	S&P500	1 minute	2 years	359
Harris, Sofianos and Shapiro (1994)	S&P500	5 minutes	2 years	91
MacKinlay and Ramaswamy (1988)	S&P500	15 minutes	3 months	56
MacKinlay and Ramaswamy (1988)	S&P500	30 minutes	3 months	26
MacKinlay and Ramaswamy (1988)	S&P500	60 minutes	3 months	16
MacKinlay and Ramaswamy (1988)	S&P500	2 hours	3 months	13
Cheung and Ng (1990)	S&P500	15 minutes	3 months	53
Park (1993)	MMI	30 minutes	2 years	12
Park (1993)	MMI	30 minutes	2 years	403
Lim (1992b)	Nikkei-Simex	5 minutes	Day	−30
Lim and Muthuswamy (1993)	Nikkei-Simex	5 minutes	Day	−16
Iihara, Kato and Tokunaga (1996)	Nikkei-OSE	5 minutes	10 months	−28.4
Iihara, Kato and Tokunaga (1996)	Nikkei-OSE	5 minutes	8 months	34.7
Iihara, Kato and Tokunaga (1996)	Nikkei-OSE	5 minutes	6 months	−6.2
Hodgson (1994)	All Ord.	15 minutes	1 year	175
Board and Sutcliffe (1995a)	FTSE100	60 minutes	Day	101
Board and Sutcliffe (1995a)	FTSE100	60 minutes	Month	85
Board and Sutcliffe (1995a)	FTSE100	60 minutes	Quarter	82
Strickland and Xu (1993)	FTSE100	60 minutes	2 years	46
Grünbichler and Callahan (1994)	DAX 30	5 minutes	10 months	27
Grünbichler and Callahan (1994)	DAX 30	15 minutes	10 months	19
Grünbichler and Callahan (1994)	DAX 30	30 minutes	10 months	18

Note: Input frequency is the time interval over which each return is computed. Output frequency is the time period over which the volatility of a set of observations is calculated.

Figure 7.1 Extra futures volatility and input frequency

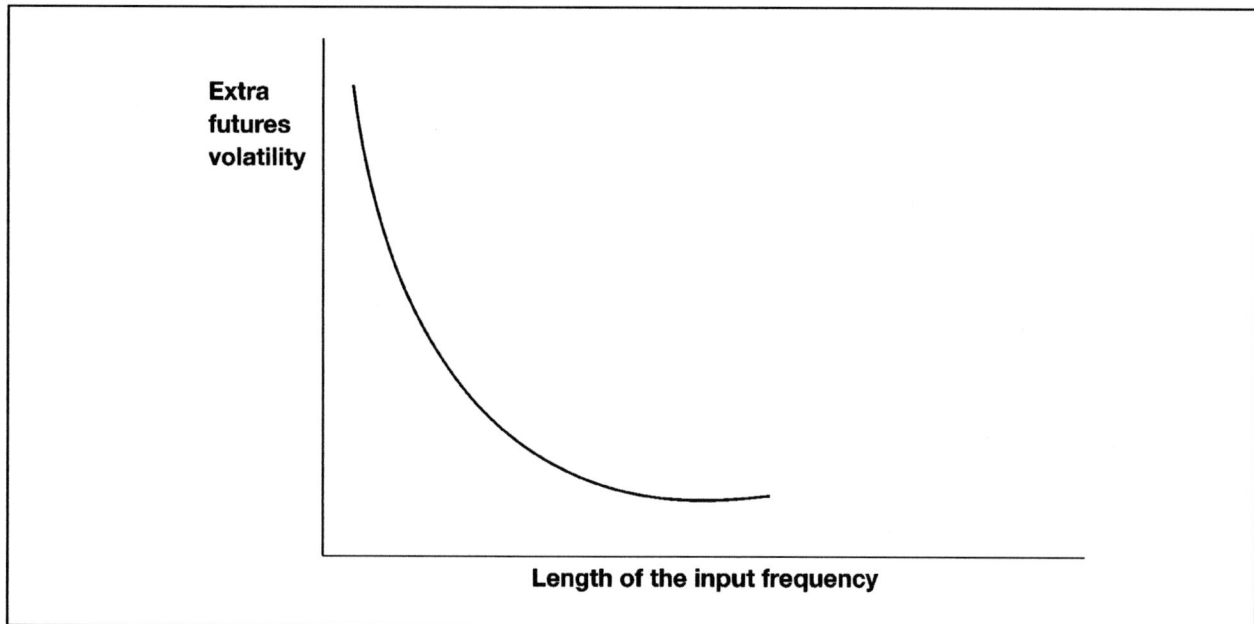

should be only about 10% less than the spot variance. For prices and price changes, if the no-arbitrage condition is met and dividends and interest rates are certain, the futures variance should be slightly larger than the spot variance. The theory predicts an extra volatility of approximately 3% for a futures contract with three months to delivery. The major theoretical results described here are explained more fully in Board and Sutcliffe (1995a).

Empirical studies using high-frequency data for the US, Japan, Australia, the UK and Germany have investigated the relative price volatility of index futures and the index. These studies are summarised in Table 7.1 and have established that index futures prices are substantially more volatile than the underlying index. Because the hypothesis being tested is concerned with the relationship between the length of the input frequency (in minutes) and the extra futures volatility, every study has used regularly spaced high-frequency data.

The studies listed in Table 7.1, together with those that have used a longer differencing interval (Sutcliffe, 1997), indicate that as the length of the input frequency shortens, the difference between futures and spot volatility increases, as shown in Figure 7.1. Thus, the extra volatility for futures markets is substantial when high-frequency data is used because the differencing interval is short. This extra volatility for high-frequency data may be due to a number of explanations: the measured volatility of the spot market being reduced by stale prices; trades outside the touch being ignored; and high transactions costs restricting price discovery. Furthermore, measured futures volatility is increased by bid–ask bounce, noise traders, a maturity effect, default risk, and interest and dividend risk.

Some studies using high-frequency data have tried to understand why index futures markets exhibit high relative volatility, and one possibility is that the bid–ask bounce in futures prices tends to cancel out in the underlying index. Smith and Whaley (1994) found that over 80% of the variance of changes in S&P500 futures transactions prices was due to bid–ask bounce. However, in an empirical study of the S&P500, Miller *et al* (1994) suggest that bid–ask bounce can only explain a 0.1% increase in the variance of futures price changes over 15-minute periods.

Another high-frequency data study sought to investigate whether large changes in the spot price (or jumps) could be explained by futures volume or open interest. Darrat and Rahman (1995) studied hourly data on the S&P500 index from May 1982 to June 1991. They investigated whether monthly futures volume or open interest was positively linked with monthly spot jump volatility (the number of hourly index returns whose absolute value exceeded a threshold). The lagged variance of the term structure and the over-the-counter (OTC) index – purged of any effects already captured by futures volume or open interest – had a positive effect on spot jump volatility. However, neither lagged changes in futures volume nor lagged changes in open interest affected spot jump volatility.

Existence of derivative markets

There have been many empirical studies of the connection between the creation of a derivative market and the volatility of the underlying asset. However, only one has used high-frequency data. Gerety and Mulherin (1991) examined hourly values of the Dow Jones index from 1933 until 1989 and found that the trading of index futures from 1982 did not lead to an increase in spot volatility.

Programme trading and volatility

Some of the critics of index futures have argued that the programme trading associated with index arbitrage and portfolio insurance may be responsible for increasing the volatility of equity prices. However, even if index arbitrage creates short-term liquidity problems in the stock market, and there is a small rise in the short-term price volatility of the shares in the index, this effect will die out as new liquidity flows into the market. Using high-frequency data, Harris *et al* (1994) did not find price reversals in the 30 minutes after index arbitrage trades, and they interpret this as evidence that such trades did not cause short-term liquidity problems leading to excess spot volatility.

It has been argued that one form of programme trading, namely portfolio insurance, is especially responsible for large increases in equity-price volatility, including the stock market crash of October 1987. If there is a demand for portfolio insurance and this is met by synthetic options (eg creating a synthetic put option by trading index futures and debt), there will be an increase in the volatility of share prices. This is because portfolio insurers wish to sell when prices fall and buy when prices rise, thereby amplifying price movements – in other words, they are momentum traders rather than value traders (or positive- rather than negative-feedback traders). If portfolio insurers use a synthetic strategy, the market is not informed in advance of their intention to sell shares if the price drops. Such unexpected trades in futures and shares tend to exhaust the capital capacity (the liquidity) of these markets. They may also appear to convey bad news about expected returns, so reducing the willingness of traders to buy from the portfolio insurers. As a result, share prices fall further, so increasing the price volatility of shares and futures. This is the "cascade theory" of the stock market crash of October 1987, ie a fall in stock market prices led portfolio insurers to sell index futures, resulting in a drop in their price, and, via index arbitrage, a further fall in stock market prices. This drop in the stock market led portfolio insurers to sell index futures, and so on.

As well as directly amplifying price movements, programme trades may lead to an apparent increase in the volatility of an index computed using the last trade prices, due to bid–ask and stale-price effects. Usually, roughly equal numbers of shares in the index were last traded at the bid and at the ask prices. In consequence, the bid–ask spread tends to cancel out, and the value of the index is equivalent to that which would have been computed if midquote prices at the time of the last trade had been used. However, just after a programme trade to buy (sell) many shares, most of the prices used in the index calculation will be ask (bid) prices. In consequence, the movement in the index will be exaggerated by about half the bid–ask spread. In addition to this bid–ask effect, a programme trade temporarily ensures that most of the last trade prices are recent or "fresh", so removing the stale-price effect. Therefore, as a result of a programme trade, most share prices reflect their current, rather than their historic, values. This situation will also tend to increase the volatility of an index computed using transactions prices, because it mitigates the reduction in measured volatility due to the use of stale prices. These effects were quantified by Harris *et al* (1994) using high-frequency data.

In their 1994 study, Harris *et al* analysed the effects of programme trading on the volatility of the S&P500 index and found that the variance

Table 7.2 Empirical studies of programme trading and equity volatility using high-frequency data

Study	Year	Spot	Data period	Time interval (minutes)	Findings
Equities spot					
Santoni	1988	S&P500	1987	1	No support for the cascade theory
Duffee, Kupiec and White	1992	NYSE	1988–89	60	Positive relationship between arbitrage programme trades and spot volatility
Neal	1993a	NYSE	1987	5	No link between portfolio insurance trades and spot volatility
Chan and Chung; Koch	1993	MMI	1984–85	5	Mispricings are followed by an increase in spot and futures volatility 5 minutes later
Kodres	1994	S&P500	1989	Futures trades	Momentum traders do not destabilise the futures market

of one-minute price changes in the S&P500 index for June 1989 was 140% larger than for price changes in the midquote index. Thus, fluctuations in the last-trade prices due to switching between the bid and ask prices led to a considerable increase in measured spot volatility. The variance of current midquote prices was about 20% larger than that of midquotes at the time of the last trade, indicating that the use of stale prices to compute the index led to a reduction in the measured variance. Thus, the increase in measured volatility for one-minute returns due to bid–ask bounce considerably exceeds the decrease in measured volatility due to stale prices. Since programme trades refresh stale prices and induce a bid–ask effect, they are expected to increase the variance by 160%. In consequence, a substantial increase in the volatility of the index when there are programme trades may be largely due to a measurement problem.

The studies of a positive link between the volume of programme trading for index arbitrage or portfolio insurance purposes and spot volatility that have used high-frequency data are summarised in Table 7.2. It is possible there could be a destabilising effect for, say, one-minute returns, but no effect for, say, 60-minute returns, because any short-term liquidity effects will have passed after an hour, while the artificial bid–ask and stale-price effects will also have been overcome. Thus the time interval used is an important feature of the test, and high-frequency data enables researchers to examine a range of differencing intervals. The small number of available studies have used a range of time intervals varying from one minute to 60 minutes. The evidence of any linkage is weak, and may be largely due to the bid–ask effect, refreshing stale prices, and correcting mispricings. Strangely, the study using 60-minute returns found evidence of a link, while most of those studies using a shorter differencing interval did not.

Price movements at expiration

At expiration, traders who have an arbitrage position between the stock and futures markets must close out their position in the spot asset at the time the futures settlement price is computed, *irrespective of the price*. Otherwise, they are taking a speculative risk. Therefore, if there is an imbalance between the size of the long and short positions held by arbitrageurs, there can be sharp movements in the price of the spot asset at expiration.

There is US, Canadian and German evidence of a short-term increase in the price volatility of the stock index when a number of different equity derivatives expire simultaneously (eg index futures, index options, options on index futures, and options on individual stocks), known as the "triple witching hour". However, the increase in volatility is small in magnitude. Table 7.3 also presents evidence of an increase in volume for both shares and futures at this time. At the expiration of interest rate futures it has been found that volatility increases, possibly due to the release of the survey-determined settlement price.

If there is an increase in volatility and volume when contracts expire, this is of relevance to traders as well as regulators. The larger price movements may create profitable opportunities – for example if the arbitrageurs in aggregate are trying to sell the index basket at any price, buying these shares and selling them within a few hours may be

Table 7.3 Empirical studies of expiration effects using high-frequency data

Study	Year	Spot	Data period	Time interval (minutes)	Findings
Equity futures and options					
Whaley	1986	S&P500	1982–85	1	Higher volatility at expiration, particularly when the S&P500 futures expire
Stoll and Whaley	1987a, 1987b	S&P500	1982–85	1	Higher volatility at expiration, particularly when the S&P500 futures expire
Stoll	1988	S&P500	1984–87	30	Higher volume and volatility at expiration
Stoll and Whaley	1990a	S&P500	1984–86	30	Volume is markedly higher, and volatility is also higher at expiration
Stoll and Whaley	1991	S&P500 S&P100 MMI	1985–89	30	The new 1987 US rules moved some of the extra volume and volatility to the Friday open
Hancock	1991, 1993	S&P500	1987–89	1	Spot volatility is higher during option expiration
Herbst and Maberly	1990	S&P500	1984–89	60	The new 1987 US rules moved some volatility and volume from the Friday close to the Friday open
Herbst and Maberly	1991	S&P500	1984–90	30	The new 1987 US rules led to some reduction in spot volatility
Sofianos	1994	NYSE	1989–92	Trades	A small increase in spot volatility at expiration
Chen and Williams	1994	Dow Jones	1984–90	60	Small increase in volatility at expiration
Chamberlain, Cheung and Kwan	1989	TSE300	1985–87	30	Increase in volatility, but not volume at expiration
Schlag	1996	DAX30	1991–94	60	Spot volume was over three times higher than normal, but no increase in volatility at expiration
Interest futures					
Park and Switzer	1995	Eurodollar	1982–92	15	There is no change in the volatility of the expiring contract, but an increase in that of the next contract

profitable. In addition, those analysing high-frequency data need to allow for expiration effects in their data.

Since the expiration effect lasts about an hour, high-frequency data is needed for its investigation. As well as investigating whether expiration causes a short-term volatility rise, empirical studies using high-frequency data have also investigated the efficacy of the US response to this situation, which was to move the expiration of S&P500 futures from the Friday close to the Friday open, as from June 1987. Starting in July 1992, the expiration of S&P500 options also moved to the Friday open. The empirical studies that have used high-frequency data to investigate these two questions are summarised in Table 7.3. There is general agreement that before June 1987 there was a small increase in spot volume and volatility at expiration, and that the 1987 rule change spread these effects over two expiration periods.

Conclusions

The use of high-frequency data for equity markets has found that, while high-frequency returns for index futures are considerably more volatile than those for the underlying spot index, there is no evidence that this has led to the futures market destabilising the spot market. The relatively high volatility of futures markets is probably due to market microstructure effects rather than some fundamental difference in volatilities.

There is evidence of a small derivatives-associated increase in short run spot volatility at expiration, but this has been dealt with in the US by altering expiration dates.

8 Regulations governing the markets

The rules and regulations that govern the way markets operate can have a powerful influence on market behaviour. There are many such regulations in existence worldwide, but it is usually only possible to measure the effects of a rule when it is varied, either over time for the same market or when different rules apply in otherwise similar markets – for instance for different securities traded on the same exchange. For some regulations, such as those governing trade publication delays and tick size, trade data is the obvious data to use as the regulations concern individual trades. For regulations that do not deal with individual trades, such as circuit breakers, trade data or regularly spaced high-frequency data is suitable for use in empirical studies.

An understanding of how regulations affect markets is important for regulators. It is also important for traders to understand how the functioning of the market is altered by the regulations. This is particularly important when regulations change and market participants have little prior experience of the new environment on which to base their trading decisions. Some of the regulations that have been studied using high-frequency data are those relating to:

✦ dual capacity;

✦ circuit breakers;

✦ short sales;

✦ transactions taxes;

✦ tick size and price clustering;

✦ trade publication delays; and

✦ expiration.

Each of these categories of regulation is discussed further below, except the last. Studies of the control of expiration volatilities appear in the relevant section in Chapter 7.

Regulation of dual capacity

"Dual capacity" exists when floor traders can both execute trades on their own account and act as a floor broker for customers. Requiring traders to have single capacity, ie to be exclusively either principals or agents, reduces "front running", which occurs when brokers trade on their own behalf ahead of their customers' orders. It also reduces the informational advantage of dual traders over customers.

However, market liquidity and the quality of the broking service may decline at times of heavy trading activity (in the form, for instance, of delayed execution) because of insufficient capacity. This occurs because traders are no longer able to switch between broking and speculating. Alternatively, if sufficient brokerage capacity exists to cope with peaks in demand, brokerage fees are higher because no profits can be made from speculation. Röell (1990) has argued that dual capacity reduces the amount of informationless trading in the market, thereby increasing the price impact of the remaining, largely information-based, orders. The evidence on the effects of dual capacity is of relevance to floor brokers as well as regulators, since the former can choose between single and dual capacity, and is also of relevance to the clients of floor brokers, who can choose between using single- or dual-capacity brokers.

There have been several empirical studies of various aspect of dual capacity using high-frequency data, and these are summarised in Table 8.1. Because these studies are concerned with the capacity in which the trader is acting, and this can vary between trades, trade data is essential for this type of investigation.

As from June 22, 1987, the "top-step rule" of the Chicago Mercantile Exchange (CME) restricted S&P500 futures traders on the top step to acting each day either as agents or proprietary traders, but not both. From May 20, 1991, the CME restricted dual trading in all liquid and mature contracts, which included S&P500 futures. These rule changes provided the requisite high-frequency data for the empirical investigation of dual capacity. The evidence on the effects of dual capacity is mixed, although there is some evidence that dual capacity increases both volume and profits for floor traders.

Circuit breakers

When established trading processes threaten to run out of control, it may be wise to activate various pre-established mechanisms that alter the procedures and pace of trading. Such mechanisms usually include a trading halt, and may involve the wider dissemination of information. "Circuit breakers", as they are called, tend to be associated with trading halts in equity markets and price limits in futures markets. Price limits do not stop all trading, only trading at prices outside the price limits (usually for the remainder of that day), while trading halts ban trading at any price, often for a period lasting anything from 10 minutes to a few hours. Circuit breakers can also take the form of preventing the sale of shares on a down-tick or the purchase of shares on an up-tick for arbitrage purposes (eg rule 80a in the US).

Table 8.1 Empirical studies of dual capacity using high-frequency data

Study	Year	Spot	Data period	Time interval	Features of dual capacity
Index futures and spot					
Park, Sarkar and Wu	1994	S&P500 Yen	1987	Trades	Lower costs to customers piggy-backing own trades Higher profits on own trades
Park and Sarkar	1992	S&P500	1986–88	Trades	No effect on mispricings or market depth
Smith and Whaley	1994	S&P500	1983–87	Trades	Lower traded bid–ask spread Higher volume
Locke, Sarkar and Wu	1994	S&P500	1987	Trades	No change in market depth Higher profits for floor traders

Table 8.2 Empirical studies of circuit breakers using high-frequency data

Study	Year	Spot	Data period	Time interval (minutes)	Findings
Index futures					
Kuhn, Kuserk and Locke	1991	S&P500	1989	Trades	No reduction in volatility An increase involatility for the related markets in MMI spot and futures
McMillan	1991	S&P500	1989	1	Gravitational effect tending to trigger halts
Kuserk, Locke and Sayers	1992	S&P500	1990	Trades	Slight increase in volatility
Overdahl and McMillan	1998	S&P500	1990–93	1	Arbitrage volume drops, as does volatility
Berkman and Steenbeek	1998	Nikkei	1992	Trades	Rejects any gravitational effect and supports the satellite market theory
Interest rates					
Arak and Cook	1997	Treasury bonds	1980–87	5	Price limits do not act as magnets

There are three main ways in which circuit breakers can be triggered:

✦ an imbalance between buy and sell orders that is big enough to create a problem for market-makers;

✦ volumes that are high enough to overwhelm the back-office procedures; and

✦ large price changes.

In each case, activation of a circuit breaker requires access to high-frequency data, and so the regulatory authorities themselves need access to high-frequency data in real time. Traders may wish to monitor whether a circuit breaker is about to be triggered as this will have implications for their trading behaviour – for example, they may then wish to bring forward trades to beat the circuit breaker, or to liquidate positions in advance of the circuit breaker limiting trading. The activation of a circuit breaker may mean that trading moves to substitutes, eg to index futures rather than shares, or to other markets (maybe abroad), or both.

The empirical questions for regulators and market participants include the effects of the initiation of a circuit breaker on the market when trading resumes. Is volatility reduced, is there a surge of pent-up volume, do price limits act as magnets, do bid–ask spreads widen, and what happens to related markets where trading continues? There have been a few studies using high-frequency data to help answer some of these questions and to determine the effects of circuit breakers (mostly trading halts in futures markets), and these studies are summarised in Table 8.2. These investigations take the form of an event study and can use regularly or irregularly spaced data.

Restrictions on short selling

The selling of shares is needed when arbitraging an underpricing of index futures; if the arbitrageur does not own the index basket then short selling is required. However, in some countries there are restrictions on short selling shares. High-frequency data can be used to investigate the effects of changing the restrictions on short selling.

On January 3, 1994, it became legal to short sell 17 of the 33 stocks in the Hang Seng index, and then from March 25, 1996, *all* the constituents of the Hang Seng could be sold short. Fung and Jiang (1999) used one-minute returns to study the effect of these two changes in the rules on leads and lags between the Hang Seng index and the value of this index implied by the current price of Hang Seng index futures. They found some evidence that the leads and lags reduced, so that the two markets became more closely integrated.

Taxes on transactions

A number of financial markets are subject to transactions taxes – for example, stamp duty of 0.5% is charged on purchases of UK equities. One issue for the regulatory authorities to consider is the effect of such taxes on trading volume. Simple economics indicates that the higher the tax, the lower the volume traded. The interesting question is the size of the reduction in volume that results from a specified transactions tax. One way to study this question is to compare trading volume before and after a change in the level of the transaction tax. However, such events are rare and so another approach has had to be developed. As far as traders are concerned, a transactions tax just increases the bid–ask spread they face. Therefore high-frequency data can be used to address this issue by studying the effect of variations in the bid–ask spread on volume. Wang, Yau and Baptiste (1997) used trade data to compute the average traded bid–ask spread per day for S&P500, Deutschmark and Treasury bond futures for 1992–94. They quantified the negative effect of a widening of the spread on volume in each case.

Tick size and price clustering

Exchanges set a tick size for each future, option and share traded. This minimum price movement is set with reference to two offsetting forces. First, the tick size rules out most possible prices, and simplifies bargaining over the price. Since "time is money", it reduces the transactions costs of trading. It also has the benefit of facilitating the trading process by reducing the requirement for close attention when recording transaction prices. Second, and in contrast, the tick size means that market prices cannot be exactly equal to the equilibrium market-clearing price unless the equilibrium price just happens to coincide with one of the permitted prices. This may lead to reduced volumes, with those who consider the security marginally adversely priced not trading. Over the course of a number of trades, these "mispricings" will tend to cancel out.

Table 8.3 Empirical studies of price clustering using high-frequency data

Study	Year	Spot	Data period	Time interval	Findings
Index futures					
Hasbrouck	1998	S&P500	1998	Trades	Low price clustering
Henker	1998	FTSE100	1994–96	Futures trades	Few half point quotes
ap Gwilym, Clare and Thomas	1998a	FTSE100	1992–95	Futures trades	Few half point quotes
Interest futures					
ap Gwilym, Clare and Thomas	1998b	Bund, JGB, Long gilt, BTP	1992–95	Trades and quotes	Clustering for BTP and JGB Greater clustering in trades than quotes
Equity options					
ap Gwilym, Clare and Thomas	1998a	FTSE100	1992–95	Trades	Few half-point quotes
Equities spot					
Niederhoffer	1965	4 US stocks	1940s	Limit orders	Price clustering for limit orders
Harris	1991	US stocks	1854, 1987	Trades and quotes	The price clustering increases with the price level and volatility
Christie and Schultz	1994	100 Nasdaq stocks	1991	Trades and quotes	Price clustering on even tick sizes
Christie, Harris and Schultz	1994	Apple, Intel, Cisco, Amgen and Microsoft	1993–94	Trades and quotes	Increased use of odd ticks and a reduction in spreads on the announcement of Christie and Schultz (1994) findings
Ahn, Cao and Choe	1996	US stocks	1992	Trades and quotes	A reduction in the tick size reduced spreads, but did not lead to an increase in volume
Godek	1996	Nasdaq	1993–94	Quotes	The price clustering is due to order preferencing not collusion
Bessembinder	1997	NYSE Nasdaq	1994	Trades and quotes	Higher execution costs are associated with the rounding of quote and trade prices
Kandel and Marx	1997	Nasdaq	1994	Quotes	Price clustering on even ticks is widespread
Aitken, Brown, Buckland, Izan and Walter	1996	267 Australian stocks	1990–93	Trades and quotes	Price clustering increases with volatility and trade size, and decreases with the number of trades and for stocks that underlie options and can be sold short
Board and Sutcliffe	1997	19 UK stocks	1994–95	Trades and quotes	While there is no tick size, quotes and trades are in round pennies

Table 8.3 – continued

Study	Year	Spot	Data period	Time interval	Findings
Forex spot					
Goodhart and Figliuoli	1991	US$, DM, £, ¥, Ffr, Sfr, L, ECU	1987	1	Clustering of the spread
Bollerslev and Melvin	1994	US$/DM	1989	Quotes	Clustering of spreads on 5, 7, 10 and 15 basis points
Goodhart and Payne	1996	US$/DM	1993	Quotes	No clustering of the inside spread
Szpiro	1998	US$/DM	1992–93	Quotes	The tick size leads to the compass rose pattern in the phase portrait of chaos theory
Hasbrouck	1999	US$/DM	1996	Quotes	Symmetric clustering, ie prices are rounded up or down to the nearest number

When a study of the relationship between two markets is undertaken, it can be important to allow for differences in their tick size. Chan, Chung and Johnson (1993) used five-minute trade and quote data on US options in order to study leads and lags between the options and stock markets. Using options trade data, they found that the stock market led the options market by 15 minutes. However, they concluded that this result was due to the much larger tick size in the options market, which prevented options prices from matching small movements in the underlying stock price.

The official tick size can sometimes be superseded by market participants choosing to use a larger tick size, which leads to "price clustering". Price clustering may be due to the attraction of prices to the nearest round number, a wish to reduce negotiation costs (particularly for small trades) by restricting the price possibilities, or it may be because the market does not wish to resolve prices to a greater degree (eg traders are not able to discern differences in value smaller than this amount). Alternatively, clustering may also be caused by implicit collusion amongst traders and, if so, price clustering becomes a regulatory issue.

The empirical studies of price clustering using high-frequency data are summarised in Table 8.3 and show that price clustering appears to be widespread.

Statistical consequences of discrete price changes

The tick size or price clustering means that trade prices, quotes and the bid–ask spread are restricted to a small number of values. This effect is particularly marked for high-frequency data because the tick size or clustering becomes large relative to the size of the price movements. If the resulting prices or spreads (or changes in price or spread) are used as the dependent variable in a linear regression, the econometric problem of limited dependent variables arises. There are estimation methods appropriate for dealing with this problem, and Hausman, Lo and MacKinlay (1992) have applied ordered-probit analysis to trade data to show that allowing for price discreteness makes a difference. However, as Hasbrouck (1996b) has argued, linear regression generally provides consistent estimates of the coefficients.

The imposition of discrete price changes on a random sequence of prices can lead to the rejection of randomness because it may introduce a small amount of negative autocorrelation (Harris, 1990b). Gottlieb and Kalay (1985) argued that it can also bias upwards the estimates of the variance. For futures with a low price and a small variance of price changes, this upward bias can be very large, even as much as 200%. Since the variance drops as the time period is shortened over which price changes are computed, the upward bias is accentuated when daily or hourly price data is used. (Using a different, and less realistic, theoretical model, Marsh and Rosenfeld, 1986, show that there is no bias.)

According to Gottlieb and Kalay (1985) and Ball (1988), any restriction to a minimum price change introduces (or accentuates) kurtosis in the distribution of price changes, particularly when changes over short time intervals are being considered. These researchers suggest

Table 8.4 Empirical studies of delayed publication using high-frequency data

Study	Year	Spot	Data period	Time interval	Findings
Equities spot					
Porter and Weaver	1998	US stocks	1990	Trades	Out-of-sequence (or late) trade reporting is substantial on Nasdaq and is consistent with market-makers deliberately delaying the release of strategic information
MacIntyre	1991	UK shares	1990–91	Trades	Delayed publication had no effect of the inside spread (or touch)
Breedon	1993	3 UK stocks	1988–91	Trades	Delayed publication increased the spread for large trades, and did not affect the speed of the price response
Board and Sutcliffe	1995b 1996	42 UK stocks	1992–94	Trades and quotes	Only modest pre- and post-positioning of large trades by market-makers suggests that delayed publication is unnecessary
Gemmill	1996	UK stocks	1987–92	Trades	Delayed publication had no effect on spreads or the speed of the price response
Board and Sutcliffe	1998	60 UK stocks	1995–96	Trades	A major increase in transparency had no detrimental effects on volume or the traded bid–ask spread

that this may account for the leptokurtic distributions for price changes over short periods of time. Volatility estimators that correct for the upward bias in the variance have been suggested by Ball (1988), Cho and Frees (1988), Ederington and Lee (1995) and Harris (1990b).

Delayed publication of trades

There has been a long debate over whether there should be delayed publication of trades in the stock market. The debate hinges around two conflicting arguments. On the one hand, it is argued that delayed publication encourages market-makers to trade large blocks of shares on request (ie immediacy in size), because it provides them with an opportunity to unwind the trade before it becomes public. As a result, if delayed publication is removed, market-makers are less prepared to undertake large trades, so that the bid–ask spreads for large trades widen, delays for trading large blocks increase, and business moves to other less transparent markets. On the other hand, delayed publication conceals information from most market participants, which harms the market by enabling market-makers to trade with an informational advantage over their counterparties. This information asymmetry may encourage trading to move to other markets by effectively requiring a subsidy from all traders to those traders who want immediacy in size.

Empirical studies of transparency in the UK and the US have generally concluded that changes in the speed of publication have had little effect on the market characteristics studied. The studies of delayed publication that have used high-frequency data for the UK stock market are summarised in Table 8.4. These show that delayed publication had little effect on the bid–ask spread or the speed of the price response to large trades. In January 1996 the London Stock Exchange effectively ended delayed publication.

Conclusions

Regulations are an important aspect of market microstructure and can have substantial implications for market behaviour. However, the empirical studies using high-frequency data have found that some of the regulations studied have had less effect than might be expected. The results for the effects of dual capacity and circuit breakers are mixed, while delayed publication appears to have had little effect. Price clustering is widespread and appears to increase the spread. While there is little evidence from high-frequency data on the effects of transactions taxes and short sales restrictions, the available evidence is consistent with theoretical expectations.

Tests of market efficiency can be classified into those testing weak, semi-strong and strong forms of efficiency. Weak-form efficiency is closely associated with the degree of dependence over time in returns, while tests of the semi-strong form of efficiency are often based on event studies looking at market reaction to the public release of a piece of information. Strong-form efficiency requires that all private information be reflected in prices, and this is unlikely to be the case in reality. (Strong efficiency is not considered further in this chapter, as there are no studies of this form of efficiency which have used high-frequency data.)

The efficient-markets approach relies on new information being immediately reflected in the market price in an unbiased manner. However, if there are short lags in the spread of information, and especially if there are trading lags, the full market response to new information may tend to occur over a short time period rather than instantly. This is particularly likely to be true in order-driven markets, while in dealer markets the market-makers can instantly reflect the new information in their quoted prices. If there is a lagged price response to new information, high-frequency data will be beneficial in identifying trading opportunities that exist for only the few minutes it takes for the new equilibrium to be reached.

Weak-form efficiency

The time-series behaviour of returns in financial markets has been of considerable interest for a long time and can be used to test weak-form efficiency. A market is efficient with respect to past prices (ie "weak-form efficient") if it is impossible to make profits by trading on the basis of knowing all past prices. Early studies of this issue used low-frequency data (eg monthly returns), but now it is possible to use high-frequency data to study the topic. Since high-frequency data may involve movements of prices from minute to minute or from trade to trade, factors such as the bid–ask spread and the tick size become important and need to be allowed for in the analysis.

In such studies a crucial decision is whether to use trade data (which is irregularly spaced in time) or data that is regularly spaced. This is because patterns in, say, minute-to-minute returns represent somewhat different phenomena from patterns in trade-to-trade returns.

Dependence in returns

If returns follow a random walk or martingale time-series process, they are independent over time and the autocorrelation of returns will be zero. If the autocorrelation is non-zero, the market may be weak-form inefficient and past returns can be used to forecast subsequent returns using a linear model. Weak-form efficiency is violated, however, if the predictive model can make profits after allowing for transactions costs and risk. Thus predictability is a necessary but not sufficient condition for violating weak-form efficiency.

Table 9.1 Empirical studies of dependence in returns using high-frequency data

Study	Year	Spot	Data period	Time interval (minutes)	Findings
Index futures					
Goldenberg	1988	S&P500	1983–84	Trades, 1	Negative first- and second-order autocorrelation Negative autocorrelation dropped as the differencing interval increased
Goldenberg	1989	S&P500	1983–84	10 seconds	Negative first- and second-order autocorrelation
Cheung and Ng	1990	S&P500	1983–87	15	Negative first-order autocorrelation of –0.03
Fung, Lo and Peterson	1994	S&P500	1987–88	1	Positive and negative dependence over 1 to 12 minutes No evidence of longer term dependence
Hasbrouck	1998	S&P500	1998	Trades	First order autocorrelation of –0.28
Andersen and Bollerslev	1997a	S&P500	1986–89	5	No autocorrelation
ap Gwilym, Brooks, Clare and Thomas	1999	FTSE100	1992–95	5	Non-linear dependence, eg Arch effects
Interest futures					
Neftci and Policano	1990	Treasury bills	1983	Trades	Negative first-order autocorrelation
Lee and Mathur	1993	Eurodollar Treasury bills	1982–89	5	Negative first-order autocorrelation
ap Gwilym, Buckle, Foord and Thomas	1996	Bund, BTP and Long Gilt	1992–93	1	Negative autocorrelation
Piccinato, Ballocchi, Dacorogna and Gençay	1998	Eurodollar, EuroSwiss, Euromark, Short sterling, three-month ECU	1994–97	3	Negative autocorrelation up to the sixth order
Ballocchi, Dacorogna, Hopman, Müller and Olsen	1998	Eurodollars, Euromark, Short sterling, Euroyen	1992–97	Trades and quotes	No autocorrelation in the implied forward rates implied by the futures prices
ap Gwilym, Brooks, Clare and Thomas	1999	Long gilt, Short sterling	1992–95	5	Both futures exhibit non-linear dependence, eg Arch effects
Equities spot					
Godfrey, Granger and Morgenstern	1964	2 US stocks	1963	Trades	Random price changes

Table 9.1 – continued

Study	Year	Spot	Data period	Time interval (minutes)	Findings
Niederhoffer and Osborne	1966	6 US stocks	1964	Trades	Negative first-order autocorrelation in price changes
Garbade and Lieber	1977	IBM and Potlatch shares	1975	Trades	Positive first-order autocorrelation of of 0.24
Smidt	1979	48 NYSE stocks	1977	Trades	Up (down) ticks tend to follow up (down) ticks
Wood, McInish and Ord	1985	Index of US equities	1971–72, 1982	1	Positive first-order autocorrelation in returns of 0.8
Hasbrouck and Ho	1987	684 NYSE stocks	1985	Trades and quotes	Negative first-order autocorrelation in transaction returns of –0.26 and in quote returns of –0.02
Jain and Joh	1988	S&P 500	1979–83	60	Positive first-order autocorrelation in returns of 0.12 and in volumes of +0.73
Stoll	1989	Nasdaq	1984	Trades	Negative first-order autocorrelation
Madhavan, Richardson and Roomans	1997	274 NYSE stocks	1990	60 (approx)	Negative first-order autocorrelation of about –0.2
Lin, Knight and Satchell	1999	IBM and Intel	1994	Trades	Negative first-order autocorrelation of about –0.2 to –0.5

Forex spot

Study	Year	Spot	Data period	Time interval (minutes)	Findings
Goodhart and Figliuoli	1991	US$, DM, £, ¥, Ffr, Sfr, L, ECU	1987	1	Negative autocorrelation, particularly around large price movements
Goodhart and Figliuoli	1992	US$, DM, £, ¥, Ffr, Sfr, L, ECU	1987	1	Negative autocorrelation is not caused by traders in different counties having different information
Goodhart and Giugale	1993	US$, £, DM, ¥	1986	60	Negative autocorrelation for Swiss franc, £ and ¥
Goodhart, McMahon and Ngama	1993	DM, ¥, £, Sfr, L, Ffr, Fls, ECU	1989 1987 1986	Quotes, 1, 60	Significant autocorrelation in returns for quotes, 1 minute and 60 minutes
Bollerslev and Melvin	1994	US$/DM	1989	Quotes	Positive autocorrelation in quote-to-quote returns
Goodhart, Ito and Payne	1996	US$/DM	1993	Trades and quotes	Negative autocorrelation for quote changes, but not for changes in trade prices
Low and Muthuswamy	1996	US$/DM, US$/¥, DM/¥	1992–93	Quotes	Negative autocorrelation for quote changes and bid–ask spread changes

Table 9.1 – continued

Study	Year	Spot	Data period	Time interval (minutes)	Findings
Drunat, Dufrénot, Dunis and Mathieu	1996	US$/DM, US$/Ffr, DM/Ffr	1993	Quotes	Not chaotic
Drunat, Dufrénot and Mathieu	1996	US$/DM, US$/Ffr, DM/Ffr	1994	Quotes	Not chaotic
Andersen and Bollerslev	1997a	US$/DM	1992–93	5	Small negative autocorrelation
Moody And Wu	1998	US$/DM	1992	Quotes	Negative first-order autocorrelation for quote to quote changes Positive autocorrelation for changes over 60 quotes (about 15 minutes)
Brooks and Hinich	1998	7 currencies	1996	30	Non-linear models using lagged returns on other currencies cannot outforecast univariate linear models
Acar and Lequeux	1999	US$/DM DM/¥	1992–93	30	Negative first-order autocorrelation

Negative autocorrelation in returns may be caused by the presence of reflecting barriers, and these may be due to bid–ask bounce or to the clustering of limit orders at specific price levels. Another possibility is that transactions prices follow a mean-reverting process, and the greater the departure from the mean price, the greater the probability of a move towards the mean, leading to negative autocorrelation in returns.

In an order-driven market, a large order may be filled by a number of limit orders at progressively worse prices. In contrast, filling a large trade in a quote-driven market may require trading with a sequence of market-makers. Such trades will tend to produce positive autocorrelation in trade-to-trade returns.

Thus the theory can explain both positive and negative autocorrelation in returns in ways that are consistent with weak-form efficiency. The empirical studies of the time series of returns are summarised in Table 9.1, and generally show negative first-order autocorrelation in trade-to-trade returns and in returns using regular time intervals. However a few studies, particularly for the spot markets in equities, have found evidence of positive autocorrelation in returns.

The study by Goldenberg (1988) is particularly interesting in that he uses both irregularly spaced trade data and regularly spaced data to analyse two versions of the same basic question: is there dependence in returns over time? The first version of the hypothesis is that the return on a trade is independent of the return on the previous trade. The second version is that the return for the current minute is independent of the return for the preceding minute.

Trading rules

When studying trading rules using high-frequency data, transactions costs become even more important than for longer time intervals, because the price movements are smaller while the size of transaction costs is undiminished. Even though trading rules that generate several buys and sells per day may not be profitable, the use of high-frequency data permits trading rules that trade infrequently to exploit intra-day price movements by trying to trade at the most advantageous price within the chosen day. Empirical studies of trading rules using high-frequency data are summarised in Table 9.2. The results are mixed, with some authors reporting net profits while others do not.

The studies summarised in Table 9.2 include some that consider an important question facing traders in many markets: should they trade via market or limit orders? Placing a limit order means offering a free option to the market, with the risk of getting "bagged". For example, a buy limit order only executes if the price moves to the limit order price or below, which may be due to the arrival of bad news after the limit order was placed (a "winner's curse" situation). In addition, a trader who places a limit order faces the risk that it may not execute. Conversely, a limit order trader benefits from price movements caused by uninformed traders, since such limit orders will tend to sell when the market temporarily rises and buy when the market temporarily falls.

The findings of trading-rule studies are difficult to interpret, as there are many potential biases operating in such research. These biases include the following.

✦ There is a tendency for academic studies to be published of trading rules that work, while studies of trading rules that fail are often not published. Hence, published research is a biased sample.

✦ The performance of the trading rule must be compared with some alternative use of the money, and there are a number of realistic alternatives from which to choose, including buy-and-hold, a market index, random selection, and zero profit.

✦ Trading inevitably generates transactions costs (including the bid–ask spread), and these must be allowed for when evaluating the performance of the trading rule and the benchmark strategy. These costs may not be a simple proportion of the value or number of trades.

✦ If the trading rule and the benchmark strategy do not involve portfolios of equal risk, allowance must be made for this when comparing their profits.

✦ Allowance must be made for a time delay between the receipt of the past share, futures or options price data and undertaking a consequential trade – in other words, a trading lag.

✦ For parametric statistical tests of the significance of the study results, a knowledge of the distribution of the profits or returns from the trading strategy (as well as the benchmark strategy) is required, and this may often be unknown. In consequence, there may be no analysis of whether the profit from the rule is significantly different from zero.

Table 9.2 Empirical studies of trading rules using high-frequency data

Study	Year	Spot	Data period	Time interval (minutes)	Findings
Index futures					
Toulson, Toulson and Sinclair	1999	FTSE100, BTP, JGB, Long gilt	1995–97	15	The portfolio of 5 futures modestly outperformed buy-and-hold
Interest futures					
Monroe and Cohn	1986	Treasury bill and gold spreads	1976–82	Trade at 10am	Profits after allowing for transactions costs
Equity options					
Harvey and Whaley	1992	S&P100	1985–89	Trades	While implied volatility is predictable, the rule cannot make net profits
Equities spot					
Harris and Hasbrouck	1996	144 US stocks	1990–91	Trades and quotes	Limit orders can outperform market orders in some circumstances
Handa and Schwartz	1996	30 US stocks	1988	Trades	Trading via limit orders is preferable to using market orders
Chow, Hsiao and Solt	1997	S&P500	1970–93	60	Exploit the weekend effect by trading during Friday afternoon
Interest rates					
Dacorogna, Gavreau, Müller, Olsen and Pictet	1996	10 interest rates	1987–93	Quotes	Significant forecasting ability for the next 2–8 hours
Forex spot					
Pictet, Dacorogna, Müller, Olsen and Ward	1992	7 Forex rates	1986–92	Quotes	Average risk-adjusted return of 12.7%
Gençay, Ballocchi, Dacorogna, Olsen and Pictet	1998	US$/DM, Sfr, Ffr, DM/¥	1990–96	5	Profits after allowing for transactions costs and market risk
Dacorogna, Müller, Jost, Pictet, Olsen and Ward	1995	US$, DM, ¥, £, Sfr, Ffr, Fls, L, DM/¥	1986–93	Quotes	Profits after allowing for transactions costs
Dacorogna, Gavreau, Müller, Olsen and Pictet	1996	9 Forex rates	1986–93	Quotes	Significant forecasting ability for the next 12–48 hours
Nabney, Dunis, Dallaway, Leong and Redshaw	1996	US$/Sfr, DM/Ffr	1992–93	Quotes	Neural networks give gross profits of 55% and 37% per year
Curcio, Goodhart, Guillaume and Payne	1997	US$, DM, ¥, £	1989 1994	Quotes	No profits

Table 9.2 – continued

Study	Year	Spot	Data period	Time interval (minutes)	Findings
Dunis, Gavridis, Harris, Leong and Nacaskul	1998	US$/DM, DM/¥	1996	Quotes	No profits
Acar and Lequeux	1999	US$/DM, DM/¥	1992–93	30	No profits after allowing for transactions costs

✦ If a trading rule generates significantly negative gross returns, this suggests that reversing the buy–sell decisions in the trading rule will lead to significantly positive gross returns, and possibly to significantly positive net returns.

✦ If a given dataset is used to optimise the choice of parameters for the trading rule, the same dataset must not be used to test the performance of the rule. Part of the dataset must be held back for use in the testing. If the same data is used both to derive and to test the trading rule, it will always be possible to find a rule that is profitable after the event.

✦ Trading rules are generally tested in isolation, whereas a trader may rely on the simultaneous use of a battery of indicators.

✦ Trading rules are applied to the test data to provide buy or sell decisions for the entire data period, whereas traders may only rely on the trading rule at certain times.

These problems suggest that the existence of a number of empirical studies reporting evidence of profitable trading rules need not mean that a profitable trading rule actually exists. In consequence, traders who discover an apparently profitable rule should carefully examine the evidence before committing substantial amounts of capital to exploiting the rule.

Semi-strong-form efficiency

A market is semi-strong-form efficient if it is impossible to make profits by trading with a knowledge of all relevant public information. One way in which semi-strong-form efficiency has been tested is by event studies, which involve studying the reaction of the market to the announcement of some piece of price-sensitive information. Because the event studies are concerned with the speed of market reaction, they typically use regularly spaced time periods; high-frequency data can be used to quantify the reaction of the market over short periods of time. However, there have been some event studies of block trades (see Chapter 10) that have used irregularly spaced trade data to investigate how many trades it takes for the market to respond.

Table 9.3 Event studies for returns using high-frequency data

Study	Year	Spot	Data period	Time interval (minutes)	Findings
Index futures					
Walsh and Quek	1999	Nikkei	1994–95	Futures trades	The Kobe earthquake and Barings Bank collapse increased volatility and the traded bid–ask spread
Interest futures					
Slovin, Sushka and Waller	1994	Treasury bills	1982–91	120	Changes in the prime rate of major US banks increase the price of treasury bill futures
Equities spot					
Patel and Wolfson	1982	96 US stocks	1976–79	60	High-frequency data is used to measure the price response to news to classify earnings and dividends as good or bad news
Patel and Wolfson	1984	96 US stocks	1976–77	5	Rapid price response to earnings and dividend announcements, with a rise in volatility and price continuations
Jennings and Starks	1986	US stocks	1981, 1982	Trades, 15	The price response of stocks on which options are traded to earnings announcements is faster
Barclay and Litzenberger	1988	303 US stocks	1981–83	Trades	Announcements of new issues lead to an increase in volume and volatility for the following 15 minutes
Woodruff and Senchack	1988	700 US stocks	1980	Trades	There is a rapid price and volume response to earnings announcements
Lee	1992	1,463 US stocks	1988	30	Small traders react differently to earnings and dividend announcements than do large traders
Lee, Mucklow and Ready	1993	209 US stocks	1988	30	Earnings announcements lead to a widening of the spread and a decrease in depth
Slovin, Sushka and Waller	1994	Dow Jones	1979–91	120	Changes in the prime rate of major US banks reduce the stock index
Chen, Mohan and Steiner	1999	Dow Jones	1973–96	60	Unexpected changes in the Federal Reserve discount rate lead to a negative price response and an increase in volatility and volume during the subsequent hour
Atkins and Basu	1995	NYSE	1984	Trades	Volume is increased by announcements
Gosnell, Keown and Pinkerton	1996	120 US stocks	1985–89	15	A positive (negative) price response for announcements of dividend increases (decreases) lasts up to 15 minutes (75 minutes)

Table 9.3 – continued

Study	Year	Spot	Data period	Time interval (minutes)	Findings
Masulis and Shivakumar	1999	573 US stocks	1990–92	15	The price response to the announcements of a secondary offering is faster on Nasdaq than the NYSE/AMEX
Smith, White, Robinson and Nason	1997	Toronto SE	1977–89	15	Volume and volatility are higher for several hours after a takeover announcement
Benos and Rockinger	1998	120 French stocks	1995–97	60	Earnings announcements increase volume and volatility
Forex spot					
Low and Muthuswamy	1996	US$/DM US$/¥, DM/¥	1992–93	Quotes	Volatility of returns and spreads increase when there is news
DeGennaro and Shrives	1997	US$/¥	1992–93	10	Volatility rises when there is expected or unexpected news

Some of the events that have been investigated using high-frequency data include:

✦ the Kobe earthquake;
✦ takeover announcements;
✦ earnings announcements;
✦ prime interest rates;
✦ macroeconomic announcements; and
✦ block trades.

Because scheduled macroeconomic announcements occur at regular times, they are discussed in Chapter 5 on intra-day seasonalities, while the studies of the information content of block trades are included in Chapter 10 on market microstructure. Table 9.3 summarises the evidence on other event studies that have used high-frequency data and shows that news events increase volatility, volume and the bid–ask spread, while the news is quickly impounded into price levels.

Conclusions

High-frequency data has been used to search for short-term price patterns that can be exploited. The evidence is that there is short-term dependence in returns, but this is probably due to market microstructure effects and does not represent a market inefficiency. There is also high-frequency data evidence that market prices and spreads react in an efficient manner to unscheduled news announcements.

10 Market making

Market making is a real-time activity, where the market-maker is constantly responding to the flow of information from trades (the number of trades, the net order flow, the trade size, the identities of traders, etc), the quotes of rival market-makers, limit orders, the depth of the market, inventory levels, and so on. Thus, to properly model the market-making process requires access to at least the same real-time data as that used by the market-makers. In consequence, the empirical analysis of market making has relied heavily on high-frequency data.

Empirical studies of the relationship between trades and the revision of quoted prices are only possible using trade and quote data. While cross-sectional studies of the determinants of bid–ask spread can be conducted using, say, daily closing quotes, a deeper understanding of the dynamics of the bid–ask spread is available from high-frequency data. Similarly, to study the price effects of very large trades, intra-day prices are highly desirable.

Revision of prices

Considerable theoretical effort has gone into developing models of how market-makers revise their quotes. There are two main approaches to understanding quote revision by market-makers, namely information asymmetry and inventory control, and these are largely complementary.

In relation to information asymmetry, the main line of argument is that the order flow contains information that is known to the trader but not the market-maker. However, the market-maker can infer whether the private information possessed by the trader implies that the current price is too low or too high, and the market-maker can then revise quotes accordingly. The other main approach is that market-makers engage in inventory control – for instance if their inventory is too low, they increase their buy and sell quotes to encourage sales and discourage buys.

Studies looking at the relationship between trades and quotes clearly require high-frequency data on both trades and quotes. Usually these studies are conducted in trade time rather than clock time, as the hypothesis to be tested is generally specified in trade time. Studies testing the inventory control model need information on the identity of the market-maker involved in each trade, so that changes in their inventories can be tracked over time. (The inventory studies by Snell and Tonks, 1995, 1998, are an exception, as they used the total inventory of all market-makers.) Using trade data to construct inventory changes, rather than having access to the actual inventory levels, leads to a number of problems. Firstly, the trade data only gives the change in inventory and not the level of inventory, and so it is not revealed whether market-makers are holding long or short inventory positions. Secondly, all the data errors in attributing trades to particular market-makers get cumulated over time into the estimated inventory.

Ederington and Lee (1993) reported that, when reacting to the scheduled announcement of employment figures, several traders in the US Treasury bond futures pit did not normally watch the screens displaying announcements but simply reacted to the order flow. This

Table 10.1 Empirical studies of price revision using high-frequency data

Study	Year	Spot	Data period	Time interval (minutes)	Findings
Index futures					
Manaster and Mann	1996	3 stock indexes	1992	Trades	Inventory is rapidly mean reverting Inventory and prices are positively related
Kempf and Korn	1999	DAX30	1993–94	1	Net order flow has a non-linear effect on price
Interest futures					
Manaster and Mann	1996	3 interest rates	1992	Trades	Inventory is rapidly mean reverting Inventory and prices are positively related
Forex futures					
Manaster and Mann	1996	6 Forex rates	1992	Trades	Inventory is rapidly mean reverting Inventory and prices are positively related
Equity options					
Ho and Macris	1984	Options on 2 stocks	1981	Trades	Quotes are adjusted by the dealer to control their inventory
Equities spot					
Hasbrouck	1988	NYSE	1985	Trades and quotes	Trades have a powerful effect on the level of quotes, with larger trades having a bigger impact
Hasbrouck	1991a	NYSE	1989	Trades and quotes	The price impact of a trade occurs with a lag Larger trades have a larger price impact
Hasbrouck	1991b	NYSE	1989	Trades and quotes	One-third of the variance of equilibrium prices is explained by trades
Madhavan and Smidt	1991	16 NYSE stocks	1987	Trades and quotes	Prices respond to trades, with larger trades having a bigger effect There is weaker evidence that prices respond to inventory levels
Jang and Venkatesh	1991	250 US stocks	1985	Trades and quotes	Quote revision is generally inconsistent with information asymmetry and inventory control
Hausman, Lo and MacKinlay	1992	6 US stocks	1988	Trades	The effect of trades on subsequent trade prices increases with trade size and frequency of trades, and is altered by the sequence of past price changes and the direction of past trades

Table 10.1 – continued

Study	Year	Spot	Data period	Time interval (minutes)	Findings
Hasbrouck and Sofianos	1993	137 US stocks	1990–91	Trades	Specialist inventories revert very slowly, while their profits come from the bid–ask spread
Madhavan and Smidt	1993	16 US stocks	1987	Trades and quotes	Specialist inventories exhibit slow mean reversion
Chan and Lakonishok	1993	US stocks	1986–88	Trades	Purchases by institutions have a bigger price effect than sells, while price impact differs with the identity of the institution
Huang and Stoll	1994	20 US stocks	1988	5	Quotes react to previous trade prices
Harris, McInish and Chakravarty	1995	IBM stock	1988	Bid and ask regimes	Prices respond to the order flow – the ask rises with buy volume and the bid falls with sell volume
Knez and Ready	1996	2 US stocks	1990–91	Trades and quotes	Price improvement (trading inside the touch) is positively related to quoted depth, and negatively related to trade size
Easley, Kiefer and O'Hara	1997a	6 US stocks	1990	Trades	Large trades have twice the price effect of small trades
Easley, Kiefer and O'Hara	1997b	Ashland Oil stock	1990	Trades	Trade size has no information content
Harris and Schultz	1997	20 Nasdaq stocks	1993–94	30 seconds	The mid-quote responds more to the net volume of SOES trades than to that of other trades
Madhavan and Sofianos	1998	US stocks	1993	Trades and quotes	Specialists control their inventories by adjusting their trade behaviour rather than their quotes
Neuberger	1992	14 UK stocks	1987–88	Trades	Market-maker inventories followed a mean reverting process
Snell and Tonks	1995	UK stocks	1990	30	Market-makers revise their quotes to control their inventories
Snell and Tonks	1998	10 UK stocks	1990	20	There are strong inventory control effects on market-makers quotes
Biais, Hillion and Spatt	1995	40 French stocks	1991	Trades and quotes	Large trades lead to the revision of the bid and ask quotes
Forex spot					
Lyons	1995	US$/DM	1992	Trades	Prices respond to both the order flow and inventory level
Lyons	1996	US$/DM	1992	Trades	Prices respond less to trades when there is a short time between trades

Table 10.1 – continued

Study	Year	Spot	Data period	Time interval (minutes)	Findings
Goodhart and Payne	1996	US$/DM	1993	Trades and quotes	Prices respond to the order flow
Goodhart, Ito and Payne	1996	US$/DM	1993	Trades and quotes	Trades lead to quote revisions

illustrates that traders in the pit need no knowledge of fundamentals in order to set prices.

The empirical studies using high-frequency data, which are summarised in Table 10.1, show that the order flow has been found to contain information in itself, with buy trades leading to a rise in the ask quote and sell trades resulting in a fall in the bid quote. There is also some evidence from the studies that the larger the trade, the greater the price response, and that the price response varies with the identity of the institution initiating the deal. Inventory control also appears to be of importance in quote revision, although some studies have found that inventory control is achieved by adjustments to the market-makers' trade behaviour, rather than their quotes.

Other aspects of financial markets

Table 10.2 shows how high-frequency data has been used to study many other aspects of market making and price behaviour in financial markets – for instance, the behaviour of Small-Order Execution System (SOES) bandits, Real Estate Investment Trusts (REITs) and specialists – as well as the manipulation of markets, preferenced and internalised trades, inter-dealer broker systems, and call-versus-continuous markets. Some studies have obtained trader identity codes, enabling them to monitor the trading behaviour of particular traders. Such analyses are only possible with high-frequency data.

Determinants of the bid–ask spread

Market-makers quote one price at which they are willing to act as counterparties to traders wishing to buy shares (the ask or offer price), and a different price to traders wishing to sell (the bid price). The difference between the bid and ask quotes is the bid–ask spread.

Theory has identified three factors that influence the size of the bid–ask spread;

✦ order-processing costs;

✦ inventory costs; and

✦ information asymmetries.

Table 10.2 Empirical studies of market making using high-frequency data

Study	Year	Spot	Data period	Time interval (minutes)	Findings
Equities spot					
Chang, Hsu, Huang and Rhee	1999	Taiwan SE	1994	10	A call market has lower volatility and the same liquidity as a continuous market
Corwin	1999	US stocks	1992	Trades and quotes	Differences in specialist behaviour result in differences between stocks in spreads, depth and trading halts
Below, Kiely and McIntosh	1995	37 US REITs	1991	Trades and quotes	Equity REITs trade less often, at lower volume, and with wider spreads than similar non-REIT securities
Harris and Schultz	1998	Nasdaq	1995–96	Trades	SOES bandits trade very frequently in a few stocks, hold positions for only a few minutes and make a small average profit per trade
Christie and Schultz	1998	Nasdaq	1991	1	The 4% drop in the market on November 15 had no effect on liquidity
Board and Sutcliffe	1995c	2 UK stocks	1995	Trades and quotes	Market-makers did not manipulate the market around the time of the secondary offering of the Genco shares (National Power and PowerGen)
Board, Sutcliffe and Vila	1997	19 UK stocks	1994–95	Trades and quotes	Some market-makers appear to be fair-weather market-makers
Hansch, Naik and Viswanashan	1998	UK Stocks	1994	Trades and quotes	Preferenced trades get worse prices, while internalised trades get better prices
Reiss and Werner	1998	45 UK stocks	1991	Trades and quotes	The inter-dealer broker systems facilitate inventory control and risk sharing amongst market-makers

Order-processing costs include rent, salaries and equipment. *Inventory costs* are made up of two main components: price risk and the cost of financing the inventory. Price risk is the risk of movements in the share price while the shares are owned by the market-maker; and the cost of financing the inventory is the opportunity cost of the funds tied up in financing the inventory, less any returns on the inventory (eg dividends or capital gains). As the expected holding period of the inventory lengthens, the price risk and financing costs increase, although the revenue from the inventory (dividends and capital gains) also increases with the holding period. The expected length of the inventory holding period decreases as the volume of trading in the stock increases, but increases as the number of market-makers increases. With regard to *information asymmetries*, in order to compensate for the risk of trading with a better-informed counterparty, a market-maker increases the bid–ask spread. The market-makers' bid–ask spread is set to cover the average cost of asymmetric information. The likelihood of an information asymmetry (and hence the bid–ask spread) may increase with the size of the trade.

The high-frequency data studies of the determinants of the bid–ask spread summarised in Table 10.3 have used time-series data rather than cross-sectional data on different stocks. This is because high-frequency data is unnecessary for a cross-sectional study, unless high-frequency data is being used in a time-series analysis to estimate some of the data for use in a cross-sectional study – such as depth, liquidity, etc. These high-frequency data studies have found that the bid–ask spread increases with volatility, and decreases with the number of trades or volume.

Some studies have compared the bid–ask spread on rival markets (eg Nasdaq and the NYSE) and have generally found significant differences in the bid–ask spread between markets. This suggests that traders may be wise to check the costs on the markets on which they choose to transact, and ensure that the higher-cost market offers other compensating benefits.

Block trades

The price effect of large trades is important to traders because a marked worsening of the price when trading in size will encourage traders to split large deals into a sequence of smaller trades. The price response to block trades is also of interest from the perspective of market efficiency. If block trades have a predictable price effect that is delayed, this may present a profitable trading rule.

There is considerable literature on the price impact of large trades, and this is distinctive in four respects. First, this empirical research started employing high-frequency data much earlier than other areas of empirical finance. Second, the approach has generally been an event study of the effects of a block trade. Since particular trades form the events, trade data on individual stocks (including trade size, so as to enable the identification of block trades) is essential. A number of these studies have used price data for only a few trades rather than the complete time series, for example the price of the immediately preceding trade and the price of the block trade itself. Third, many of these event studies have chosen to use event (or trade) time rather than clock time. Finally, these studies are only for equity markets. The lack of widespread availability of forex trade data precludes such academic studies in forex spot markets, while there are also data-collection difficulties for spot interest rates. The absence of similar studies for index and interest-rate futures markets, and for interest rate options markets, is harder to explain.

There are three main views in the literature that aim to explain how a large trade may affect the share price.

✦ *Liquidity effect*. A large trade has a liquidity (or immediacy or inventory) cost, and a slightly worse price is required to compensate the equity market-maker. This is a temporary effect that should have disappeared within one trade, and will be related to block size.

✦ *Information effect*. A large trade may also have an information effect, in that it signals good or bad news about the company's fundamentals, leading to a permanent rise or fall in the share price.

Table 10.3 Empirical studies of the bid–ask spread using high-frequency data

Study	Year	Spot	Data period	Time interval (minutes)	Findings
Interest futures					
Breedon and Holland	1998	Bund (Liffe and DTB)	1995	Quotes, 1	Volatility is associated with an increase in the bid–ask spread
Frino, McInish and Toner	1998	Bund (Liffe and DTB)	1997	1	Spreads increase with volatility and decrease with the number of trades
Forex futures					
Ding	1999	US$/DM US$/¥	1990	Trades	Spreads increase with volatility and decrease with the number of trades
Equity options					
Neal	1992	CBOE and AMEX	1986	Trades and quotes	Spreads increase with options volatility, and decrease with options volume and being traded on AMEX
ap Gwilym, Clare and Thomas	1998c	FTSE100	1993–94	Quotes	Bid–ask spread increases with spot volatility and decreases with volume
Jameson and Wilhelm	1992	40 US options	1985	Quotes	Bid–ask spreads are widened due to the risks of inventory management
George and Longstaff	1993	S&P100	1989	Quotes	Average spread for 2–2.15pm has a negative relationship with the average time between trades
Berkman	1992	22 Dutch options	1989	60	The spread increases with spot volatility, stock price and hedge ratio, and decreases with the number of trades and competition from the limit order book
Equities spot					
Glosten and Harris	1988	270 US stocks	1981–83	Trades	The bid–ask spread is partly due to asymmetric information
Stoll	1989	Nasdaq	1984	Trades and quotes	The bid–ask spread is primarily due to asymmetric information and order processing, with only a modest inventory holding cost
Hasbrouck	1991a	NYSE	1989	Trades and quotes	Large trades lead to a widening of the bid–ask spread
McInish and Wood	1992	NYSE	1989	Quotes	Bid–ask spreads decrease with volume and number of trades, and increase with volatility and trade size
Lee, Mucklow and Ready	1993	209 US stocks	1988	30	Spreads increase with volume and decrease with depth
Harris	1994	US stocks	1989	Quotes	Spreads increase with volatility and decrease with volume

Table 10.3 – continued

Study	Year	Spot	Data period	Time interval (minutes)	Findings
Christie and Huang	1994	Nasdaq NYSE AMEX	1990	Trades and quotes	Quoted and traded spreads decline when stocks shift from Nasdaq to AMEX or the NYSE
Petersen and Fialkowski	1994	NYSE	1990–91	Trades and quotes	The effective spread is about half the posted (or quoted) spread
Affleck-Graves, Hegde and Müller	1994	NYSE Nasdaq	1985	Trades and quotes	Compares the order processing, adverse selection and inventory costs of these two markets
Easley, Kiefer, O'Hara and Paperman	1996	90 US stocks	1990	Trades	The risk of information-based trades is larger for high volume stocks, giving a reason for their lower spreads
Krinsky and Lee	1996	US stocks	1989–90	30	Adverse selection costs increase around earnings announcements, while inventory and order processing costs decline
Huang and Stoll	1996	NYSE Nasdaq	1991	Trades and quotes	The Nasdaq bid–ask spread is twice as large as that for the NYSE
Kim and Ogden	1996	NYSE AMEX	1993	Trades and quotes	The main determinant of the bid–ask spread is asymmetric information
Cao, Choe and Hatheway	1997	NYSE	1993	Trades and quotes	Order processing costs are higher for actively traded stocks
Neal and Wheatley	1998	17 closed-end funds	1988	1	The adverse selection costs of the funds are puzzlingly large – not much smaller than for stocks
Saporta, Trebeschi and Vila	1999	7 UK stocks	1995–96	Trades	Order processing costs are a major component of the realised bid–ask spread
de Jong, Nijman and Röell	1994	French stocks	1991	Trades and quotes	Lower in Paris than London for small trades In Paris the spread does not vary with trade size, while in London it drops
de Jong, Nijman and Röell	1996	10 French stocks	1991	Trades and quotes	The main determinants of the bid–ask spread are asymmetric information and order processing costs
Interest rates					
Chakravarty and Sarkar	1999	US bonds	1995–97	Trades	The realised bid–ask spread decreases as volume increases, and increases with credit risk and time to maturity
Forex spot					
Bollerslev and Domowitz	1993	US$/DM	1989	Quotes	No relationship between the bid–ask spread and the number of quotes

Table 10.3 – continued

Study	Year	Spot	Data period	Time interval (minutes)	Findings
Moody and Wu	1998	US$/DM	1992	Quotes	Bid–ask spread increases with volatility
Bollerslev and Melvin	1994	US$/DM	1989	Quotes	Bid–ask spread increases with volatility
Goodhart and Payne	1996	US$/DM	1993	Quotes	Inside spread increases with volatility Negative autocorrelation in the inside spread
Demos and Goodhart	1996	US$/DM US$/¥	Not stated	Quotes	Bid–ask spread increases with quote frequency and spot volatility

The size of this effect may be related to the size of the trade and the identity of the initiator of the trade.

✦ *Price pressure effect.* A large trade may have a price effect because the degree to which investors are prepared to substitute between shares in different companies is not infinite. Thus, to encourage investors to buy shares in a company may require a lower price. This price pressure effect is usually argued to be temporary, although some authors have suggested it may be permanent.

The available studies are primarily for the US equity markets. A block trade has been defined by the NYSE as a trade of 10,000 or more shares, but US studies have used a variety of definitions, including:

✦ the number of shares (a single trade of 5,000+ shares, 10,000+ shares, 20,000+ shares or 50,000+ shares have been used in various studies) or a percentage of the shares' average daily volume;

✦ the proportion of a company's outstanding equity involved in the trade (eg 0.1%);

✦ the dollar value of the trade (eg US$100,000 or US$1 million);

✦ the largest 50 trades for each company; or

✦ the trade having been negotiated in the upstairs market.

For large deals, traders must negotiate with the dealer in a quote-driven market or move further up the order book in an order-driven market. Therefore, the price impact of large trades is not directly observable from the published quote information, as quotes are usually only firm up to some specified size.

The high-frequency data studies have analysed the effects of block buys and sells separately, and have looked for temporary and permanent price effects. Temporary price effects may be caused by liquidity costs or price pressure, while a permanent price change is due to information effects. The high-frequency data studies summarised in Table 10.4 generally support the view that block trades have a permanent price impact and so contain information. This is supported by the finding that buys increase the price while sells decrease the price, and that the larger

Table 10.4 Empirical studies of the price impact of large trades using high-frequency data

Study	Year	Spot	Data period	Time interval (minutes)	Findings
Equity options					
Vijh	1990	US stocks	1985	Trades and quotes	Large option trades have little price impact
Berkman	1996	EOE stocks	1989	Quotes	Large option trades have no permanent price effect when a market-maker is the counterparty, but do have a permanent effect when a block trade hits a limit order
Equities spot					
Kraus and Stoll	1972	US stocks	1968–69	Trades	Permanent and temporary price effects
Nielsen and Joehnk	1973–74	US stocks	1965–71	Trades	Permanent and temporary price effects
Grier and Albin	1973	US stocks	1968–69	15	Gross profits from a trading rule based on block trades
Dann, Mayers and Raab	1977	US stocks	1968–69	Trades	Net profits cannot be made from a trading rule based on block trades by non-members of the NYSE
Carey	1977	US stocks	1971–72	Trades	Substantial net profits can be made by members of the NYSE from a trading rule based on block trades
Holthausen, Leftwich and Mayers	1987	US stocks	1982	Trades	Permanent and temporary price effects Block size influences the price effect
Holthausen, Leftwich and Mayers	1990	US stocks	1982–84	Trades	Permanent and temporary price effects Block size influences the price effect
Aggarawal and Chen	1990	US stocks	1977	Trades	No permanent price effect
Madhavan and Smidt	1991	16 NYSE stocks	1987	Trades and quotes	Larger trades have a bigger price impact than do smaller trades
Kumar, Sarin and Shastri	1992	US stocks	1983	15	Options prices respond to a block trade in the stock market 30 before the spot trade
Seppi	1992	US stocks	1982	Trades	Block trades shortly before an earnings announcement reveal private information in the announcement
Keim and Madhavan	1996	US stocks	1985–92	Trades	Permanent and temporary price effects Block size influences the price effect
LaPlante and Muscarella	1997	US stocks	1990	Trades	Price impact of block trades is lower on the NYSE than on Nasdaq
Gemmill	1996	UK stocks	1987–92	Trades	Purchases had a permanent price effect Trade size had little effect on the size of the price response

Table 10.4 – continued

Study	Year	Spot	Data period	Time interval (minutes)	Findings
Hansch and Neuberger	1993	26 UK stocks	1991–92	Trades	Traded bid–ask spread increased slightly with trade size
Ball and Finn	1989	Australian stocks	1974–77	Block price	Permanent price effect, but no temporary effect Size has no effect

the trade the bigger the price effect. There is also evidence that block trades have a temporary price effect, which indicates the existence of a liquidity effect.

Conclusions

High-frequency data has an important role in the empirical analysis of market-making behaviour. Understanding the way market-makers behave is obviously important in testing theories of market microstructure. It can also be important in devising trading strategies in relation to, for instance, how much a large trade will move the price of a stock, or how quickly such a response will occur. Other important issues include the following: if a large trade is split into a number of smaller trades, will the price response be different? And what can be inferred about the order flow and market-maker inventories from observing quote revisions?

11 Conclusions and future developments

Advances in information technology over recent years have resulted in improved data availability on financial markets, which implies significant benefits for those geared to exploiting the potential in terms of trading, research and risk management. The ongoing analysis of high-frequency data is continually improving understanding of how financial markets work, while the breadth of application areas testifies to the usefulness of such data.

The use of intra-day data creates a major new problem for analysts, with the need to take account of the important intra-day seasonalities that exist in such data – in returns, volatilities, autocorrelations, volumes, spreads, etc. If these patterns in the data are not allowed for, the results of any analysis using intra-day data are likely to be biased. There is still debate on the appropriate method of controlling such effects – for example, via dummy variables, the fast Fourier framework, time deformation, trigonometric terms, cubic splines, etc. However, there is general agreement that such seasonalities must be allowed for in *some* way.

While there are well developed techniques for analysing regularly spaced data, techniques for the analysis and modelling of irregularly spaced time-series data are still being developed – and at a rapid pace. It is likely that future modelling will simultaneously use data on trade prices and volumes, on quote prices and quantities, and also on the time gaps between successive trades and quotes.

An influential current trend is the increasing abandonment of trading floors in favour of electronic systems where trades are conducted via terminals and no personal contact is necessary. A by-product of this will be improved data from some exchanges as electronic audit trails replace partly manual, paper-based systems (eg open-outcry futures trading).

High-frequency data will be an enduring phenomenon. Future datasets cannot be recorded at increased frequency because the currently available data is already at the highest possible frequency. However, future developments are likely in two respects. First, there will be greater breadth of coverage, in that high-frequency data will become available across more markets and assets. In particular, there will be increasing demands for more reliable and comprehensive datasets on the foreign exchange market, and for expansion of the very limited data availability on fixed income markets. The current lack of data in these markets means that there is far less understanding of the fine detail of the trading process in these markets, relative to equity and derivatives markets. Second, there will be increasing demands for data at the microstructure level, which will include increased detail on individual transactions, such as traders' and principals' identities and motivation, and market-maker inventory positions.

Data suppliers are likely to increasingly focus on making data available on-line, including updating via Internet sites. They will face demands from users for ever more sophistication in their filtering and cleaning algorithms. As increasing numbers of market participants come to rely on high-frequency data, its quality and reliability will become increasingly important. This report has illustrated the many issues involved in collecting, maintaining and manipulating high-frequency data, and it is important to note that more data is not necessarily advantageous in every situation.

The analysis of high-frequency data is still relatively new and hence is continuously evolving. New issues and problems will continue to appear as understanding of the trading process evolves, and these will be followed by innovative solutions and further theoretical, methodological and modelling advances. The empirical evidence that has emerged from the analysis of high-frequency data has greatly enhanced understanding of how markets function and resulted in significant advances in bridging the gap between theory and market reality.

References

Abhyankar, A.H., 1995a, "Return and volatility dynamics in the FT-SE 100 stock index and stock index futures markets", *Journal of Futures Markets*, 15(4), pp. 457–88.

Abhyankar, A.H., 1998, "Linear and nonlinear Granger causality: evidence from the UK stock index futures market", *Journal of Futures Markets*, 18(5), August, pp. 519–40.

Abhyankar, A.H., L.S. Copeland and W. Wong, 1995, "Liffe cycles: intraday evidence from the FT-SE 100 stock index futures market", Department of Accountancy and Finance, University of Stirling, Discussion paper no. 95/04, 24 pages (*European Journal of Finance,* forthcoming).

Abhyankar, A., D. Ghosh, E. Levin and R.J. Limmack, 1997, "Bid–ask spreads, trading volume and volatility: intra-day evidence from the London Stock Exchange", *Journal of Business Finance and Accounting*, 24(3/4), April, pp. 343–62.

Acar, E. and P. Lequeux, 1999, "Trading rules profits and the underlying time series properties", in P. Lequeux (ed), *Financial Markets Tick by Tick*, John Wiley and Sons, Chichester, pp. 255–301.

Acar, E., P. Lequeux and S. Ritz, 1996, "Timing the highs and lows of the day", *Liffe Equity Products Review*, 2nd Quarter, pp. 1–3.

Admati, A.R. and P. Pfleiderer, 1988, "A theory of intraday patterns: volume and price variability", *Review of Financial Studies*, 1(1), Spring, pp. 3–40.

Afleck-Graves, J., S.P. Hegde and R.E. Miller, 1994, "Trading mechanisms and the components of the bid–ask spread", *Journal of Finance*, 49(4), September, pp. 1,471–88.

Aggarawal, R. and S.N. Chen, 1990, "The adjustment of stock returns to block trading information", *Quarterly Journal of Business and Economics*, 29, pp. 46–56.

Ahn, H.J., C.Q. Cao and H. Choe, 1996, "Tick size, spread and volume", *Journal of Financial Intermediation*, 5, pp. 2–22.

Aitken, M., P. Brown, C. Buckland, H.Y. Izan and T. Walter, 1996, "Price clustering on the Australian Stock Exchange", *Pacific Basin Finance Journal*, 4(2–3), July, pp. 297–314.

Aitken, M. and A. Frino, 1996, "The accuracy of the tick test: evidence from the Australian Stock Exchange, *Journal of Banking and Finance*, 20, pp. 1,715–29.

Aitken, M., A. Frino and E. Jarnecic, 1997, "Intraday returns and the frequency of trading at the ask on the Sydney Futures Exchange: a research note", *Abacus*, 33(2), pp. 228–35.

Almeida, A., C.A.E. Goodhart and R. Payne, 1998, "The effects of macroeconomic news on high frequency exchange rate behaviour", *Journal of Financial and Quantitative Analysis*, 33(3), September, pp. 383–408.

Andersen, T.G. and T. Bollerslev, 1997a, "Intraday periodicity and volatility persistence in financial markets", *Journal of Empirical Finance*, 4(2–3), June, pp. 115–58.

Andersen, T.G. and T. Bollerslev, 1997b, "Heterogeneous information arrivals and return volatility dynamics: uncovering the long run in high frequency returns", *Journal of Finance*, 52(3), July, pp. 975–1,005.

Andersen, T.G. and T. Bollerslev, 1998a, "Towards a unified framework for high and low frequency return volatility modelling", *Statistica Neerlandica*, 52(3), November, pp. 273–302.

Andersen, T.G. and T. Bollerslev, 1998b, "Deutsche mark dollar volatility: intraday activity patterns, macroeconomic announcements and longer run dependencies", *Journal of Finance*, 53(1), February, pp. 219–65.

Antoniou, A. and I. Garrett, 1989, "Long run equilibrium and short run dynamics: the case of the FT-SE 100 share index and futures contract", Department of Economics, Brunel University, Discussion paper 89–06, 32 pages.

Antoniou, A. and I. Garrett, 1992, "Are financial markets effectively functioning? Some evidence from the UK stock index futures markets", Centre for Empirical Research in Finance, Department of Economics, Brunel University, Discussion paper 92–05, 32 pages.

Antoniou, A. and I. Garrett, 1993, "To what extent did stock index futures contribute to the October 1987 stock market crash?", *Economic Journal*, 103(421), pp. 1,444–61.

Antoniou, A. and P. Holmes, 1995a, "Futures market efficiency, the unbiasedness hypothesis and variance bounds tests: the case of the FT-SE 100 futures contract", Centre for Empirical Research in Finance, Department of Economics, Brunel University, Discussion paper 95–12, 23 pages.

ap Gwilym, O., C. Brooks, A. Clare and S.H. Thomas, 1999, "Tests of non-linearity using LIFFE futures transactions price data", *The Manchester School*, 67(2), March, pp. 167–86.

ap Gwilym, O., M. Buckle, A. Clare and S.H. Thomas, 1998, "The transaction-by-transaction adjustment of interest rate and equity index futures markets to macroeconomic announcements", *Journal of Derivatives*, 6(2), Winter, pp. 7–17.

ap Gwilym, O., M. Buckle, T. Foord and S.H. Thomas, 1996, "The intraday behaviour of European bond futures", *Journal of Fixed Income*, 6(2), September, pp. 49–66.

ap Gwilym, O., M. Buckle and S.H. Thomas, 1997, "The intraday behaviour of bid–ask spreads, returns and volatility for FTSE-100 stock index options", *Journal of Derivatives*, 4(4), Summer, pp. 20–32.

ap Gwilym, O., M. Buckle, S.H. Thomas, 1999, "The intraday behaviour of key market variables for LIFFE derivatives". In *Financial Markets Tick by Tick*, edited by P. Lequeux, John Wiley and Sons, Chichester, pp. 151–89.

ap Gwilym, O., A. Clare and S.H. Thomas, 1998a, "Extreme price clustering in the London equity index futures and options markets", *Journal of Banking and Finance*, 22(9), September, pp. 1,193–206.

ap Gwilym, O., A. Clare and S.H. Thomas, 1998b, "Price clustering and bid–ask spreads in international bond futures", *Journal of International Financial Markets, Institutions and Money*, 8(3–4), November, pp. 377–91.

ap Gwilym, O., A. Clare and S.H. Thomas, 1998c, "The bid–ask spread on stock index options: an ordered probit analysis", *Journal of Futures Markets*, 18(4), June, pp. 467–85.

ap Gwilym, O. and S. H. Thomas, 1998, "An empirical comparison of quoted and implied bid–ask spreads on futures contracts under floor and electronic trading", Proceedings of 8th Annual Derivatives Securities Conference, Boston, USA.

Arai, T., T. Akamatsu and A. Yoshioka, 1993, "Stock index futures in Japan: problems and prospects", *NRI Quarterly* 2(1), Spring, pp. 28–57. A slightly edited version of the final section appears in the *Journal of International Securities Markets*, 7 (Autumn), pp. 159–64.

Arak, M. and R.E. Cook, 1997, "Do daily limits act as magnets? The case of treasury bond futures", *Journal of Financial Services Research*, 12(1), August, pp. 5–20.

Arshanapalli, B. and J. Doukas, 1994, "Common volatility in S&P500 stock index and S&P500 index futures prices during October 1987", *Journal of Futures Markets*, 14(8), pp. 915–25.

Atkins, A.B. and S. Basu, 1995, "The effect of after-hours announcements on the intraday U-shaped volume pattern", *Journal of Business Finance and Accounting*, 22(6), Summer, pp. 789–809.

Bae, K.H., K. Chan and Y.L. Cheung, 1998, "The profitability of index futures arbitrage: evidence from bid–ask quotes", *Journal of Futures Markets*, 18(7), October, pp. 743–63.

Baillie, R.T. and T. Bollerslev, 1990, "Intraday and inter-market volatility in foreign exchange rates", *Review of Economic Studies*, 58, pp. 565–85.

Ball, C.A., 1988, "Estimation bias induced by discrete security prices", *Journal of Finance*, 43(4), pp. 841–65.

Ball, R. and F.J. Finn, 1989, "The effect of block transactions on share prices: Australian evidence", *Journal of Banking and Finance*, 13(3), July, pp. 397–419.

Ballocchi, G., M.M. Dacorogna, C.M. Hopman, U.A. Müller and R.B. Olsen, 1998, "The intraday multivariate structure of the Eurofutures markets", Working paper, Olsen and Associates, 29 pages.

Bamberg, G. and K. Röder, 1994a, "The intraday ex ante profitability of DAX futures arbitrage for institutional investors in Germany: the case of early and late transactions", *Financial Markets and Portfolio Management*, (Austria), 8(1), pp. 50–62.

Bamberg, G. and K. Röder, 1994b, "Seasonality in ex ante German stock index futures arbitrage; where do reverse cash and carry arbitrage profits in Germany come from?", Paper presented to the Seventh Annual European Futures Research Symposium, Chicago Board of Trade, Bonn.

Barclay, M.J. and R.H. Litzenberger, 1988, "Announcement effects of new equity issues and the use of intraday price data", *Journal of Financial Economics*, 21, pp. 71–99.

Bassett, G.W., V.G. France and S.R. Pliska, 1989, "The MMI cash-futures spread on October 19, 1987", *Review of Futures Markets*, 8(1), pp. 118–46.

Becker, K.G., J.E. Finnerty and J. Friedman, 1995, "Economic news and equity market linkages between the US and UK", *Journal of Banking and Finance*, 19(7), pp. 1191–210.

Becker, K.G., J.E. Finnerty and K.J. Kopecky, 1993, "Economic news and intraday volatility in international bond markets", *Financial Analysts Journal*, 49(5–6), May–June, pp. 81–6, 65.

Becker, K.G., J.E. Finnerty and K.J. Kopecky, 1996, "Macroeconomic news and the efficiency of international bond futures markets", *Journal of Futures Markets*, 16(2), April, pp. 131–45.

Becker, K.G., J.E. Finnerty and A.L. Tucker, 1992, "The intraday independence structure between US and Japanese equity markets", *Journal of Financial Research*, 15(1), Spring, pp. 27–37.

Below, S.D., J.K. Kiely and W. McIntosh, 1995, "An examination of informed traders and the market microstructure of real estate investment trusts", *Journal of Real Estate Research*, 10(3), pp. 335–61.

Benos, A. and M. Rockinger, 1998, "Market response to earnings announcements and interim reports: an analysis of SBF 120 companies", Working paper, Department of Finance, HEC School of Management, June, 36 pages.

Berkman, H., 1992, "The market spread, limit orders and options", *Journal of Financial Services Research*, 6(4), January, pp. 399–415.

Berkman, H., 1996, "Large option trades, market makers and limit orders", *Review of Financial Studies*, 9(3), Fall, pp. 977–1,002.

Berkman, H. and O.W. Steenbeek, 1998, "The influence of daily price limits on trading in Nikkei futures", *Journal of Futures Markets*, 18(3), May, pp. 265–79.

Bessembinder, H., 1997, "The degree of price resolution and equity trading costs", *Journal of Financial Economics*, 45(1), July, pp. 9–34.

Bhattacharya, M., 1983, "Transaction data tests of efficiency of the Chicago Board Options Exchange", *Journal of Financial Economics*, 12, pp. 161–85.

Bhattacharya, M., 1987, "Price changes of related securities: the case of call options and stocks", *Journal of Financial and Quantitative Analysis*, 22(1), March, pp. 1–15.

Biais, B., Hillion, P. and Spatt, C., 1995, "An empirical analysis of the limit order book and the order flow in the Paris Bourse", *Journal of Finance*, 50(5), December, pp. 1655–89.

Blume, M.E. and M.A. Goldstein, 1997, "Quotes, order flow and price discovery", *Journal of Finance*, 52(1), March, pp. 221–44.

Blume, M.E., A.C. MacKinlay and B. Terker, 1989, "Order imbalances and stock price movements on October 19 and 20, 1987", *Journal of Finance*, 44(4), pp. 827–48.

Board, J.L.G. and C.M.S Sutcliffe, 1995a, "The relative volatility of the markets in equities and index futures", *Journal of Business Finance and Accounting*, 22(2), pp. 201–23.

Board, J.L.G. and C.M.S. Sutcliffe, 1995b, *The Effects of Trade Transparency in the London Stock Exchange: A Summary*, Financial Markets Group Special Paper no. 67, London School of Economics, January, 30 pages.

Board, J.L.G. and C.M.S Sutcliffe, 1995c, "Market manipulation of the secondary offering of Genco shares", *Stock Exchange Quarterly*, Summer edition, April–June, pp. 16–22.

Board, J.L.G. and C.M.S. Sutcliffe, 1996, "Transparency and the London Stock Exchange", *European Financial Management*, 2(3), November, pp. 355–65.

Board, J.L.G. and C.M.S. Sutcliffe, 1997, "The proof of the pudding: the effects of increased trade transparency in the London Stock Exchange", Financial Markets Group Special Paper no. 95, London School of Economics and Political Science, 33 pages, March.

Board, J.L.G. and C.M.S. Sutcliffe, 1998, "Options trading when the underlying market is not transparent", *Journal of Futures Markets*, 18(2), April, pp. 225–42.

Board, J.L.G., C.M.S. Sutcliffe and A. Vila, 1997, "Market maker performance: the search for fair weather market makers", Financial Markets Group Discussion Paper No. 276, London School of Economics and Political Science, 27 pages, September.

Bolland, P.J., J.T. Connor and A-P.N. Refenes, 1998, "Application of neural networks to forecast high frequency data: foreign exchange", in C. Dunis and B. Zhou (eds), *Nonlinear Modelling of High Frequency Financial Time Series*, John Wiley and Sons, Chichester, pp. 225–46.

Bollerslev, T., 1986, "Generalized autoregressive conditional heteroscedasticity", *Journal of Econometrics*, 31, pp. 307–27.

Bollerslev, T. and I. Domowitz, 1993, "Trading patterns and prices in the interbank foreign exchange market", *Journal of Finance*, 48(4), September, pp. 1,421–43.

Bollerslev, T. and M. Melvin, 1994, "Bid–ask spreads and volatility in the foreign exchange market", *Journal of International Economics*, 36, pp. 355–72.

Brailsford, T.J. and A.J. Cusack, 1997, "A comparison of futures pricing models in a new market: the case of individual share futures", *Journal of Futures Markets*, 17(5), pp. 515–41.

Breedon, F.J., 1993, "Intraday price formation on the London Stock Exchange", London School of Economics Financial Markets Group, Discussion Paper no. 158, March, 38 pages.

Breedon, F.J. and A. Holland, 1998, "Electronic versus open outcry markets: the case of the bund futures contract", Working paper No. 76, Bank of England, January, 34 pages.

Brennan, M.J. and E.S. Schwartz, 1990, "Arbitrage in stock index futures", *Journal of Business*, 63(1)(2), pp. 27–31.

Brennan, M.J. and A. Subrahmanyam, 1996, "Market microstructure and asset pricing: on the compensation for illiquidity in stock returns", *Journal of Financial Economics*, 41(3), July, pp. 441–64.

Brock, W.A. and A,W, Kleidon, 1992, "Periodic market closure and trading volume: a model of intraday bids and asks", *Journal of Economic Dynamics and Control*, 16(3&4), pp. 451–89.

Brockman, P. and D.Y. Chung, 1998, "Inter and intra-day liquidity patterns on the Stock Exchange of Hong Kong", *Journal of International Financial Markets, Institutions and Money*, 8(3–4), November, pp. 277–98.

Brooks, C. and M.J. Hinich, 1998, "Forecasting high frequency exchange rates using cross-bicorrelations". In *Decision Technologies for Computational Finance: Proceedings of the Fifth International Conference Computational Finance*, A.P.N. Refenes, A.N. Burgess and J.E. Moody (eds), *Advances in Computational Management Science*, 2, Kluwer Academic Publishers, pp. 61–72.

Buckle, M., O. ap Gwilym, S.H. Thomas and M.S. Woodhams, 1998, "Intraday empirical regularities in interest rate equity index futures markets and the effect of macroeconomic announcements", *Journal of Business Finance and Accounting*, 25(7/8), September–October, pp. 921–44.

Bühler, W. and A. Kempf, 1995, "DAX index futures: mispricing and arbitrage in German markets", *Journal of Futures Markets*, 15(7), pp. 833–59.

Campbell, J. Y., A. W. Lo and A. C. MacKinlay, 1997, *The Econometrics of Financial Markets*, Princeton University Press, Princeton, NJ.

Carey, K.J., 1977, "Non-random price changes in association with trading in large blocks: evidence of market efficiency in the behaviour of investor returns", *Journal of Business*, 50(4), October, pp. 407–14.

Cao, C., H. Choe and F. Hatheway, 1997, "Does the specialist matter; differential execution costs and intersecurity subsidization on the New York Stock Exchange", *Journal of Finance*, 52(4), September, pp. 1,615–40.

Chakravarty, S. and A. Sarkar, 1999, "Liquidity in US fixed income markets: a comparison of the bid–ask spread in corporate, government and municipal bond markets", Working paper, Purdue University, March, 41 pages.

Chamberlain, T.W., C.S. Cheung and C.C.Y. Kwan, 1989, "Expiration-day effects of index futures and options: some Canadian evidence", *Financial Analysts Journal*, 45(5), pp. 67–71.

Chan, L.K.C. and J. Lakonishok, 1993, "Institutional trades and intraday stock price behaviour", *Journal of Financial Economics*, 33(2), April, pp. 173–99.

Chan, K., 1992, "A further analysis of the lead–lag relationship between the cash market and stock index futures market", *Review of Financial Studies*, 5(1), pp. 123–52.

Chan, K., K.C. Chan and G.A. Karolyi, 1991, "Intraday volatility in the stock index and stock index futures markets", *Review of Financial Studies*, 4(4), pp. 657–84.

Chan, K.C., W.G. Christie and P.H. Schultz, 1995, "Market structure and the intraday pattern of bid–ask spreads for NASDAQ securities", *Journal of Business*, 68(1), January, pp. 35–60.

Chan, K. and Y.P. Chung, 1993, "Intraday relationships among index arbitrage, spot and futures price volatility and spot market volume: a transactions data test", *Journal of Banking and Finance*, 17(4), pp. 663–87.

Chan, K., Y.P. Chung and H. Johnson, 1993, "Why option prices lag stock prices: a trading-based explanation", *Journal of Finance*, 48(5), December, pp. 1,957–67.

Chan, K., Y.P. Chung and H. Johnson, 1995, "The intraday behaviour of bid–ask spreads for NYSE stocks and CBOE options", *Journal of Financial and Quantitative Analysis*, 30(3), September, pp. 329–46.

Chang, E.C., P.C. Jain and P.R. Locke, 1995, "Standard and Poor's 500 index futures volatility and price changes around the New York Stock Exchange close", *Journal of Business*, 68, pp. 1, 61–84.

Chang, R.P., T. Fukuda, S.G. Rhee and M. Takano, 1993, "Intraday and interday behaviour of the TOPIX", *Pacific Basin Finance Journal*, 1(1), March, pp. 67–95.

Chang, R.P., S.T. Hsu, N.K. Huang and S.G. Rhee, 1999, "The effects of trading methods on volatility and liquidity: evidence from the Taiwan Stock Exchange", *Journal of Business Finance and Accounting*, 26(1&2), January–March, pp. 139–70.

Chen, C. and J. Williams, 1994, "Triple witching hour, the change in expiration timing and the stock market reaction", *Journal of Futures Markets*, 14(3), pp. 275–92.

Chen C.R., N.J. Mohan and T.L. Steiner, 1999, "Discount rate changes, stock market returns, volatility and trading volume: evidence from intraday data and implications for market efficiency", *Journal of Banking and Finance*, 23, pp. 897–924.

Cheng, M. and A. Madhavan, 1994, "In search of liquidity: Block trades in the upstairs and downstairs markets", NYSE Working paper no. 94–02.

Cheung, Y.L., 1995, "Intraday returns and the day-end effect: evidence from the Hong Kong equity market", *Journal of Business Finance and Accounting*, 22(7), October, pp. 1,023–34.

Cheung, Y.W. and L.K. Ng, 1990, "The dynamics of S&P500 index and S&P500 futures intraday price volatilities", *Review of Futures Markets*, 9(2), pp. 458–86.

Cho, D.C. and E.W. Frees, 1988, "Estimating the volatility of discrete stock prices", *Journal of Finance*, 43(2), pp. 451–66.

Chow, E.H., P. Hsiao and M.E. Solt, 1997, "Trading returns for the weekend effect using intraday data", *Journal of Business Finance and Accounting*, 24(3/4), April, pp. 425–44.

Christie, W., J.H. Harris and P. Schultz, 1994, "Why did NASDAQ market makers stop avoiding odd-eighth quotes?", *Journal of Finance*, 49(5), December, pp. 1,841–60.

Christie, W.G. and R.D. Huang, 1994, "Market structures and liquidity: a transactions data study of exchange listings", *Journal of Financial Intermediation*, 3, June, pp. 300–26.

Christie, W.G. and P.H. Schultz, 1994, "Why do NASDAQ market makers avoid odd-eighth quotes?", *Journal of Finance*, 49(5), December, pp. 1,813–40.

Christie, W.G. and P.H. Schultz, 1998, "Dealer markets under stress: the performance of Nasdaq market makers during the November 15, 1991 market break", *Journal of Financial Services Research*, 13(3), pp. 205–29.

Chung, Y.P., 1991, "A transaction data test of stock index futures market efficiency and index arbitrage profitability", *Journal of Finance*, 46(5), pp. 1,791–809.

Chung, Y.P., J.K. Kang and S.G. Rhee, 1994a, "The lead–lag relationship between the stock market and stock index futures market in Japan", PACAP Research Centre, University of Rhode Island, Working paper, 27 pages.

Chung, Y.P., J.K. Kang and S.G. Rhee, 1994b, "Index arbitrage in Japan", PACAP Research Centre, University of Rhode Island, Working paper, 35 pages.

Clark, P. K., 1973, "A subordinated stochastic process model with finite variance for speculative prices", *Econometrica*, 41, pp. 135–59.

Crain, S.J. and J.H. Lee, 1995, "Intraday volatility in interest rate and foreign exchange spot and futures markets", *Journal of Futures Markets*, 15(4), June, pp. 395–421.

Cornett, M.M., T.V, Schwarz and A.C. Szakmary, 1995, "Seasonalities and intraday return patterns in the foreign currency futures market", *Journal of Banking and Finance*, 19(5), August, pp. 843–69.

Corwin, S.A., 1999, "Differences in trading behaviour across NYSE specialist firms", *Journal of Finance*, 54(2), April, pp. 721–45.

Curcio, R., C.A.E. Goodhart, D. Guillaume and R. Payne, 1997, "Do technical trading rules generate profits? Conclusions from the intraday foreign exchange market", *International Journal of Finance and Economics*, 2, October, pp. 267–80.

Dacco', R. and S. Satchell, 1998, "High frequency switching regimes: A continuous-time threshold process", in C. Dunis and B. Zhou (eds), *Nonlinear Modelling of High Frequency Financial Time Series*, John Wiley and Sons, Chichester, pp. 177–200.

Dacorogna, M.M., C.L. Gauvreau, U.A. Müller, R.B. Olsen and O.V. Pictet, 1996, "Changing time scale for short term forecasting in financial markets", *Journal of Forecasting*, 15(3), April, pp. 203–27.

Dacorogna, M.M., U.A. Müller, C. Jost, O.V. Pictet, R.B. Olsen and J.R. Ward, 1995, "Heterogeneous real-time trading strategies in the foreign exchange market", *European Journal of Finance*, 1(4), pp. 383–403. Reprinted C. Dunis (ed), *Forecasting Financial Markets: Exchange Rates, Interest Rates and Asset Management*, John Wiley, pp. 69–92.

Dacorogna, M.M., U.A. Müller, R.J. Nagler, R.B. Olsen and O.V. Pictet, 1993, "A geographical model for the daily and weekly seasonal volatility in the foreign exchange market", *Journal of International Money and Finance*, 12, pp. 413–38.

Dacorogna, M.M., U.A. Müller, R.B. Olsen and O.V. Pictet, 1998, "Modelling short-term volatility with GARCH and HARCH models", in C. Dunis and B. Zhou (eds), *Nonlinear Modelling of High Frequency Financial Time Series*, John Wiley and Sons, Chichester, pp. 161–76.

Dacorogna, M.M., U.A. Müller, O.V. Pictet and C.G. De Vries, 1995, "The distribution of extremal foreign exchange returns in extremely large data sets", Working paper, Olsen and Associates, June, 28 pages.

Daigler, R.T., 1993a, *Financial Futures Markets: Concepts, Evidence and Applications*, Harper Collins College Publishers, New York.

Daigler, R.T., 1993b, *Managing Risk with Financial Futures: Hedging, Pricing and Arbitrage*, Probus Publishing Co., Chicago, Illinois.

Daigler, R.T., 1997, "Intraday futures volatility and theories of market behaviour", *Journal of Futures Markets*, 17(1), February, pp. 45–74.

Dann, L.Y., D. Mayers and R.J. Raab, 1977, "Trading rules, large blocks and the speed of price adjustment", *Journal of Financial Economics*, 4(1), January, pp. 3–22.

Darrat, A.F. and S. Rahman, 1995, "Has futures trading activity caused stock price volatility?" *Journal of Futures Markets*, 15(5), pp. 537–57.

DeGennaro, R.P. and R.E. Shrives, 1997, "Public information releases, private information arrival and volatility in the foreign exchange market", *Journal of Empirical Finance*, 4(4), December, pp. 295–315.

de Jong, F. and M.W.M. Donders, 1998, "Intraday lead–lag relationships between the futures, options and stock market", *European Finance Review*, 1, pp. 337–59.

de Jong, F. and T. Nijman, 1997, "High frequency analysis of lead–lag relationships between financial markets", *Journal of Empirical Finance*, 4(2–3), June, pp. 259–77.

de Jong, F., T. Nijman and A. Röell, 1994, "A comparison of the cost of trading French shares on the Paris Bourse and on SEAQ International", *European Economic Review*, 39(7), August, pp. 1,277–301.

de Jong, F., T. Nijman and A. Röell, 1996, "Price effects of trading and components of the bid–ask spread on the Paris Bourse", *Journal of Empirical Finance*, 3(2), June, pp. 193–213.

Demos, A.A. and C.A.E. Goodhart, 1996, "The interaction between the frequency of market quotations, spread and volatility in the foreign exchange market", *Applied Economics*, 28(3), March, pp. 377–86.

Diamond, D.W. and R.E. Verrecchia, 1987, "Constraints on short selling and asset price adjustments to private information", *Journal of Financial Economics*, 18, pp. 277–311.

Ding, D.K., 1999, "The determinants of bid–ask spreads in the foreign exchange futures market: a microstructure analysis", *Journal of Futures Markets*, 19(3), May, pp. 307–24.

Docking, D.S., I.G. Kawaller and P.D. Koch, 1999, "Mid-day volatility spikes in US futures markets", *Journal of Futures Markets*, 19(2), April, pp. 195–216.

Drunat, J., G. Dufrénot, C. Dunis and L. Mathieu, 1996a, "Stochastic or chaotic dynamics in high frequency exchange rates?", in C. Dunis (ed), *Forecasting Financial Markets: Exchange Rates, Interest Rates and Asset Management*, John Wiley, pp. 33–49.

Drunat, J., G. Dufrénot and L. Mathieu, 1996b, "Stochastic nonlinearities in high frequency exchange rates", *Rivista Internazionale di Scienze Economiche e Commerciali*, 43(4), October–December, pp. 897–926.

Dufour, A. and R.F. Engle, 1997, "Time and the price impact of a trade". Discussion Paper, Department of Economics, University of California, San Diego, November, 39 pages.

Duffee, G., P. Kupiec and A.P. White, 1992, "A primer on program trading and stock price volatility: a survey of the issues and the evidence". In G.G. Kaufman (ed), *Research in Financial Services: Private and Public Policy*, 4, Jai Press Inc., Greenwich, Connecticut, pp. 21–49.

Dunis, C., M. Gavridis, A. Harris, S. Leong and P. Nacaskul, 1998, "An application of genetic algorithms to high frequency trading models: a case study", in C. Dunis and B. Zhou (eds), *Nonlinear Modelling of High Frequency Financial Time Series*, John Wiley and Sons, Chichester, pp. 247–78.

Dunis, C. and B. Zhou (eds), 1998, *Nonlinear Modelling of High Frequency Financial Time Series*, John Wiley & Sons, Chichester.

Dwyer, G.P., P.R. Locke and W. Yu, 1996, "Index arbitrage and nonlinear dynamics between the S&P500 futures and cash", *Review of Financial Studies*, 9(1), Spring, pp. 301–32.

Eagle, D. and E. Nelson, 1991, "Index arbitrage and the concentration effect", *Review of Futures Markets*, 10(2), pp. 212–47.

Easley, D., N.M. Kiefer and M. O'Hara, 1997a, "The information content of the trading process", *Journal of Empirical Finance*, 4(2–3), June, pp. 159–86.

Easley, D., N.M. Kiefer and M. O'Hara, 1997b, "One day in the life of a very common stock", *Review of Financial Studies*, 10(3), Fall, pp. 805–35.

Easley, D., N.M. Kiefer, M. O'Hara and J.B. Paperman, 1996, "Liquidity, information and infrequently traded stocks", *Journal of Finance*, 51(4), September, pp. 1,405–36.

Easley, D. and M. O'Hara, 1992, "Time and the process of security price adjustment, *Journal of Finance*, 47, pp. 577–605.

Ederington, L.H. and J.H. Lee, 1993, "How markets process information: news releases and volatility", *Journal of Finance*, 48(4), September, pp. 1,161–91.

Ederington, L.H. and J.H. Lee, 1994, "The response of the dollar/yen exchange rate to economic announcements", *Financial Engineering and the Japanese Markets*, 1, pp. 111–28.

Ederington, L.H. and J.H. Lee, 1995, "The short run dynamics of the price adjustment to new information", *Journal of Financial and Quantitative Analysis*, 30(1), pp. 117–34.

Ekman, P.D., 1992, "Intraday patterns in the S&P500 index futures market", *Journal of Futures Markets*, 12(4), pp. 365–81.

Engle, R. F., 1982, "Autoregressive conditional heteroscedasticity with estimates of the variance of United Kingdom inflation", *Econometrica*, 50, pp. 987–1,007.

Engle, R.F., 1996, "The econometrics of ultra-high frequency data", Discussion Paper, Department of Economics, University of California, San Diego, no. 96–15, May, 19 pages.

Engle, R. F. and A. Lunde, 1998, "Trades and quotes: a bivariate point process", Discussion Paper, Department of Economics, University of California, San Diego, no. 98–07, February, 26 pages.

Engle, R.F. and J.R. Russell, 1997, "Forecasting the frequency of changes in quoted foreign exchange prices with the autoregressive conditional duration model", *Journal of Empirical Finance*, 4(2–3), June, pp. 187–212.

Engle, R.F. and J.R. Russell, 1998, "Autoregressive conditional duration: a new model for irregularly spaced transaction data", *Econometrica* 66(5), September, pp. 1,127–62.

Epps, T., 1979, "Co-movements in stock prices in the very short run", *Journal of the American Statistical Society*, 74, pp. 291–8.

Finnerty, J.E. and H.Y. Park, 1987, "Stock index futures: does the tail wag the dog?", *Financial Analysts Journal*, 43(2), pp. 57–61.

Finnerty, J.E. and H.Y. Park, 1988, "How to profit from program trading", *Journal of Portfolio Management*, 14(2), Winter, pp. 40–6.

Finucane, T., 1999, "A new measure of the direction and timing of information flow between markets", *Journal of Financial Markets*, 2(2), May, pp. 135–51.

Fleming, J., B. Ostdiek and R.E. Whaley, 1996, "Trading costs and the relative rates of price discovery in stock, futures and option markets", *Journal of Futures Markets*, 16(4), pp. 353–87.

Followill, R. A. and A. J. Rodriguez, 1991, "The estimation and determinants of bid–ask spreads in futures markets", *Review of Futures Markets*, 10, pp. 1–11.

Foster, F.D. and S. Viswanathan, 1993, "Variations in trading volume, return volatility and trading costs: evidence on recent price formation models", *Journal of Finance*, 48(1), March, pp. 187–211.

Franke, G. and D. Hess, 1995, "Anonymous electronic trading versus floor trading", Working paper, University of Konstanz, November 1995.

Franses, P.H., R.V. Ieperen, P. Kofman, M. Martens and B. Menkveld, 1994, "Volatility patterns and spillovers in bund futures", Working paper no 16/94, Department of Econometrics, Monash University, July 1994.

Frino, A., T.H. McInish and M. Toner, 1998, "The liquidity of automated exchanges: new evidence from German bund futures", *Journal of International Financial Markets, Institutions and Money*, 8(3–4), November, pp. 225–41.

Froot, K.A., J.F. Gammill and A.F. Perold, 1990, "New trading practices and the short-run predictability of the S&P500", in *Market Volatility and Investor Confidence*, New York Stock Exchange, Appendix G1.

Fung, H.G., W.C. Lo and J.E. Peterson, 1994, "Examining the dependency in intra-day stock index futures", *Journal of Futures Markets*, 14(4), pp. 405–19.

Fung, J.K.W., L.T.W. Cheng and K.C. Chan, 1997, "The intraday pricing efficiency of Hong Kong Hang Seng index options and futures markets", *Journal of Futures Markets*, 17(7), October, pp. 797–815.

Fung, J.K.W. and A.K.W. Fung, 1997, "Mispricing of index futures contracts: a study of index futures versus index options", *Journal of Derivatives*, 5(2), Winter, 37–45.

Fung, J.K.W. and L. Jiang, 1999, "Restrictions on short selling and spot-futures dynamics", *Journal of Business Finance and Accounting*, 26(1–2), January–March, pp. 227–48.

Furbush, D., 1989, "Program trading and price movement: evidence from the October 1987 market crash", *Financial Management*, 18(3), Autumn, pp. 68–83.

Gannon, G.L., 1994, "Simultaneous volatility effects in index futures", *Review of Futures Markets*, 13(4), pp. 1,027–68.

Gannon, G.L., 1995, "Volatility spillovers and transmission effects: currency futures and equity index futures", Working paper no. 1995–4, Centre in Finance, Department of Economics and Finance, Faculty of Business, Royal Melbourne Institute of Technology, Australia, 48 pages.

Garbade, K. and Z. Lieber, 1977, "On the independence of transactions on the New York Stock Exchange", *Journal of Banking and Finance*, 1, pp. 151–72.

Gavridis, M., 1998, "Modelling with high frequency data: a growing interest for financial economists and fund managers". In C. Dunis and B. Zhou (eds), *Nonlinear Modelling of High Frequency Financial Time Series*, John Wiley and Sons, Chichester, pp. 3–21.

Gavridis, M., R.N. Markellos and T.C. Mills, 1999, "High frequency random walks?", in P. Lequeux (ed), *Financial Markets Tick by Tick*, John Wiley and Sons, Chichester, pp. 227–54.

Geiss, C.G., 1995, "Distortion-free futures price series", *Journal of Futures Markets*, 15(7), pp. 805–31.

Gemmill, G., 1996, "Transparency and liquidity: a study of large trades on the London Stock Exchange under different publication rules", *Journal of Finance*, 51(5), December, pp. 1,765–90.

Gençay, R., G. Ballocchi, M. Dacorogna, R. Olsen and O. Pictet, 1998, "Real time trading models and the statistical properties of foreign exchange rates", Working paper, Olsen and Associates, December, 61 pages.

George, T.J. and F.A. Longstaff, 1993, "Bid–ask spreads and trading activity in the S&P 100 index options market", *Journal of Financial and Quantitative Analysis*, 28(3), September, pp. 381–97.

Gerety, M.S. and J.H. Mulherin, 1991, "Patterns in intraday stock market volatility, past and present", *Financial Analysts Journal*, 47(5), September–October, pp. 71–9.

Gerety, M.S. and J.H. Mulherin, 1992, "Trading halts and market activity: an analysis of volume at the open and the close", *Journal of Finance*, 47(5), December, pp. 1,765–84.

Ghosh, A., 1993a, "Cointegration and error correction models: intertemporal causality between index and futures prices", *Journal of Futures Markets*, 13(2), pp. 193–8.

Ghosh, A., 1993b, "Hedging with stock index futures: estimation and forecasting with error correction model", *Journal of Futures Markets*, 13(7), pp. 743–52.

Ghysels, E., C. Gourieroux and J. Jasiak, 1998, "High frequency financial time series data: some stylized facts and models of stochastic volatility", in C. Dunis and B. Zhou (eds), *Nonlinear Modelling of High Frequency Financial Time Series*, John Wiley and Sons, Chichester, pp. 127–60.

Glosten, L.R. and L.E. Harris, 1988, "Estimating the components of the bid–ask spread", *Journal of Financial Economics*, 21, pp. 123–42.

Godek, P.E., 1996, "Why NASDAQ market makers avoid odd-eighth quotes", *Journal of Financial Economics*, 41(3), July, pp. 465–74.

Godfrey, M.D., C.W.J. Granger and O. Morgenstern, 1964, "The random walk hypothesis of stock market behaviour", *Kyklos*, 17, pp. 1–29.

Goldenberg, D.H., 1988, "Trading frictions and futures price movements", *Journal of Financial and Quantitative Analysis*, 23(4), pp. 465–81.

Goldenberg, D.H., 1989, "Memory and equilibrium futures prices", *Journal of Futures Markets*, 9(3), pp. 199–213.

Goodhart, C.A.E., 1986, "Interaction between Wall Street and the London Stock Exchange: a test of the efficient market hypothesis", *Economics Letters*, 22(4), pp. 359–60.

Goodhart, C.A.E., 1999, Foreword, in P. Lequeux (ed), *Financial Markets Tick by Tick: Insights in Financial Markets Microstructure*, John Wiley, pp. ix–x.

Goodhart, C.A.E., Y. Chang and R. Payne, 1997, "Calibrating an algorithm for estimating transactions from FXFX exchange rate quotes", *Journal of International Money and Finance*, 16(6), December, pp. 921–30.

Goodhart, C.A.E. and L. Figliuoli, 1991, "Every minute counts in financial markets", *Journal of International Money and Finance*, 10, pp. 23–52.

Goodhart, C.A.E. and L. Figliuoli, 1992, "The geographical location of the foreign exchange market: a test of an 'islands' hypothesis", *Journal of International and Comparative Economics*, 1, pp. 13–27.

Goodhart, C.A.E. and M. Giugale, 1993, "From hour to hour in the foreign exchange market", *The Manchester School*, 61(1), March, pp. 1–34.

Goodhart, C.A.E., S.G. Hall, S.G.B. Henry and B. Pesaran, 1993, "News effects in a high frequency model of the sterling-dollar exchange rate", *Journal of Applied Econometrics*, 8, pp. 1–13.

Goodhart, C.A.E., T. Ito and R. Payne, 1996, "One day in June 1993: a study of the working of the Reuters 2000–2 electronic foreign exchange trading system". In J.A. Frankel, G. Galli and A. Giovannini (eds), *The Microstructure of Foreign Exchange Markets*, University of Chicago Press, pp. 107–82.

Goodhart, C.A.E., P.C. McMahon and Y.L. Ngama, 1993, "Testing for unit roots with very high frequency spot exchange rate data", *Journal of Macroeconomics*, 15(3), Summer, pp. 424–38.

Goodhart, C.A.E. and M. O'Hara, 1997, "High frequency data in financial markets: issues and applications", *Journal of Empirical Finance*, 4(2–3), June, pp. 73–114.

Goodhart, C.A.E. and R. Payne, 1996, "Micro-structural dynamics in a foreign exchange electronic broking system", *Journal of International Money and Finance*, 15(6), December, pp. 829–52.

Gosnell, T.F., A.J. Keown and J.M. Pinkerton, 1996, "The intraday speed of stock price adjustment to major dividend changes: bid–ask bounce and order flow imbalances", *Journal of Banking and Finance*, 20, pp. 247–66.

Gottlieb, G. and A. Kalay, 1985, "Implications of the discreteness of observed stock prices", *Journal of Finance*, 40(1), pp. 135–53.

Granger, C.W.J., 1998, "Extracting information from mega-panels and high frequency data", Department of Economics, University of California, San Diego, no. 98-01, January, 24 pages.

Grier, P.C. and P.S. Albin, 1973, "Non-random price changes in association with trading in large blocks", *Journal of Business*, 46(3), July, pp. 425–33.

Griffiths, M.D. and R.W. White, 1993, "Tax induced trading and the turn of the year anomaly: an intraday study", *Journal of Finance*, 48(2), June, pp. 575–98.

Grünbichler, A. and T.W. Callahan, 1994, "Stock index futures arbitrage in Germany: the behaviour of the DAX index futures price", *Review of Futures Markets*, 13(2), pp. 661–94.

Grünbichler, A., F.A. Longstaff and E.S. Schwartz, 1994, "Electronic screen trading and the transmission of information: an empirical examination", *Journal of Financial Intermediation*, 3(2), pp. 166–87.

Guillaume, D.M., M.M. Dacorogna, R.R. Davé, U.A. Müller, R.B. Olsen and O.V. Pictet, 1997, "From the bird's eye to the microscope: a survey of new stylized facts of the intra-daily foreign exchange markets", *Finance and Stochastics*, 1, pp. 95–129.

Habeeb, G., J.M. Hill and A.J. Rzad, 1991, "Potential rewards from path-dependent index arbitrage with S&P500 futures", *Review of Futures Markets*, 10(1), pp. 180–203.

Handa, P. and R.A. Schwartz, 1996, "Limit order trading", *Journal of Finance*, 51(5), December, pp. 1,835–61.

Hancock, G.D., 1991, "Futures option expirations and volatility in the stock index futures market", *Journal of Futures Markets*, 11(3), pp. 319–30.

Hancock, G.D., 1993, "Whatever happened to the triple witching hour?", *Financial Analysts Journal*, 49(3), pp. 66–72.

Hansch, O., N.Y. Naik and S. Viswanathan, 1998, "Preferencing, Internalization, Best Execution and Dealer Profits", *Journal of Finance*, 53(5), October, pp. 1623–56.

Hansch, O. and A. Neuberger, 1993, "Block trading on the London Stock Exchange", Institute of Finance and Accounting, London Business School, Working paper 182, November, 22 pages.

Harris, F.H.D., T.H. McInish and R.R. Chakravarty, 1995, "Bids and asks in disequilibrium market microstructure: the case of IBM", *Journal of Banking and Finance*, 19(2), May, pp. 323–45.

Harris, J.H. and P.H. Schultz, 1997, "The importance of firm quotes and rapid executions: evidence from the January 1994 SOES rules change", *Journal of Financial Economics*, 45(1), July, pp. 135–66.

Harris, J.H. and P.H. Schultz, 1998, "The trading profits of SOES bandits", *Journal of Financial Economics*, 50, pp. 39–62.

Harris, L.E. 1986, "A transaction data study of weekly and intradaily patterns in stock returns", *Journal of Financial Economics*, 16(1), May, pp. 99–117.

Harris, L.E., 1989a, "The October 1987 S&P500 stock-futures basis", *Journal of Finance*, 44(1), pp. 77–90.

Harris, L.E., 1989b, "A day-end transaction price anomaly", *Journal of Financial and Quantitative Analysis*, 24(1), March, pp. 29–45.

Harris, L.E., 1990b, "Estimation of stock price variances and serial covariances from discrete observations", *Journal of Financial and Quantitative Analysis*, 25(3), pp. 291–306.

Harris, L.E., 1991, "Stock price clustering and discreteness", *Review of Financial Studies*, 4(3), pp. 389–415.

Harris, L.E., 1994, "Minimum price variations, discrete bid–ask spreads and quotation sizes", *Review of Financial Studies*, 7(1), Spring, pp. 149–78.

Harris, L.E. and J. Hasbrouck, 1996, "Market vs. limit orders: the SuperDOT evidence on order submission strategy", *Journal of Financial and Quantitative Analysis*, 31(2), June, pp. 213–31.

Harris, L., G. Sofianos and J.E. Shapiro, 1994, "Program trading and intraday volatility", *Review of Financial Studies*, 7(4), Winter, pp. 653–85.

Harvey, C.R. and R.D. Huang, 1991, "Volatility in the foreign currency futures market", *Review of Financial Studies*, 4(3), pp. 543–69.

Harvey, C.R. and R.E. Whaley, 1992, "Market volatility prediction and the efficiency of the S&P 100 index option market", *Journal of Financial Economics*, 31(1), February, pp. 43–73.

Hasbrouck, J., 1987, "Order arrival, quote behaviour and the return generating process", *Journal of Finance*, 42(4), pp. 1,035–48.

Hasbrouck, J., 1988, "Trades, quotes, inventories and information", *Journal of Financial Economics*, 22(2), December, pp. 229–52.

Hasbrouck, J., 1991a, "Measuring the information content of stock trades", *Journal of Finance*, 46(1), March, pp. 179–207.

Hasbrouck, J., 1991b, "The summary informativeness of stock trades: an econometric analysis", *Review of Financial Studies*, 4(3), pp. 571–95.

Hasbrouck, J., 1996a, "Order characteristics and stock price evolution: an application to program trading", *Journal of Financial Economics*, 41(1), pp. 129–49.

Hasbrouck, J., 1996b, "Modelling market microstructure time series", in G.S. Maddala and C.R. Rao (eds), *Statistical Methods in Finance*, Handbook of Statistics, 14, Elsevier, pp. 647–92.

Hasbrouck, J., 1998, "Liquidity in the futures pits: inferring market dynamics from incomplete data", Working paper, New York University, September, 56 pages.

Hasbrouck, J., 1999, "Security bid–ask dynamics with discreteness and clustering: simple strategies for modelling and estimation", *Journal of Financial Markets*, 2(1), February, pp. 1–28.

Hasbrouck, J. and T.S.Y. Ho, 1987, "Order arrival, quote behaviour and the return-generating process", *Journal of Finance*, 42(4), September, pp. 1,035–48.

Hasbrouck, J. and G. Sofianos, 1993, "The trades of market makers: an empirical analysis of NYSE specialists", *Journal of Finance*, 48(5), December, pp. 1,565–93.

Hausman, J.A., A.W. Lo and A.C. MacKinlay, 1992, "An ordered probit analysis of transaction stock prices", *Journal of Financial Economics*, 31, pp. 319–79.

Henker, T., 1998, "The bid–ask spread of the FTSE 100 futures contract", Working paper, University of Massachusetts, November, 30 pages.

Henry, M. and R. Payne, 1997, "An investigation of long range dependence in intraday foreign exchange rate volatility", Financial Markets Group, Discussion Paper, May 1997, 25 pages.

Herbst, A.F. and E.D. Maberly, 1990, "Stock index futures, expiration day volatility and the 'special' Friday opening: a note", *Journal of Futures Markets*, 10(3), pp. 323–5.

Herbst, A.F. and E.D. Maberly, 1991, "An alternative methodology for measuring expiration day price effects at Friday's close: the expected price reversal – a note", *Journal of Futures Markets*, 11(6), pp. 751–4.

Herbst, A.F. and E.D. Maberly, 1992, "The informational role of end-of-the-day returns in stock index futures", *Journal of Futures Markets*, 12(5), pp. 595–601.

Herbst, A.F., J.P. McCormack and E.N. West, 1987, "Investigation of a lead-lag relationship between spot stock indices and their futures contracts", *Journal of Futures Markets*, 7(4), pp. 373–81.

Hilliard, J.E. and A.L. Tucker, 1992, "A note on weekday, intraday and overnight patterns in the interbank foreign exchange and listed currency options markets", *Journal of Banking and Finance*, 16(6), December, pp. 1,159–71.

Hiraki, T., E.D. Maberly and N. Takezawa, 1995, "The information content of end of the day index futures returns: international evidence from the Osaka Nikkei 225 futures contract", *Journal of Banking and Finance*, 19(5), pp. 921–36.

Ho, R.Y. and R.S. Lee, 1998, "Market closure effects on return, volatility and turnover patterns in the Hong Kong index futures market", *Journal of International Financial Markets Institutions and Money*, 8(3–4), November, pp. 433–51.

Ho, R.Y.K., J.Z. Fang and C.K. Woo, 1992, "Intraday arbitrage opportunities and price behaviour of the Hang Seng index futures", *Review of Futures Markets*, 11(3), pp. 413–45.

Ho, T.S.Y. and R.G. Macris, 1984, "Dealer bid–ask quotes and transaction prices: an empirical study of some AMEX options", *Journal of Finance*, 39(1), March, pp. 23–45.

Ho, Y.K. and Y.L. Cheung, 1991 "Behaviour of intra-daily stock return on an Asian emerging market – Hong Kong", *Applied Economics*, 23(5), May, pp. 957–66.

Hodgson, A., 1994, "The evolution of intraday prices and information shocks", Working paper, 25 pages.

Hodgson, A., C. Kendig and M. Tahir, 1993, "Intraday price movements in related markets: futures and cash prices", Working paper, Australian National University, 25 pages.

Holland, A., 1999, "Price discovery and market integration in European government bond markets", in P. Lequeux (ed), *Financial Markets Tick by Tick*, John Wiley and Sons, Chichester, pp. 190–206.

Holthausen, R.W., R.W. Leftwich and D. Mayers, 1987, "The effect of large block transactions on security prices: a cross-sectional analysis", *Journal of Financial Economics*, 19(2), December, pp. 237–67.

Holthausen, R.W., R.W. Leftwich and D. Mayers, 1990, "Large block transactions, the speed of response and temporary and permanent stock price effects", *Journal of Financial Economics*, 26(1), July, pp. 71–95.

Hsieh, D.A. and A.W. Kleidon, 1996, "Bid–ask spreads in foreign exchange markets: implications for models of asymmetric information", in J.A. Frankel, G. Galli and A. Giovannini (eds), *The Microstructure of Foreign Exchange Markets*, University of Chicago Press, pp. 183–206.

Huang, R.D. and H.R. Stoll, 1994, "Market microstructure and stock return predictions", *Review of Financial Studies*, 7(1), Spring, pp. 179–213.

Huang, R.D. and H.R. Stoll, 1996, "Dealer versus auction markets: a paired comparison of execution costs on NASDAQ and the NYSE", *Journal of Financial Economics*, 41(3), July, pp. 313–57.

Iihara, Y., K. Kato and T. Tokunaga, 1996, "Intraday return dynamics between the cash and the futures markets in Japan", *Journal of Futures Markets*, 16(2), pp. 147–62.

Ito, T. and W.L. Lin, 1992, "Lunch break and intraday volatility of stock returns", *Economics Letters*, 39(1), May, 1992, pp. 85–90.

Jain, P.C. and G.H. Joh, 1988, "The dependence between hourly prices and trading volume", *Journal of Financial and Quantitative Analysis*, 23(3), September, pp. 269–83.

Jameson, M. and W. Wilhelm, 1992, "Market making in the options markets and the costs of discrete hedge rebalancing", *Journal of Finance*, 47(2), June, pp. 765–79.

Jang, H. and P.C. Venkatesh, 1991, "Consistency between predicted and actual bid–ask quote revisions", *Journal of Finance*, 46(1), March, pp. 433–46.

Jennings, R. and L. Starks, 1986, "Earnings announcements, stock price adjustment and the existence of option markets", *Journal of Finance*, 41(1), March, pp. 107–25.

Jones, J.D., R. Nachtmann and F. Phillips-Patrick, 1993, "Linkage between S&P and non-S&P stocks on the NYSE", *Applied Financial Economics*, 3(2), pp. 127–44.

Kandel, E. and L.M. Marx, 1997, "NASDAQ market structure and spread patterns", *Journal of Financial Economics*, 45(1), July, pp. 61–89.

Kawaller, I.G., P.D. Koch and T.W. Koch, 1987, "The temporal price relationship between S&P500 futures and the S&P500 index", *Journal of Finance*, 42(5), pp. 1,309–29.

Kawaller, I.G., P.D. Koch and T.W. Koch, 1988, "The relationship between the S&P500 index and S&P500 index futures prices", *Federal Reserve Bank of Atlanta Economic Review*, 73, May–June, pp. 2–10.

Kawaller, I.G., P.D. Koch and T.W. Koch, 1990, "Intraday relationships between volatility in S&P500 futures prices and volatility in the S&P index", *Journal of Banking and Finance*, 14 (2/3), pp. 373–97.

Kawaller, I.G., P.D. Koch and T.W. Koch, 1993, "Intraday market behaviour and the extent of feedback between S&P500 futures prices and the S&P500 index", *Journal of Financial Research*, 16(2), Summer, pp. 107–21.

Kawaller, I.G., P.D. Koch and J.E. Peterson, 1994, "Assessing the intraday relationship between implied and historical volatility", *Journal of Futures Markets*, 14(3), pp. 323–46.

Keim, D.B., 1989, "Trading patterns, bid–ask spreads and estimated security returns: the case of common stocks at calendar turning points", *Journal of Financial Economics*, 25(1), November, pp. 75–97.

Keim, D.B. and A. Madhavan, 1996, "The upstairs market for large block transactions: analysis and measurement of price effects", *Review of Financial Studies*, 9(1), Winter, pp. 1–36.

Kempf, A., 1998, "Short selling, unwinding and mispricing", *Journal of Futures Markets*, 18(8), December, pp. 903–23.

Kempf, A. and O. Korn, 1998, "Trading system and market integration", *Journal of Financial Intermediation*, 7, pp. 220–39.

Kempf. A. and O. Korn, 1999, "Market depth and order size", *Journal of Financial Markets*, 2(1), February, pp. 29–48.

Kim, M., A.C. Szakmary and T.V. Schwarz, 1999, "Trading costs and price discovery across stock index futures and cash markets", *Journal of Futures Markets*, 19(4), June, pp. 475–98.

Kim, S.H. and J.P. Ogden, 1996, "Determinants of the components of bid–ask spreads on stocks", *European Financial Management*, 1(1), March, pp. 127–45.

King, M.A. and S. Wadhwani, 1990, "Transmission of volatility between stock markets", *Review of Financial Studies*, 3(1), pp. 5–33.

Kleidon, A.W., 1992, "Arbitrage, nontrading and stale prices: October 1987", *Journal of Business*, 65(4), pp. 483–507.

Kleidon, A.W. and R.E. Whaley, 1992, "One market? Stocks, futures and options during October 1987", *Journal of Finance*, 47(3), pp. 851–77.

Klemkosky, R.C. and J.H. Lee, 1991, "The intraday ex post and ex ante profitability of index arbitrage", *Journal of Futures Markets*, 11(3), pp. 291–311.

Knez P.J. and M.J. Ready, 1996, "Estimating the profits from trading strategies", *Review of Financial Studies*, 9(4), pp. 1,121–64.

Koch, P.D., 1993, "Re-examining intraday simultaneity in stock index futures markets", *Journal of Banking and Finance*, 17(6), pp. 1,191–205.

Kodres, L.E., 1994, "The existence and impact of destabilizing positive feedback traders: evidence from the S&P500 index futures market", Working paper, International Monetary Fund, 42 pages.

Kofman, P., T. Bouwman and J.T. Moser, 1994, "Is there LIF(F)E after DTB? Competitive aspects of cross listed futures contracts on synchronous markets", Working paper no 9/94, Department of Econometrics, Monash University, July.

Kofman, P. and M. Martens, 1997, "Interaction between stock markets: an analysis of the common trading hours at the London and New York Stock Exchange", *Journal of International Money and Finance*, 16(3), pp. 387–414.

Kofman, P. and J.T. Moser, 1997, "Spreads, information flows and transparency across trading systems", *Applied Financial Economics*, 7(3), June 1997, pp. 281–94.

Koutmos, G. and M. Tucker, 1996, "Temporal relationships and dynamic interactions between spot and futures stock markets", *Journal of Futures Markets*, 16(1), pp. 55–69.

Kraus, A. and H.R. Stoll, 1972, "Price impacts of block trading on the New York Stock Exchange", *Journal of Finance*, 27(3), June, pp. 569–88.

Krinsky, I. and J. Lee, 1996, "Earnings announcements and the components of the bid–ask spread", *Journal of Finance*, 51(4), September, pp. 1,523–35.

Kuhn, B.A., G.J. Kuserk and P.R. Locke, 1991, "Do circuit breakers moderate volatility? Evidence from October 1989", *Review of Futures Markets*, 10(1), pp. 136–75.

Kumar, R., A. Sarin and K. Shastri, 1992, "The behaviour of option prices around large block transactions in the underlying security", *Journal of Finance*, 47(3), July, pp. 879–89.

Kuserk, G.J., P.R. Locke and C.L. Sayers, 1992, "The effects of amendments to rule 80a on liquidity, volatility and price efficiency in the S&P500 futures", *Journal of Futures Markets*, 12(4), pp. 383–409.

Kutner, G.W. and R.J. Sweeney, 1991, "Causality tests between the S&P500 cash and futures markets", *Quarterly Journal of Business and Economics*, 30(2), Spring, pp. 51–74.

Laatsch, F.E. and T.V. Schwarz, 1988, "Price discovery and risk transfer in stock index cash and futures markets", *Review of Futures Markets*, 7(2), pp. 272–89.

LaPlante, M. and C.J. Muscarella, 1997, "Do institutions receive comparable execution in the NYSE and NASDAQ markets? A transaction study of block trades", *Journal of Financial Economics*, 45(1), July, pp. 97–134.

Lauterbach, B. and M. Monroe, 1989, "A transaction data examination of the weekend effect in futures markets", *Review of Futures Markets*, 8(3), pp. 370–82.

Laux, P. and A. Senchack, 1992, "Bid–ask spreads in financial futures", *Journal of Futures Markets*, 12, pp. 621–34.

Lee, C.I. and I. Mathur, 1993, "Analysis of intertemporal dependence in intraday Eurodollar and treasury bill futures returns", *Journal of Multinational Financial Management*, 3(1–2), pp. 111–33.

Lee, C.M.C., 1992, "Earnings news and small traders", *Journal of Accounting and Economics*, 15, pp. 265–302.

Lee. C.M.C., B. Mucklow and M.J. Ready, 1993, "Spreads, depths and the impact of earnings information: an intraday analysis", *Review of Financial Studies*, 6(2), pp. 345–74.

Lee, C. M. C. and M. J. Ready, 1991, "Inferring trade direction from intraday data", *Journal of Finance*, 46, pp. 733–46.

Lee, J.H. and S.C. Linn, 1994, "Intraday and overnight volatility of stock index and stock index futures returns", *Review of Futures Markets*, 13(1), pp. 1–38.

Lee, J.H. and N. Nayar, 1993, "A transactions data analysis of arbitrage between index options and index futures", *Journal of Futures Markets*, 13(8), pp. 889–902.

Lehmann, B.N. and D.M. Modest, 1994, "Trading and liquidity on the Tokyo Stock Exchange: a bird's eye view", *Journal of Finance*, 49(3), July, pp. 951–84.

Leng, H., 1996, "Announcement versus non-announcement: a study of intraday price paths of Deutsche mark and Japanese yen futures", *Journal of Futures Markets*, 16(7), October, pp. 829–57.

Lequeux, P., 1997, "On the impact of high frequency data in the financial markets", *Derivatives, Use, Trading and Regulation*, 3(2), pp. 154–61.

Lequeux, P., 1999a, "Introduction", in P. Lequeux (ed), *Financial Markets Tick by Tick: Insights in Financial Markets Microstructure,* John Wiley & Sons, Chichester, pp. xxi–xxv.

Lequeux, P., 1999b, "A practical approach to information spillover at high frequency: empirical study of the gilt and FTSE LIFFE contracts", in P. Lequeux (ed), *Financial Markets Tick by Tick,* John Wiley & Sons, Chichester, pp. 207–26.

Lequeux, P. and E. Acar, 1996, "Tick by tick: an empirical study of BTP/bund spread trading", *Smart Spreads* (LIFFE), no. 5, June, pp. 2–4.

Levin, E.J. and R.E. Wright, 1999, "Explaining the intraday variation in the bid–ask spread in competitive dealership markets: a research note", *Journal of Financial Markets,* 2(2), May, pp. 179–91.

Lim, K.G., 1992a, "Arbitrage and price behaviour of the Nikkei stock index futures", *Journal of Futures Markets,* 12(2), pp. 151–61.

Lim, K.G., 1992b, "Speculative, hedging and arbitrage efficiency of the Nikkei index futures", in S.G. Rhee and R.P. Chang (eds), *Pacific Basin Capital Markets Research,* 3, North Holland, Amsterdam, pp. 441–61.

Lim, K.G. and J. Muthuswamy, 1993, "The impact of transaction costs on Nikkei index futures arbitrage", *Review of Futures Markets,* 12(3), pp. 717–43.

Lin, S.J., J. Knight and S. Satchell, 1999, "Modelling intraday equity prices and volatility using information arrivals – a comparative study of different choices of informational proxies", in P. Lequeux (ed), *Financial Markets Tick by Tick,* John Wiley and Sons, Chichester, pp. 27–64.

Lo, A. W. and A. C. MacKinlay, 1988, "Stock market prices do not follow random walks: evidence from a simple specification test", *Review of Financial Studies,* 1, pp. 41–66.

Lo, A. W. and A. C. MacKinlay, 1990, "An econometric analysis of non-synchronous trading", *Journal of Econometrics,* 40, pp. 181–212.

Locke, P.R., A. Sarkar and L. Wu, 1994, "Did the good guys lose? Regulatory restrictions of dual trading", Working paper, Federal Reserve Bank of New York, 32 pages.

Locke, P.R. and C.L. Sayers, 1993, "Intra-day futures price volatility: information effects and variance persistence", *Journal of Applied Econometrics,* 8, pp. 15–30.

Low, A.H.W. and J. Muthuswamy, 1996, "Information flows in high frequency exchange rates", in C. Dunis (ed), *Forecasting Financial Markets: Exchange Rates, Interest Rates and Asset Management,* John Wiley, pp. 3–32.

Lundin, M., M.M. Dacorogna and U.A. Müller, 1999, "Correlation of high frequency financial time series", in P. Lequeux (ed), *Financial Markets Tick by Tick,* John Wiley and Sons, Chichester, pp. 91–126.

Lyons, R.K., 1995, "Tests of micro-structural hypotheses in the foreign exchange market", *Journal of Financial Economics,* 39(2–3), October–November, pp. 321–51.

Lyons, R.K., 1996, "Foreign exchange volume: sound and fury signifying nothing?", in J.A. Frankel, G. Galli and A. Giovannini (eds), *The Microstructure of Foreign Exchange Markets*, University of Chicago Press, pp. 183–206.

Lyons, R.K. and A.K. Rose, 1995, "Explaining forward exchange bias... intraday", *Journal of Finance*, 50(4), September, pp. 1,321–29.

Ma, C.K., R.L. Peterson and R.S. Sears, 1992, "Trading noise, adverse selection and intraday bid–ask spreads in futures markets", *Journal of Futures Markets*, 12(5), October, pp. 519–38.

MacGregor, P., 1999, "The sources, preparation and use of high frequency data in the derivatives markets", in P. Lequeux (ed), *Financial Markets Tick by Tick*, John Wiley and Sons, Chichester, pp. 305–23.

MacIntyre, D., 1991, "Review of the January 14th rule changes", *Quality of Markets Review*, Summer edition, April–June, pp. 35–7.

MacKinlay, A.C. and K. Ramaswamy, 1988, "Index-futures arbitrage and the behaviour of stock index futures prices", *Review of Financial Studies*, 1(2), Summer, pp. 137–58.

Madhavan, A., M. Richardson and M. Roomans, 1997, "Why do security prices change? A transaction-level analysis of NYSE stocks", *Review of Financial Studies*, 10(4), Winter, pp. 1,035–64.

Madhavan, A. and S. Smidt, 1991, "A Bayesian model of intraday specialist pricing", *Journal of Financial Economics*, 30(1), November, pp. 99–134.

Madhavan, A. and S. Smidt, 1993, "An analysis of changes in specialist inventories and quotations", *Journal of Finance*, 48(5), December, pp. 1,595–628.

Madhavan, A. and G. Sofianos, 1998, "An empirical analysis of NYSE specialist trading", *Journal of Financial Economics*, 48, pp. 189–210.

Manaster, S. and S.C. Mann, 1996, "Life in the pits: competitive market making and inventory control", *Review of Financial Studies*, 9(3), Fall, pp. 953–75.

Marsh, T.A. and E.R. Rosenfeld, 1986, "Non-trading, market making and estimates of stock price volatility", *Journal of Financial Economics*, 15(3), pp. 359–72.

Martens, M., 1998, "Price discovery in high low volatility periods: open outcry versus electronic trading", *Journal of International Financial Markets, Institutions and Money*, 8(3–4), November, pp. 243–60.

Masulis, R.W. and L. Shivakumar, 1999, "Intraday market response to equity offering announcements: a NYSE/AMEX-NASDAQ comparison", Working paper no. 287, London Business School, March, 47 pages.

McInish, T.H. and R.A. Wood, 1990a, "A transactions data analysis of the variability of common stock returns during 1980–1984", *Journal of Banking and Finance*, 14(1), March, pp. 99–112.

McInish, T.H. and R.A. Wood, 1990b, "An analysis of transactions data for the Toronto Stock Exchange", *Journal of Banking and Finance*, 14(2/3), August, pp. 441–58.

McInish, T.H. and R.A. Wood, 1991, "Autocorrelation of daily index returns: intraday to intraday versus close to close intervals", *Journal of Banking and Finance*, 15(1), February, pp. 193–206.

McInish, T.H. and R.A. Wood, 1992, "An analysis of intraday patterns in bid/ask spreads for NYSE stocks", *Journal of Finance*, 47(2), June, pp. 753–64.

McMillan, H., 1991, "Circuit breakers in the S&P500 futures market: their effects on volatility and price discovery in October 1989", *Review of Futures Markets* 10(2), pp. 248–81.

Mercer, J.M., 1997, "An alternative specification for intraday simultaneity in spot and futures markets", *Quarterly Review of Economics and Finance*, 37(3), Fall, pp. 667–82.

Merton, R.C., 1980, "On estimating the expected return on the market", *Journal of Financial Economics*, 8, pp. 323–61.

Miller, M.H., J. Muthuswamy and R.E. Whaley, 1994, "Mean reversion of Standard & Poor's 500 index basis changes: arbitrage induced or statistical illusion?", *Journal of Finance*, 49(2), pp. 479–513.

Min, J.H. and M. Najand, 1999, "A further investigation of the lead–lag relationship between the spot market and stock index futures: early evidence from Korea", *Journal of Futures Markets*, 19(2), April, pp. 217–32.

Monroe, M.A. and R.A. Cohn, 1986, "The relative efficiency of the gold and treasury bill futures markets", *Journal of Futures Markets*, 6(3), Fall, pp. 477–93.

Moody, J. and L. Wu, 1998, "High frequency foreign exchange rates: price behaviour analysis and 'true price' models", in C. Dunis and B. Zhou (eds), *Nonlinear Modelling of High Frequency Financial Time Series*, John Wiley and Sons, Chichester, pp. 23–47.

Moriarty, E.J., J.D. Gordon, G.J. Kuserk and G.H.K. Wang, 1990, "Statistical analysis of price and basis behaviour: October 12–26, 1987, S&P500 futures and cash", in G.P. Dwyer and R.W. Hafer (eds), *The Stock Market: Bubbles, Volatility and Chaos*, Kluwer Academic Publishers, Dordrecht, pp. 141–79.

Mucklow, B., 1994, "Market microstructure: an examination of the effects on intraday event studies", *Contemporary Accounting Research*, 10(2), Spring, pp. 355–82.

Müller, U.A., M.M. Dacorogna, R.D. Davé, R.B. Olsen, O.V. Pictet and J.E. Von Weizäcker, 1997, "Volatilities of different time resolutions – analyzing the dynamics of market components", *Journal of Empirical Finance*, 4(2–3), June, pp. 213–39.

Müller, U.A., M.M. Dacorogna, R.D. Davé, O.V. Pictet, R.B. Olsen and J.R. Ward, 1995, "Fractals and intrinsic time – a challenge to econometricians", Working paper, Olsen and Associates, June, 23 pages.

Müller, U.A., M.M Dacorogna, R.B. Olsen, O.V. Pictet, M. Schwarz and C. Morgenegg, 1990, "Statistical study of foreign exchange rates, empirical evidence of a price change scaling law and intraday analysis", *Journal of Banking and Finance*, 14, pp. 1,189–208.

Müller, U.A., M.M. Dacorogna and O.V. Pictet, 1998, "Heavy Tails in High-Frequency Financial Data", in R.J. Adler, R.E. Feldman and M.S. Taqqu (eds), *A Practical Guide to Heavy Tails: Statistical Techniques and Applications*, Birkhaüser, Boston, pp. 55–77.

Nabney, I., C. Dunis, R. Dallaway, S. Leong and W. Redshaw, 1996, "Leading edge forecasting techniques for exchange rate prediction", in C. Dunis (ed), *Forecasting Financial Markets: Exchange Rates, Interest Rates and Asset Management*, John Wiley, pp. 227–43.

Neal, R., 1992, "A comparison of transaction costs between competitive market maker and specialist market structures", *Journal of Business*, 65(3), July, pp. 317–34.

Neal, R., 1993a, "The intra day effects of program trades on stock returns: evidence from October 1987", *Review of Futures Markets*, 12(1), pp. 143–65.

Neal, R., 1993b, "Is program trading destabilizing?", *Journal of Derivatives*, 1, Winter, pp. 64–77.

Neal, R., 1996, "Direct tests of index arbitrage models", *Journal of Financial and Quantitative Analysis*, 31(4), December, pp. 541–62.

Neal, R. and S.M. Wheatley, 1998, "Adverse selection and bid–ask spreads: evidence from closed-end funds", *Journal of Financial Markets*, 1(1), April, pp. 121–49.

Neftci, S.N. and A.J. Policano, 1990, "On some sample path properties of intra-day futures prices", *Review of Economics and Statistics*, 72(3), August, pp. 529–36.

Neuberger, A.J., 1992, "An empirical examination of market maker profits on the London Stock Exchange", *Journal of Financial Services Research*, 6(4), January, pp. 343–72.

Niederhoffer, V., 1965, "Clustering of stock prices", *Operations Research*, 13(2), March–April, pp. 258–65.

Niederhoffer, V. and M.F.M. Osborne, 1966, "Market making and reversal on the stock exchange", *Journal of the American Statistical Association*, 61(316), December, pp. 897–916.

Nielsen, J.F. and M.D. Joehnk, 1973–74, "Further evidence on the effects of block transactions on stock price fluctuations", *Mississippi Valley Journal of Business and Economics*, Winter, pp. 27–34.

Niemeyer, J., 1994, "An analysis of the lead–lag relationship between the OMX index forwards and the OMX cash index", Paper presented to the Seventh Annual European Futures Symposium, Bonn, 28 pages.

Niemeyer, J. and P. Sandås, 1995, "An empirical analysis of the trading structure at the Stockholm Stock Exchange", Working paper no. 44, Stockholm School of Economics, January, 35 pages.

Overdahl, J. and H. McMillan, 1998, "Another day, another collar: an evaluation of the effects of NYSE rule 80A on trading costs and intermarket arbitrage", *Journal of Business*, 71(1), January, pp. 27–53.

Park, H.Y. 1993, "Trading mechanisms and the price volatility: spot versus futures", *Review of Economics and Statistics*, 75(1), pp. 175–79.

Park, H.Y. and A. Sarkar, 1992, "Market depth, liquidity and the effect of dual trading in futures markets", Bureau of Economic and Business Research, College of Commerce and Business Administration, University of Illinois at Urbana-Champaign, Bureau of Economic and Business Research, Faculty Working paper 92–0134, 50 pages.

Park, H.Y., A. Sarkar and L. Wu, 1994, "The costs and benefits of endogenous market making: the case of dual trading", Working paper, Federal Reserve Bank of New York, 30 pages.

Park, T.H. and L.N. Switzer, 1995, "Settlement method of Eurodollar futures and expiration day effects: an analysis of intraday price volatility", *Journal of Multinational Financial Management*, 5(2–3), pp. 33–46.

Patel, J.M. and M.A. Wolfson, 1981, "Ex ante and ex post price effects of quarterly earnings announcements reflected in option and stock prices", *Journal of Accounting Research*, 19(2), Autumn, pp. 434–58.

Patel, J.M. and M.A. Wolfson, 1982, "Good news, bad news and the intraday timing of corporate disclosures", *Accounting Review*, 57(3), July, pp. 509–27.

Patel, J.M. and M.A. Wolfson, 1984, "The intraday speed of adjustment of stock prices to earnings and dividend announcements", *Journal of Financial Economics*, 13, pp. 223–52.

Payne, R., 1997, "Announcement effects and seasonality in the intraday foreign exchange market, Financial Markets Group", Discussion Paper no. 238, May 1997, 38 pages.

Petersen, M.A. and D. Fialkowski, 1994, "Posted versus effective spreads", *Journal of Financial Economics*, 35(3), June, pp. 269–92.

Piccinato, B., G. Ballocchi and M. Dacorogna, 1998, "A closer look at the Eurofutures market: intraday statistical analysis", Working paper, Olsen & Associates, 20 pages.

Piccinato, B., G. Ballocchi, M. Dacorogna and R. Gençay, 1998, "Intraday statistical properties of Eurofutures", Working paper, Olsen and Associates, 51 pages.

Pictet, O.V., M.M. Dacorogna, U.A. Müller, R.B. Olsen and J.R. Ward, 1992, "Real-time trading models for foreign exchange rates", *Neural Network World*, 2(6), pp. 713–44.

Pirrong, C., 1996, "Market liquidity and depth on computerized and open outcry trading systems: a comparison of DTB and LIFFE bund contracts", *Journal of Futures Markets*, 16(5), August, pp. 519–43.

Pizzi, M.A., A.J. Economopoulos and H.M. O'Neill, 1998, "An examination of the relationship between stock index cash and futures markets: a cointegration approach", *Journal of Futures Markets*, 18(3), pp. 297–305.

Pope, P.F. and P.K. Yadav, 1992, "Transaction cost thresholds, arbitrage activity and index futures pricing", mimeo, 51 pages, included as Chapter 4 in *Studies on Stock Index Futures Pricing: A UK Perspective*, by P.K. Yadav, PhD Thesis, University of Strathclyde.

Porter, D.C., 1992, "The probability of a trade at the ask: an examination of interday and intraday behaviour", *Journal of Financial and Quantitative Analysis*, 27(2), pp. 209–27.

Porter, D.C. and D.G. Weaver, 1998, "Post-trade transparency on NASDAQ's national market system", *Journal of Financial Economics*, 50(2), November, pp. 231–52.

Reiss, P.C. and I.M. Werner, 1998, "Does risk sharing motivate interdealer trading?", *Journal of Finance*, 53(5), October, pp. 1,657–703.

Robinson, M., 1988, "Block trades on the major Canadian and US stock exchanges: A study of pricing behaviour and market efficiency", Doctoral dissertation, School of Business Administration, University of Western Ontario, London.

Röell, A., 1990, "Dual capacity trading and the quality of the market", *Journal of Financial Intermediation*, 1(2), pp. 105–24.

Roll, R., 1984, "A simple measure of the effective bid–ask spread in an efficient market", *Journal of Finance*, 39, pp. 1,127–39.

Rougier, J., 1996, "An optimal price index for stock index futures contracts", *Journal of Futures Markets*, 16(2), pp. 189–99.

Santoni, G.J., 1988, "The October crash: some evidence on the cascade theory", *Federal Reserve Bank of St. Louis Review*, 70, May–June, pp. 18–33.

Saporta, V., G. Trebeschi and A. Vila, 1999, "Price formation and transparency on the London Stock Exchange", Working paper series no. 95, Bank of England, April, 42 pages.

Schlag, C., 1996, "Expiration day effects of stock index derivatives in Germany", *European Financial Management*, 1(1), pp. 69–95.

Schmidt, H. and P. Iversen, 1992, "Automating German equity trading: bid–ask spreads on competing systems, *Journal of Financial Services Research*, 6(4), January, pp. 373–97.

Schnidrig, R., 1998, "ADRENALIN: A distributed realtime environment for the intraday analysis of financial markets", Dissertation no. 12890 submitted to the Swiss Federal Institute of Technology, Zurich.

Seppi, D.J., 1992, "Block trading and information revelation around quarterly earnings announcements", *Review of Financial Studies*, 5(2), pp. 281–305.

Sheikh, A.M. and E.I. Ronn, 1994, "A characterization of the daily and intraday behaviour of returns on options", *Journal of Finance*, 49(2), June, pp. 557–79.

Shyy, G. and J.H. Lee, 1995, "Price transmission and information asymmetry in bund futures markets: LIFFE vs. DTB", *Journal of Futures Markets*, 15(1), February, pp. 87–99.

Shyy, G. and C.H. Shen, 1997, "A comparative study on interday market volatility and intraday price transmission of Nikkei/JGB futures markets between Japan and Singapore", *Review of Quantitative Finance and Accounting*, 9(2), September, pp. 147–63.

Shyy, G., V. Vijayraghavan and B. Scott-Quinn, 1996, "A further investigation of the lead-lag relationship between the cash market and stock index futures market with the use of bid–ask quotes: the case of France", *Journal of Futures Markets*, 16(4), pp. 405–20.

Sim, A.B. and R. Zurbreugg, 1999, "Intertemporal volatility and price interactions between Australian and Japanese spot and futures stock index markets", *Journal of Futures Markets*, 19(5), August, pp. 523–40.

Slovin, M.B., M.E. Sushka and E.R. Waller, 1994, "Is there news in the prime rate?", *Journal of Financial and Quantitative Analysis*, 29(4), December, pp. 633–46.

Smidt, S., 1979, "Continuous versus intermittent trading on auction markets", *Journal of Financial and Quantitative Analysis*, 14(4), November, pp. 837–66.

Smith, B.F., R. White, M. Robinson and R. Nason, 1997, "Intraday volatility and trading volume after takeover announcements", *Journal of Banking and Finance*, 21(3), March, pp. 337–68.

Smith, D.G. and R.I. Webb, 1993, "The volatility of Eurodollar futures prices around Fed time", *Journal of Fixed Income*, 2(4), March, pp. 58–73.

Smith, T. and R.E. Whaley, 1994, "Estimating the effective bid–ask spread from time and sales data", *Journal of Futures Markets*, 14(4), pp. 437–55.

Snell, A. and I. Tonks, 1995, "Determinants of price quote revisions on the London Stock Exchange", *Economic Journal*, 105, January, pp. 77–94.

Snell, A. and I. Tonks, 1998, "Testing for asymmetric information and inventory control effects in market maker behaviour on the London Stock Exchange", *Journal of Empirical Finance*, 5(1), January, pp. 1–25.

So, R.W., G.G. Booth and O. Loistl, 1997, "An examination of intraday common volatility in the German index derivatives markets", *Journal of Multinational Financial Management*, 7(4), December, pp. 305–16.

Sofianos, G., 1991, "Potential rewards from path-dependent index arbitrage with S&P500 futures: commentary", *Review of Futures Markets*, 10(1), pp. 204–06.

Sofianos, G., 1993, "Index arbitrage profitability", *Journal of Derivatives* 1, Fall, pp. 6–20.

Sofianos, G., 1994, "Expirations and stock price volatility", *Review of Futures Markets*, 13(1), pp. 39–113.

Stephan, J.A. and R.E. Whaley, 1990, "Intraday price change and trading volume relationships in the stock and stock options markets", *Journal of Finance*, 45(1), March, pp. 191–220.

Sternberg, J.S., 1994, "A re-examination of put-call parity on index futures", *Journal of Futures Markets*, 14(1), August, pp. 79–101.

Stoll, H.R., 1988, "Index futures, program trading and stock market procedures", *Journal of Futures Markets*, 8(4), pp. 391–412.

Stoll, H.R., 1989, "Inferring the components of the bid–ask spread: theory and empirical tests", *Journal of Finance*, 44(1), March, pp. 115–34.

Stoll, H.R. and R.E. Whaley, 1987a, *Expiration Day Effects of Index Options and Futures*, Monograph Series in Finance and Economics, Monograph 86–3, New York University.

Stoll, H.R. and R.E. Whaley, 1987b, "Program trading and expiration day effects", *Financial Analysts Journal*, 43(2), pp. 16–28.

Stoll, H.R. and R.E. Whaley, 1990a, "Program trading and individual stock returns: ingredients of the triple-witching brew", *Journal of Business*, 63(1)(2), pp. S165–92.

Stoll, H.R. and R.E. Whaley, 1990b, "The dynamics of stock index and stock index futures returns", *Journal of Financial and Quantitative Analysis*, 25(4), pp. 441–68.

Stoll, H.R. and Whaley, 1991, "Expiration-day effects: what has changed?", *Financial Analysts Journal*, 47(1), pp. 58–72.

Stoll, H.R. and R.E. Whaley, 1993, *Futures and Options: Theory and Applications*, South-Western Publishing Co., Cincinnati, Ohio.

Strickland, C. and X. Xu, 1993, "Behaviour of the FT-SE 100 basis", *Review of Futures Markets*, 12(2), pp. 459–502.

Susmel, R. and R.F. Engle, 1994, "Hourly volatility spillovers between international equity markets", *Journal of International Money and Finance*, 13, pp. 3–25.

Sutcliffe, C.M.S., 1997, *Stock Index Futures: Theories and International Evidence*, Second edition, International Thomson Business Press, London.

Swinnerton, E.A., R.J. Curcio and R.E. Bennett, 1988, "Index arbitrage program trading and the prediction of intraday stock index price changes", *Review of Futures Markets*, 7(2), pp. 300–23.

Szpiro, G.G., 1998, "Tick size, the compass rose and market nanostructure", *Journal of Banking and Finance*, 22(12), December, pp. 1,559–69.

Tanner, G., 1997, "A note on economic news and intraday exchange rates", *Journal of Banking and Finance*, 21, pp. 573–85.

Tauchen, G.E. and M. Pitts, 1983, "The price variability volume relationship in speculative markets", *Econometrica*, 51, pp. 484–505.

Thompson, S. and M. Waller, 1988, "Determinants of liquidity costs in commodity futures markets", *Review of Futures Markets*, 7, pp. 110–26.

Toulson, D., S. Toulson and A. Sinclair, 1999, "Constructing a managed portfolio of high frequency LIFFE futures positions", in P. Lequeux (ed), *Financial Markets Tick by Tick*, John Wiley and Sons, Chichester, pp. 347–75.

Tse, Y., 1999, "Market microstructure of FTSE 100 index futures: an intraday empirical analysis", *Journal of Futures Markets*, 19(1), February, pp. 31–58.

Umlauf, S.R., 1991, "Information asymmetries and security market design: an empirical study of the secondary market for US Government securities", *Journal of Finance*, 46(3), July, pp. 929–53.

Vaidyanathan, R. and T. Krehbiel, 1992, "Does the S&P500 futures mispricing series exhibit nonlinear dependence across time?", *Journal of Futures Markets*, 12(6), pp. 659–77.

Vijh, A.M., 1988, "Potential biases from using only trade prices of related securities on different exchanges: a comment", *Journal of Finance*, 43(4), September, pp. 1,049–55.

Vijh, A.M., 1990, "Liquidity of the CBOE equity options", *Journal of Finance*, 45(3), July, pp. 1,157–79.

Vila, A.F. and G. Sandmann, 1995, "Floor trading versus electronic screen trading: an empirical analysis of market liquidity and information transmission in the Nikkei stock index futures market", Financial Markets Group, London School of Economics, Discussion paper no. 218, 49 pages.

Walsh, D.M. and J. Quek, 1999, "An empirical examination of the SIMEX Nikkei 225 futures contract around the Kobe earthquake and the Barings collapse", *Journal of Futures Markets*, 19(1), February, pp. 1–29.

Wang, G.H.K., R.J. Michalski, J.V. Jordan and E.J. Moriarty, 1994, "An intraday analysis of bid–ask spreads and price volatility in the S&P500 index futures market", *Journal of Futures Markets*, 14(7), pp. 837–59.

Wang, G.H.K., E.J. Moriarty, R.J. Michalski and J.V. Jordan, 1990, "Empirical analysis of the liquidity of the S&P500 stock index futures market during the October 1987 market break", in F.J. Fabozzi (ed), *Advances in Futures and Options Research: A Research Annual*, 4, JAI Press, Greenwich, Connecticut, pp. 191–218.

Wang, G.H.K. and J. Yau, 1994, "A time series approach to testing for market linkage: unit root and cointegration tests", *Journal of Futures Markets*, 14(4), pp. 457–74.

Wang, G.H.K., J. Yau and T. Baptiste, 1997, "Trading volume and transaction costs in futures markets", *Journal of Futures Markets*, 17(7), October, pp. 757–80.

Wegman, E.J., 1995, "Huge data sets and the frontiers of computational feasibility", *Journal of Computational and Graphical Statistics*, 4(4), pp. 281–95.

Werner, I.M. and A.W. Kleidon, 1996, "UK and US trading of British cross-listed stocks: an intraday analysis of market integration", *Review of Financial Studies*, 9(2), Summer, pp. 619–64.

Whaley, R.E., 1986, "Expiration-day effects of index futures and options – empirical results", *Review of Research in Futures Markets*, 5(3), pp. 292–308.

Wood, R. and M. McCorry, 1994, "Inferring trade direction from intra-day data: a note", Working paper (Memphis State University, Memphis, Tn.).

Wood, R.A., T.H. McInish and J.K. Ord, 1985, "An investigation of transactions data for NYSE stocks", *Journal of Finance*, 40(3), July, pp. 723–41.

Woodruff, C.S. and A.J. Senchack, 1988, "Intradaily price-volume adjustments of NYSE stocks to unexpected earnings", *Journal of Finance*, 43(2), June, pp. 467–91.

Yadav, P.K. and P.F. Pope, 1992a, "Intraweek and intraday seasonalities in stock market risk premia: cash and futures", *Journal of Banking and Finance*, 16(1), pp. 233–72.

Yadav, P.K. and P.F. Pope, 1992b, "Mean reversion in stock index futures mispricing: evidence from the US and the UK", mimeo, 44 pages, included as Chapter 7 in P.K. Yadav, *Studies on Stock Index Futures Pricing: A UK Perspective*, PhD Thesis, University of Strathclyde.

Yadav, P.K. and P.F. Pope, 1992c, "Pricing of stock index futures spreads: theory and evidence", mimeo, 69 pages, included as Chapter 8 in P.K. Yadav, *Studies on Stock Index Futures Pricing: A UK Perspective*, PhD Thesis, University of Strathclyde.

Yadav, P.K. and P.F. Pope, 1994, "Stock index futures mispricing: profit opportunities or risk premia?", *Journal of Banking and Finance*, 18(5), pp. 921–53.

Zhou, B., 1996, "Forecasting foreign exchange rates subject to de-volatilization", in C. Dunis (ed), *Forecasting Financial Markets: Exchange Rates, Interest Rates and Asset Management*, John Wiley, pp. 51–67.

Zhou, B., 1998, "F-consistency, de-volatization and normalization of high frequency financial data", in C. Dunis and B. Zhou (eds), *Nonlinear Modelling of High Frequency Financial Time Series*, John Wiley and Sons, Chichester, pp. 109–23.

Zumbach, G., 1998, "Considering time as the random variable: the first hitting time", Working paper, Olsen & Associates, 9 pages.